The Service Providers

The Service Providers

Dana Yagil

First published 2008 by
PALGRAVE MACMILLAN
Houndmills, Basingstoke, Hampshire RG21 6XS and
175 Fifth Avenue, New York, N.Y. 10010
Companies and representatives throughout the world

PALGRAVE MACMILLAN is the global academic imprint of the Palgrave Macmillan division of St. Martin's Press, LLC and of Palgrave Macmillan Ltd. Macmillan® is a registered trademark in the United States, United Kingdom and other countries. Palgrave is a registered trademark in the European Union and other countries.

ISBN 13: 978–0–230–51497–3   hardback
ISBN 10: 0–230–51497–9   hardback

This book is printed on paper suitable for recycling and made from fully managed and sustained forest sources. Logging, pulping and manufacturing processes are expected to conform to the environmental regulations of the country of origin.

A catalogue record for this book is available from the British Library.

A catalogue record for this book is available from the Library of Congress.

10   9   8   7   6   5   4   3   2   1
17   16   15   14   13   12   11   10   09   08

Printed and bound in Great Britain by
CPI Antony Rowe, Chippenham and Eastbourne

To my parents with love and gratitude

Contents

List of Tables and Figures

List of Tables

List of Figures

Preface

Customer service is often described as involving three participants: the customer, the service provider and the organization. The organization's role in service as well as the customer's perspective have been reviewed in numerous books. Yet, while a number of studies have explored issues relating to service providers, no book has so far integrated the knowledge regarding these participants in the service process. This book is designed to fill this gap by discussing distinctive issues relevant to service providers, while linking them to extant research on customers and service in organizations.

Employees in customer service jobs merit study not only because they comprise a large sector of the employment market, but also because their role is significant both theoretically and practically. From a conceptual viewpoint, all customer service jobs share distinctive fascinating characteristics generated by two basic features of the work: service providers are positioned at the organization's boundary with the public, and they perform their job through interpersonal interactions. The boundary position implies that the service providers' role involves a mediation function between organization and customer, and while they are part of the organization's work force, their work is performed mostly with people outside the organization. This organizational position involves issues relating to the object of the service providers' commitment and identification; their involvement in customer-organization conflicts; and the way these two sets of relationships affect each other. The second feature inherent in the customer service job is its social nature, as it involves constant management of interactions with customers. While these interactions consist of universal interpersonal processes (e.g., social exchange), they are also strictly defined in regard to each party's role, the verbal content of the interaction, and the progress of the service process. Service providers are expected to manage these complicated social interactions which vary with each customer, and their performance in this respect involves many challenging interpersonal and intrapersonal processes.

Not surprisingly, from a practical viewpoint, it is commonly acknowledged that the success of service organizations ultimately depends on the performance of service employees. They represent the organization in the perception of the customer; largely determine the quality of the 'moment of truth' when the customer encounters the organization; and are responsible for recovery of service failures. Their performance affects all aspects of customer attitudes and behavior, namely satisfaction, emotions, evaluation of service quality, and word of mouth. Most importantly, service providers significantly affect customer loyalty to the organization, with clear financial consequences.

However, providing service through interpersonal interaction is not restricted to customer service jobs; it is a component of almost every job in contemporary organizations. Users of computer software programs are defined as customers of the developer, students as customers of the teacher, and subordinates as customers of the supervisor. Regardless of type of organization or job, in today's organizations most employees have internal and/or external customers and spend part of their working time providing services. Thus, most of the issues reviewed in the book are relevant to a great many jobs which are not defined as service jobs, as they describe the processes involved when the employee turns into a service provider.

Acknowledgments

I am grateful to all the researchers whose theories and studies about service providers are integrated in this book. I am indebted to the following scholars who commented on various parts of the manuscript: Barry Babin of the Louisiana Tech University, Simon Bell of the University of Cambridge, Alicia Grandey of the Pennsylvania State University, Christian Gronroos of the Swedish School of Economics, Barbara Gutek of the University of Arizona, Kevin Gwinner of Kansas State University, Patrice Rosenthal of the University of London, Wilmar Schaufeli of Utrecht University and Benjamin Schneider of the University of Maryland. My thanks to Virginia Thorp at Palgrave for her assistance throughout the publishing process. I thank the Research Authority of the University of Haifa for providing financial support. I owe a debt of gratitude to Judy Krautz for her exceptional involvement and help in editing the manuscript. I thank Ela Konikov for her assistance in the preparation of the manuscript. My deepest gratitude to Yoad my husband, for his infinite caring and invaluable suggestions, and to Alon and Noga my children, for being all that they are.

Introduction

The guiding discipline in the book is social psychology, reflected in its focus on individuals and their interpersonal interactions. The boundary role of service providers is reflected in sections which discuss their relationship with the organization as well as with customers. In as much as service providers are the focus of this book, the other participants in service – the customers and the organization – are discussed primarily in reference to the service providers.

Part I of the book focuses on fundamental interpersonal processes that underlie the service encounter. Chapter 1 discusses the notion of service as an act performed by service providers for the customer's benefit, presents the similarities of the service encounter with a theatre performance and integrates literature about the notion of emotional regulation. Chapter 2 discusses organizational control over and empowerment of service providers, the struggle for control in the interaction with customers, and the power relations among the three parties involved. Chapter 3 examines the issue of social exchange in the service providers' relationship with the customers and the organization.

Part II of the book covers issues relating to service providers' attitudes and behaviors and to customers' behaviors toward them. Chapters 4 and 5 describe positive and negative interpersonal behaviors of customers and service providers, respectively. Chapter 6 discusses personality characteristics of service providers and Chapter 7 reviews the organizational perspectives of the service role. Chapter 8 discusses the role of service providers in achieving the ultimate purpose of service, namely customer satisfaction and loyalty and Chapter 9 summarizes managerial implications.

While service jobs share many common characteristics, the heterogeneity of the service sector implies that service providers may differ in such major parameters as professional background, required skills, type of interaction with customers and organizational status. In order to identify the shared characteristics as well as the heterogeneity of service jobs, a review of definitions of services, which address the common characteristics of serviced jobs is presented below, followed by several classifications which address the heterogeneity of the service sector and posit parameters for analyzing it.

Definitions and classifications of customer services

The simplest definitions of service view it as actions, processes and performance.[1,2] More broadly, service is mostly defined in comparison to production in an attempt to differentiate between the two. Consequently, the definitions emphasize what service is not – it is not about tangible products. Service is described as a process consisting of more or less intangible activities;[3] an act which does not result in the ownership of anything; a situation in which benefits rather than goods are delivered to the customer;[4] a process in which the method of delivery is as important as what is delivered;[5] economic activities that provide intangible added values to the customer;[2] and relatively quickly perishable activities.[6] Bowen and Ford (2002)[7] suggest that 'an intangible service includes all the elements that come together to create a memorable experience for a customer at a point in time, namely a service product, a service setting and a service delivery system' (p. 449). Nevertheless, very few products are purely or totally tangible. While services may be seen not as absolutely intangible they are more intangible than manufactured products.[2] Since services are often offered in addition to goods they may be described as being in the central area of the tangible-intangible continuum.[6]

Two additional characteristics of service are described in several of the definitions: the interactions that take place between the service providers and the customers[3,6,8] and the simultaneous nature of the delivery and consumption of service.[2,6,8] However, production may take place before the service has started, while consumption may continue after the interaction with the service provider has ended.

A summary of the definitions of service (Gronroos, 2001)[3] reveals three characteristics common to most services: they consist of activities rather than things, they are produced and consumed simultaneously, and customers participate in the service production process. Based on these definitions, the following job description of service providers is suggested: *The role of service providers is to interact with customers in order to provide mostly intangible outputs that are consumed at the time of the process.*

Due to the heterogeneity of customer services, many authors have developed their own classification of services. Indeed, there is no single accepted classification.[6] Two examples of comprehensive classifications which cover a broad range of aspects are those presented by Lovelock (1983)[9] and Kasper *et al.* (1999).[6] Both classifications include the parameters of the nature of the service, market characteristics, characteristics of the service process, customer-organization relationship and physical aspects of the service.

Lovelock's well-known classification is based on five components of service:

(1) The nature of the service act in terms of tangibility and the object of the service (i.e., things or people).
(2) The type of the customer relationship with the organization in terms of reoccurrence of contact and relationship formality.
(3) The ability of service providers to exercise judgment and the customization of the service.
(4) Demand for service relative to supply.
(5) The method of the service delivery in terms of location of interaction and availability of outlets.

Kasper *et al.* (1999)[6] proposed the following nine parameters for the classification of services:

(1) Services and goods.
(2) Services provided in the profit and non-profit sector.
(3) Markets and industries.
(4) Internal and external services.
(5) Individual customers and organizations as customers.
(6) The relationship between the service provider and the customer in terms of ongoing relationships or discrete encounters and the customer's loyalty to a particular service provider.
(7) Characteristics of the service provider such as knowledge, skill, capacity, and the dependence of the organization on a particular person.
(8) The service delivery process in terms of service delivery operations, equipment-based vs. people-based services, number of contacts during the service process, and the presence of the customer during the process.
(9) The physical site of service delivery.

While the classifications posited by Lovelock and Kasper *et al.* are broad and intend to cover all aspects of service, several classifications have focused on the social aspects of the service process specifically.

Service encounters and relationships

Gutek (1995)[10] and colleagues (1999,[11] 2000[12]) developed a classification based on the continuity of the service provider-customer relationship, differentiating between three types of relationships: service relationships, encounters and pseudorelationships. Service relationships are formed when a customer has repeated contact with the same provider. The customer and the service provider get to know each other and develop a history of shared interactions. In service relationships the expectation of further interactions in the future enhances the parties' self-interest in cooperating with each other, and, from the point of view of the service provider, in producing high-quality service.

By contrast, service encounters consist of a single interaction between a customer and a service provider, with no expectations of future interactions. In such encounters there is no intrinsic motivation to cooperate and therefore management operates to achieve high-quality service by designing structured interactions, providing uniform training to all service providers, and monitoring their behavior.

Service pseudorelationships are formed when customers identify with the organization rather than with a specific service provider and maintain a long-term relationship with the organization. Since customers interact with a different provider in the organization each time, they are not close with any individual service provider but are familiar with the organization's characteristics.

The criteria for classifying the service organization into one of the three groups are: the ability of the service provider and the customer to identify each other, their history of interactions, and their expectations regarding future interactions.[11]

Other classifications based on type of relationship between service provider and customer refer to a continuum between one-time transactions and continuing relationships. Service interactions therefore may be classified according to duration of the interaction, affective content of the interaction, and level of proximity among participants. This typology may be associated with Gutek's model, with brief, unemotional and public interactions defined as encounters, and continuous interactions that involve emotions and intimacy defined as relationships.[13] A similar classification[14] is based on the extent to which service providers interact with customers, type of interaction (face to face or telephone/other), and type of service outcome (standard or custom). The combinations of these variables result in eight types of service providers. The authors point out that the effect of service predisposition and job characteristics on customer service behavior may vary with the type of service provider.

Professional relationships and friendships

Analyzing the service interaction from the customer's viewpoint, it has been suggested that the more interactions between service provider and the customer, the greater the opportunity for the 'bond' between them to grow stronger and more personal (Coulter & Ligas, 2004).[15] As a result, the customer may develop a more enhanced view of the relationship, with the emergence of feelings of trust and commitment, in much the same way that they occur in personal friendships. The authors propose a classification scheme consisting of four distinct relationship types based on the customer's view of the relationship: professional relationships, casual acquaintances, personal acquaintances and friendships. These relationships range along a continuum of low to high professionalism. Professional relationships are described as instrumental, in the sense that the customer is focused on obtaining the service and functional benefits from the provider rather than on developing a personal contact. Casual acquaintanceship also revolve primarily around the functional aspects of the service provided, although the customer is willing to disclose personal information and might develop an emotional attachment to the service provider, while the exchange is less business-like and more informal. In the personal acquaintance category, besides the customer's willingness to provide personal information to the service provider and the development of an emotional attachment toward the provider, he/she is also interested in socializing with the service provider. Lastly, friendships are characterized by the customer's comfort in providing personal information, as well as his/her emotional and social attachment to the provider. The exchanges, while structured around the service, are more intimate, and the customer is interested in spending more time with the service provider. In this type of relationship the customer is open to socializing with the provider outside the service setting.[15]

Simple and complex interactions

Another salient characteristic of service organizations, in addition to the intangibility of services, is the complexity of the service.[16] The interaction between the customer and the service provider may be seen as an open system in which there is mutual influence between the organization and the customer segment of the environment. Accordingly, three classes of service organizations with different customer-service provider relationships have been identified:[16]

(1) Maintenance-interactive organizations, such as banks and insurance companies. These are characterized by a superficial relationship

between service providers and customers, in which the emphasis is on trust-building as a means to maintain customer loyalty. The interaction between the service provider and the customer is brief, distant and polite, and they exchange a relatively limited amount of information. The informational input of customers is highly important, thus the dependence of customers on service providers is low and both parties perceive little power disparity. Service providers engage in routine activities which generate an image of stability, and their major role is to ensure a smooth workflow. Customers display predictable behaviors, are usually loyal to the organization, and there is little uncertainty for the service providers.

(2) Task-interactive organizations, such as advertising agencies. These involve complex interactions that focus on the technical aspects of the service and the best way to accomplish the customer's goals. The parties exchange the information needed for task completion. Customers are knowledgeable about their goals but not about the techniques required to achieve them, while the service provider is an expert in the techniques. The information provided by the customers is not highly significant and therefore customers are dependent on service providers.

(3) Personal-interactive services, such as legal, medical and counseling services. These are organizations offering professional services to solve personal problems presented by customers to service providers, with interaction focusing on improving the customer's well-being. Customers have little knowledge of either the desirable goals or the means to achieve them and are therefore highly dependent on the service providers. The perceived power gap is especially large in this type of interaction and the customer is in a subordinate role (e.g., a teacher-student relationship). Service providers make complex decisions, operate with considerable autonomy in light of few guidelines, and engage in transformation of the information provided by customers into knowledge. In these organizations service providers may identify more with the customer and less with the organization because a central part of their role is to ensure the customer's welfare.

In addition, a series of interface variables affect the service interaction: information, which is the raw material with which service organizations work, and which is classified by quantity, quality and confidentiality; the nature of the decisions made by service providers; the time spent in the interaction; the customer's awareness of the nature of the problems they bring to the service interaction; the ease of replacing service providers; the perceived expertise of service providers; and service providers' commitment to the organization.[16]

Professional and non professional service jobs

Lastly, several classifications have focused on characteristics of the service provider's job. One such classification refers to the differences between the 'emotional proletariat' – the front-line service providers, and para-professionals engaged in interactive work.[8] This classification is based on the observation that industries produce two kinds of jobs: large numbers of low-skill low-pay jobs, and a smaller number of high-skill high-income jobs, with very few jobs that could be classified in the middle. As a result, service jobs fall into two broad categories: those likely to be production-line jobs, and those likely to be empowered jobs. The categories differ in level of responsibility, autonomy expected of workers, wages, benefits, job security and potential for advancement. Empowered service jobs are associated with full-time work and satisfactory wages and benefits, while production-line jobs offer none of these.[8] Paradoxically, service organizations are often dependent on customer-contact employees – often the lowest-paid members of the organization – for the organization's reputation and cash flow.[17] A somewhat similar distinction is based on the complexity of the service,[18] namely service characterized by low-complexity and a routine service process involving mostly call center employees; sales or a medium-complexity process defined as less predictable and relying on the skills of the sales people; and knowledge or a high-level complexity process characterized by a high degree of customization as employees with special expertise seek to identify and address the clients' highly diverse problems.

Notes

1 Berry, Leonard L. (1980). Services marketing is different. *Business*, 30, 24–33.
2 Zeithaml, V. A. & Bitner, M. J. (1996). *Service Marketing*. New York: McGraw-Hill.
3 Gronroos, C. (2001). *Service Management and Marketing: A Customer Relationship Management Approach*. Chichester: Wiley.
4 Bateson, J. & Hui, M. (1992). The ecological validity of photographic slides and videotapes in simulating the service setting. *Journal of Consumer Research*, 19, 271–282.
5 Schneider, B. & Bowen, D. E. (1995). *Winning the Service Game*. Boston: Harvard Business School Press.
6 Kasper, H., van Helsdingen, P. & De Vries, V. (1999). *Services Marketing Management: An International Perspective*. New York: John Wiley.

7   Bowen, J. & Ford, R. C. (2002). Managing service organizations: Does having a 'thing' make a difference? *Journal of Management*, 28, 447–469.

8   Macdonald, C. L. & Sirianni, C. (1996). The service society and the changing experience of work. In C. L. Macdonald & C. Sirianni (eds) *Working in the Service Society*. Philadelphia: Temple University Press.

9   Lovelock, C. H. (1983). Classifying services to gain strategic marketing insights. *Journal of Marketing*, 47, 9–21.

10 Gutek, B. (1995). *The Dynamics of Service: Reflections on the Changing Nature of Customer/Provider Interactions*. San Francisco: Jossey-Bass.

11 Gutek, B. A., Bhappu, A. D., Liao Troth, M. A. & Cherry, B. (1999). Distinguishing between service relationships and encounters. *Journal of Applied Psychology*, 84, 218–233.

12 Gutek, B. A., Cherry, B., Bhappu, A. D., Schneider, S. & Woolf, L. (2000). Features of service relationships and encounters. *Work and Occupations*, 27, 319–352.

13 Vilnai-Yavetz, I. & Rafaeli, A. (2003). Organizational interactions: A basic skeleton with spiritual tissue. In R. A. Giacalone & C. L. Jurkiewicz (eds), *Handbook of Workplace Spirituality and Organizational Performance*, pp. 76–93. Armonk, New York: Sharpe Publications.

14 Rogelberg, S. G., Barnes-Farrell, J. L. & Creamer, V. (1999). Customer service behavior: The interaction of service predisposition and job characteristics. *Journal of Business and Psychology*, 13, 421–435.

15 Coulter, R. & Ligas, M. (2004). A typology of customer-service provider relationships: The role of relational factors in classifying customers. *Journal of Services Marketing*, 18, 482–493.

16 Mills, P. & Margulies, N. (1980). Toward a core typology of service organizations. *Academy of Management Review*, 5, 255–265.

17 Weatherly, K. A. & Tansik, D. A. (1993). Tactics used by customer-contact workers: Effects of role stress, boundary spanning and control. *International Journal of Service Industry Management*, 4, 4–17.

18 Frenkel, S. J., Korczynski, M., Shire K. A. & Tarn, M. (1999). *On the Front Line: Organization of Work in the Information Economy*. Ithaca, NY: Cornell University Press.

Part I

Basic Processes in the Service Context

1

Pretending and Dissembling: The Act of Service

The chapter introduces the notion that service involves many elements found in the theater. Typically, service providers are encouraged by their organization to present a performance to the customers, who generally accept and approve of the artificial nature of the service situation. In the dramaturgical context, the service interaction is analyzed in terms of roles, with the service provider as an actor and the customer as audience. The norms underlying the development of the service process, which mold the parties' expectations and behaviors, are discussed in terms of the service script. The physical environment in which the interaction takes place is viewed as a theater set, meant to stimulate desired emotions and behaviors on the part of the audience.

A central theme in the service role is related to projecting emotions. Service organizations often convey specific rules to their employees regarding the emotions they are allowed or even required to display to customers, as well as the emotions they should avoid showing. Often, service providers engage in emotion regulation when the emotions they are required to display are inconsistent with their authentic inner emotions. The issue of emotion regulation in service, the causes of this significant job requirement and its effects on service providers are discussed.

Service interaction as theater

The drama metaphor, introduced to the field of service research by Grove and Fisk[1] (1983; later Grove, Fisk & Bitner, 1992)[2] provides an apt framework that conceptualizes the service encounter as theater. Since service is a process, these authors suggest, the theatrical elements coalesce during the duration of the service act to create a performance.

As in theater, coordination and consistency between the various elements is necessary since together they contribute to the reality of service, with the customer's experience dependent on the organization's skill in combining actor, audience and setting to produce a successful performance.

Additional similarities between the service and theater contexts are the transitory nature of the production and the reliance on human relationship between actor and audience.[3] Both in service and theater, no two performances are identical. Moreover, the human relationships are essential whether to recreating a reality or bringing fantasy to life. Thus, the perception of service encounters as theatrical in nature is most applicable for those services that involve face-to-face contact between service provider and customer.[2]

Service and the theater are also associated in terms of impression management.[4] According to impression management theory, interpersonal interaction takes place in two regions: backstage and front stage. The audience usually sees only the front stage, while the backstage is usually hidden. Backstage people can perform actions that if seen would foil the desired effect because backstage is where people prepare for the front stage appearance. The border between backstage and front stage is managed with the help of scripts that are used to save face and maintain a positive image. The front stage appearance affects the audience's willingness to accept the actor in a particular role, as demonstrated in research showing that men who perform service roles traditionally performed by women (e.g., nurses) report that customers have difficulty accepting them as legitimate performers of these roles.[5]

The use of the dramaturgical context to describe the service field serves the purpose of differentiating service from production and highlighting the role of the customer in the service process. An analysis of the drama metaphor in comparison with the factory metaphor which was previously applied to service is instructive.[6] The factory metaphor was widely used by early service researchers who wanted to differentiate the study of services from the study of production. It focused on operations that can be performed by interchangeable employees who are valued not as individuals but as contributors to the process and the final product. The factory metaphor is replete with such terms as inputs, processing, outputs and productivity. In contrast, the drama metaphor helps to conceptualize the elements of service delivery that differ from production, sees customers as an audience, and presents service strategies in terms of scripting and staging. While early research tried to remove the troublesome human customers from the factory, recent research attempts to integrate customer needs with the interests of the organization, viewing the role of metaphor in service as 'moving the drama into the factory' (Goodwin, 1996, p. 13).[6]

The model presented in the research by Grove and Fisk[1] (1983) and Grove, Fisk and Bitner (1992)[2] describes the following similarities between the components of the service encounter and theater: (1) service providers as actors (2) customers as audience (3) physical environment in which the service takes place as setting (4) the service enactment itself as performance. An addition theatrical element underlying the service interaction is the service script.[7,8] Each of these components is described below.

Service providers as actors

The drama metaphor has been found to be most appropriate when service quality is based on performance related to the service provider, who is trained by the organization to present a scene that customers will recognize as staged.[6] Customers are expected to assign credit to the organization and the service provider for taking the trouble to stage a performance. In other words, customers generally favor a staged performance: they take for granted that the service provider's behavior is artificial, and that he/she is being paid to act out certain service scripts.[4] The service providers themselves might also benefit from the artificial nature of their role: service providers sometimes distance themselves from the service role by acting, which allows them to attribute their behavior to their organizational role rather than to their 'real' self.[9] A waiter, for example might imagine that he is onstage performing a restaurant scene rather than in a real-world situation.

Every aspect of the service provider's appearance determines the service impression which molds the customers' evaluation of service and loyalty. However, the weight of these components in determining the customer's evaluation varies according to service content. The appearance and manner of the service provider in hair styling services for example, is the primary determinant of the image of the organization. However, customers of education or medicine services are mainly interested in the service provider's skill and dedication.[10,11]

The performance of service

The theatrical concept of performance refers to the set of activities that take place before an audience.[12] Like a play in a theater, service itself exists only during the time of its enactment on the front stage, whereas the planning and design occur backstage. The goal of the service organization is thus the same as that of a theater – to mount a performance that will create a favorable impression before an audience.[11] As in the theater, the performance of service fails if the audience feels that the presentation does not achieve its goal or if it perceives some misrepresentation, such as a service deception. Nevertheless, whereas in the theater the role of the actors is always prominent, the role of the service provider is varied and may be less visible. By way of example,[13] the customer might be unaware of the role of the service provider in the service process (e.g., cash machines); customers might be aware that the service process involves a person (e.g., a waitress in a restaurant); or the customer might be aware that enactment occurs specifically so that it can be observed (e.g., an open kitchen in a restaurant).

The dramaturgical metaphor has been found to be particularly appropriate in analyzing the performance of consultants, since the core feature of consultancy is creating and maintaining an illusion that will persuade clients of the consultant's effectiveness, in the same way that actors seek to create a 'theatrical reality'.[14] The intangibility of the consultancy role prevents customers from measuring service quality before they receive the service, so that they are basically asked to buy a promise of a certain level of quality. Consequently, intangibility impels consultants to use impression management prior to providing the service, namely manipulating the images, impressions and perceptions of their quality, convincing customers of their know-how, and conveying that they have something of value to offer – specifically that they have the solution needed to attain the customer's goals.

Impression management continues to be important throughout the provision of the service, as the interpersonal interaction with customers largely determines the outcome of a consultancy service. In order to create the impression of qualitative service, consultants engage in active management of the interaction with customers. An example of such impression management is embodied in the role of executive search consultants, who function as directors and stage managers. Since customers evaluate the value of an executive search service according to the quality of the candidates presented to them, consultants seek to enhance the impression of their service by managing the meeting between client and candidates. In the dramaturgical metaphor, the work of executive search consultants is a 'backstage' activity in which the interaction process with clients is managed indirectly. The crucial skill of these consultants is to manage the steps that lead to the final interview, so that candidates are able to present themselves effectively in terms of the role demanded by the organizational script.[14] Thus, the first task of the consultant is to become familiar with the organizational script so that it can be performed effectively by the candidates at the interview. Consultants conduct a detailed study of the organization and the vacant job and then prepare the candidates for the interview. In this way, consultants and candidates work together to create an illusion by playing the role according to the demands of the organizational script. Paradoxically, consultants achieve an appearance of spontaneity and naturalness through careful 'backstage' direction and stage management applied to the candidates' verbal and physical actions as well as to their appearance. Executive search consultants therefore have two key tasks: first to 'read' the organizational script and second to prepare the candidates so that their appearance and performance comply with the demands of the script.

The service setting

The setting component in the theater metaphor refers to the physical environment in which the play occurs, and to its staging.[12] In the theater, the setting enhances the plot presented to the audience; in the service situation, the setting serves a similar function – it consists of elements such as space and furnishings that shape the service reality and are designed to create a specific desired impression on customers.[11] The theater model is most relevant for understanding customer experiences in 'servicescapes' (Bitner, 1992),[15] or man-made physical settings such as restaurants, airlines, banks or hair salons, which are physically complex and are the scene of both customer and employee actions.[10]

Retail settings also include elements of theater that are incorporated into store design and merchandise presentation.[16] Retail managers attempt to create exciting environments that involve opportunities for audience participation and interaction and are presented as a 'fun' experience involving spectacle and excitement. The theater metaphor has been adopted by retailers as a way of creating new consumer interest in stores and merchandise.

Customers as audience

The importance of the audience – or customers – in the realm of service performance results from the inseparability of production and consumption that is characteristic of most services. The customers often affect the service delivery and outcome through their behaviors, whether they are passive or active in the process.[10] Yet, the role of the audience is especially important when customers are instrumental in determining the service outcome, e.g., participants in a weight-loss program or customers of psychological services.[11]

Perception of performance

As in the gradual comprehension of the theme in a play in the theater, which develops over time as the plot unfolds, the comprehension and evaluation of service emerges over time.[11] In both cases the audience evaluates performance based on subjective and often affective responses.[6]

In the retail setting customer roles differ according to the purpose of the performance: in some cases the setting is formal, with a deliberate attempt to create distance between the service providers, the performance and the audience. In other cases there is little attempt to disguise that the audience is present at a performance in a kind of theater – a retail environment – with customers having the opportunity on-site to be critical of the merchandise and the way it is presented. In yet other cases customers are bombarded with stimuli designed to stimulate various levels of physiological response. In other cases customers perform a role associated with theater of the absurd, namely their personal interpretation of the merchandise counts most. In such a situation there is no right or wrong way to judge the merchandise; it depends entirely on the customer's prior knowledge and experience.[16]

Participation in the performance

Another similarity between theater and service is that the input of the audience, or the participation of the customer, affects the performance.[11,13] A key aspect of customer participation in service is the passive-active dimension. Service encounters may be classified as 'producer-paced performances' when the service provider is the more active performer, and as 'customer-paced' performances when the customer is the more active.[13] In the most passive role, the customer contributes to the production of a performance simply by showing up. In such a role, customers are treated as a managed component of service delivery who support the script, and are referred to as an 'audience' rather than as 'actors'.[17] In a more active role, for example in financial services, the customer functions as both audience and co-performer. In its most active form, for example in wedding organization services, the customer's role is as director of the production and as performer.[13]

Active customer participation in the performance is acknowledged as creating positive experiences by enabling customers to take part in the drama.[17] Customers play an increasingly active role in service encounters, with many service organizations implementing a participatory theater paradigm that offers opportunities for consumers to interact and take part in the service experience.[18] Based on such a participatory theater concept, customers may be engaged in different aspects of the theater production. A customer may be a lead actor (playing a central role in the consumption of the service) or a director (providing direction for how the consumption process is to proceed).

Roles in the service encounter

According to Goffman (1959),[19] behavior in social situations is strongly guided by the norms or role expectations defining how people should behave in each interaction and reflected as well in the reactions of others present in the situation. Role expectations have been described as the privileges, duties and obligations accompanying social positions.[7] Since each role player's behavior is dependent on the behavior of those in complementary roles, each party must be sensitive to the role behavior of the other and must be able to predict the behavior of others in order to gauge his/her own behavior. Each participant in a social situation, therefore attempts to identify the other's role early in the interaction to facilitate prediction and to adjust his/her personal behavior accordingly. In this sense, the early stages of the encounter are more important to the success of the interaction than later stages.

In service encounters, role expectations which form the basis for these predictions are often highly defined in that the service interaction is conducted with a specific purpose that is agreed upon by the participants. In light of this agreement, the interaction follows ritualized behavior patterns. Each party plays a role that reflects a learned set of behaviors appropriate for the situation.[7] The social exchange which occurs between the participants is perceived as demonstrating certain patterns that are determined to a large extent by role expectations.[7,20]

The highly defined nature of the roles in the service encounter implies that while specific aspects of the roles may be determined by the participants in each particular interaction, basically, any customer can go to any service provider in a defined role (e.g., a doctor) with the assumption that they will be able to jointly engage in a familiar social exchange (e.g., examination, questions etc.). The mutual assumption that the other is prepared for such exchanges constitutes the motivation for participants to enter into the encounter in the first place.[21]

Role expectations have different functions at different stages of the service process.[20] In the pre-service stage, both the service provider and the customer have specific role expectations. During service, these expectations determine the role performance of both parties although service providers are expected to satisfy additional role expectations of customers related to dealing with unexpected customer problems that might emerge.[22] In the post-service stage, customers evaluate the degree to which their expectations were met, namely the extent of role fulfillment/discrepancy.[20] Furthermore, the enactment of roles in a service encounter largely determines future interactions. The appropriateness of the behavior displayed in the current service encounter is related to the likelihood of success in future service encounters.[20]

The evaluation of service roles, however, may result in ambiguity.[7] The evaluation of the appropriateness of the service provider's behavior is determined by management, co-workers and customers. Service providers attempt to adjust to the feedback received from all these components of the audience, but if they receive contradictory feedback they experience role ambiguity.

Another potential source of ambiguity, for service providers as well as customers, relates to the degree to which the players in the service encounter share a common definition of service roles. The service provider and the customer have complementary roles which are defined during the initial encounter and sustained throughout subsequent service encounters. The outcome of role assignment affects the interaction: each partner, in identifying his/her primary role, implicitly defines the complementary role of the other. Problems arise when there are role discrepancies or inconsistencies in the parties' expectations which may be exhibited in one of two ways: (1) The employee's perceptions of job duties or qualifications differ from the customer's expectations of these duties or (2) The customer's conception of the customer role differs from the employee's notion of this role. By contrast, congruent role expectations enhance predictability, decrease the effort that must be expended to complete the service transaction, and increase both parties' satisfaction with the service encounter.[7]

The service script

Cognitive scripts enhance the comprehension of situations and help predict the sequence of behaviors in interpersonal interactions. Scripts reflect the individual's learned or imagined conception of behavior and generate expectations that function both as behavioral guides (by providing information about one's own expected behavior) and as norms for the evaluation of the expected complementary behavior of others. Expectations may vary over time as a script becomes redefined, though acceptance of a new script is facilitated by integration with an old one. A strong script is a structure that clearly defines appropriate sequences of role behaviors in a particular context.[7]

In reviewing the literature, a distinction may be found between a basic type of interpersonal interaction, and a more extensive type, or between a 'business' or a 'professional' script and an 'interpersonal relations' or 'personal' script.[8] Applying this distinction to the service context, results in a differentiation between two components of the service script: the 'skeleton' and the 'tissue'. The skeleton of an interaction is the foundation, which contains the content essential in service interactions and which is taken for granted by the parties. The second aspect of the script, the tissue, consists of social interactions which may spin off from essential behaviors called for in the basic script. The tissue is an informal script which adds spiritual qualities to the service interaction and affects the quality of the experience of the parties. Both skeleton and tissue behaviors are important to service interactions. The skeleton directly addresses organizational goals and tasks, while the tissue indirectly promotes these goals by affecting service providers' and customers' emotions, satisfaction, commitment and citizenship behaviors.

Service providers have been found to need flexible scripts in order to respond effectively, because a rigid script may result in a non-fulfillment of the customer's expectations.[23] However, the more flexible the script, the more ambiguous the role, and consequently the more anxious the service provider might become. Consequently, some service providers may project artificiality, mouthing words dictated by a service script as theater actors. Empowerment is therefore necessary to enable service providers to adapt a script or invent a new script according to the demands of the situation.

Ultimately, the relative importance of the core of the service script and its additional parts depends on the type of the service.[7] Parties who encounter each other in familiar situations often interact mindlessly with little conscious attention. This is true for most routine service encounters which take place in an almost automatic style with a minimum of cognitive activity. As long as the structure of the service script is followed, the encounter is characterized by mindlessness. It is only when the experience somehow deviates from the service script that the participants are mindful of the event because a departure from expected role behavior requires active processing. In simple interactions, the important characteristics of the service are consistency, speed and fulfillment of formal role expectations. In a more complicated encounter, the informal components and the personal touch become more important.

Table 1.1   Dramaturgical concepts and their meaning in the service context

Dramaturgical concepts	Meaning in the service context
Actors	Usually the service provider, sometimes the customers as well
Audience	Customers
Performance	The behaviors of the service provider within the service interaction
Setting	The physical aspects of service
Backstage	The part of the service organization which the customer does not encounter
Front stage	The part of the service organization which the customer encounters
Roles	The behaviors that are expected of both the service provider and the customer within the service interaction
Script	Expectations regarding the progress of the service process

Table 1.1 summarizes the applications of the dramaturgical concepts to the service context.

Enacting emotions

Given that service organizations direct and control the way employees present themselves to customers, a key component of the work performed by many service providers has become the presentation of emotions that are specified by their organizations.[24] The psychological processes necessary to manage organizationally desired emotions as part of one's job are defined as emotional work or emotional labor. Hochschild (1983),[24] who introduced the term, defined it as the 'management of feeling to create a publicly observable facial and bodily display' (p. 7). Accordingly, jobs involving emotional labor are characterized by (1) voice or face-to-face contact with customers; (2) the requirement to elicit a certain emotional state in customers; and (3) opportunities for the employer to control the emotional activities of the employee.[24] The public display of emotions as part of the job is considered a form of labor because it requires effort, planning, anticipation and adjustment to situational factors.

Several other conceptualizations of emotional labor have been formulated (see Grandey, 2000,[25] Zapf 2002, for reviews).[26] While there is some ambiguity regarding the concept, all the research shares the underlying assumption that emotional labor involves managing the display of emotions, regardless of whether they reflect true internal feelings.[25,27] Generally, theoretical treatments of emotional labor involve the themes of internal states, internal processes and external behavioral displays, albeit with differences in focus. A focus on behavior rather than on the presumed emotions underlying behavior[28] define emotional labor as 'the act of displaying appropriate emotions' (p. 90) and a form of impression management reflected in the employees' attempt to create a certain social perception of themselves as well as a certain interpersonal climate. A focus on the underlying behavior,[29] by contrast, defines emotional labor as 'the effort, planning, and control needed to express organizationally desired emotion during interpersonal transactions' (Morris & Feldman, 1996, p. 987), based on the assumption that even in situations of congruence between the employee's true emotion and the displayed emotion, employees still invest effort in expressing these emotions. The notion of emotional labor as a process (Grandey, 2000)[25] defines such labor as 'the process of regulating both feelings and expressions for the organizational goals' (p. 98) or as 'the psychological processes necessary to regulate organizationally desired emotions' (Zapf, 2002, p. 239).[26]

The confusing nature of the definitions of emotional labor may be addressed by locating the similarities across conceptualizations.[25] Despite different perspectives, different definitions, and foci on different outcomes, all the conceptualizations have a single underlying theme: individuals can regulate their emotional expressions at work in order to meet the display rules stated by the organization. Rather than being in opposition, the varying theoretical perspectives may be viewed as complementary.[27]

Although the display of emotions as an organizational requirement is not limited to the service context, emotional labor is especially relevant to service jobs where social interactions with customers are a significant part of the work. Expressing appropriate emotions during service interactions is a job demand for many employees in the service industry.[30] Several characteristics of service have been shown to make the service provider's emotional expressions especially important:[28] service providers represent the organization to customers; their interactions with customers are often unpredictable and have a dynamic quality; and the services provided to customers are intangible, thus making the service provider's behavior more influential.

The presentation of emotions through 'deep acting' and 'surface acting'

Hochschild (1983)[24] differentiated between two processes that underlie emotional labor: deep acting and surface acting (see Figure 1.1). Deep acting may be divided into passive and active acting. Passive deep acting takes place when employees spontaneously feel what they are required to feel, although even when employees display their true feelings, effort is still involved in the display.[24] In active deep acting, individuals try to influence what they feel in order to 'become' the role they are asked to display.[24] This can be achieved in two ways: (1) exhorting feeling, reflected in the employee's attempts to evoke or suppress an emotion and (2) trained imagination, reflected in the active stimulation of thoughts, images and memories to produce the associated emotion. In much the same way that actors deliberately 'psyche themselves' for a role, service providers actively psyche themselves into experiencing the desired emotion. In this type of emotional labor, internal emotions are regulated in addition to the external emotional display. The intent of the service provider in deep acting is to seem authentic to the audience.[31] Such acting has been described as 'faking in good faith'[32] (Rafaeli & Sutton, 1987, p. 32).

Surface acting means that employees try to manage their displayed emotions in order to comply with organizational display rules, while their inner feelings remain unchanged.[24] Surface acting involves simulating or faking emotions that are not actually experienced, through verbal and nonverbal behaviors such as facial expressions, gestures and voice tone. Such acting performed by employees in order to keep their jobs rather than to help the customer or contribute to the organization[31] has been described as 'faking in bad faith' (Rafaeli & Sutton, 1987, p. 32).[32] Two types of surface acting have been identified.[28] One takes place when the service provider is truly concerned about the welfare of the customers, but a discrepancy occurs between felt and displayed emotion because various factors prevent service providers from feeling the emotions they display. The other type of surface acting occurs when the service provider is not concerned with the welfare of his/her customers and expresses emotions in a mechanical manner.

Surface acting may be desirable to organizations who want customers to always see the appropriate emotional expressions, even when the service provider feels differently. However, such acting may be a problematic strategy when customers expect more than superficial emotions. Furthermore, while faking emotions may be relatively easy for employees in highly standardized situations, in more complicated or unpredictable situations, the employee's true emotions may be unintentionally revealed to customers.[26]

Grandey (2000)[25] developed a model that describes how employees use emotion regulation processes to accomplish emotional labor, positing two main types of emotion regulation involved in emotional labor: antecedent-focused and response-focused regulation. These are similar to the concepts of deep and surface acting, respectively. Antecedent-focused regulation is related to the modification of a person's perception of a situation. The two main techniques accomplishing this are attention deployment and cognitive change. Attention deployment involves changing the focus of one's thoughts to things that induce the required emotions. Cognitive change involves evaluating situations in a different way in order to alter the emotions they induce. Response-focused regulation relates to the regulation of emotional responses by modulating reactions to situations, namely faking the intensity of the displayed emotion or faking the emotion entirely. In this emotion management technique, employees work to display more emotion than they feel, or to suppress true feelings and show acceptable emotional displays. This emotional regulation technique involves modifying the emotional display rather than internal feelings, as in deep acting.[25]

The extent to which individuals generally use deep acting and surface acting was found to be mirrored by the extent to which they used

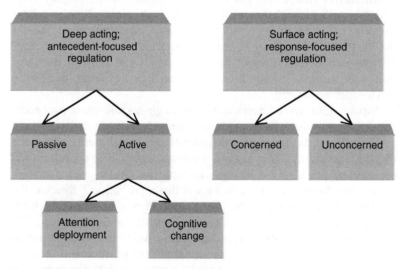

Figure 1.1 Deep acting and surface acting

'perspective taking' (antecedent-focused regulation) and faking emotions (response-focused regulation).[33]

Antecedents of emotional labor

Two types of factors affect service providers' displayed emotions: (1) societal, occupational and organizational norms, and (2) service provider's characteristics and inner feelings on the job.[34]

Organizational variables

Display rules. The service provider's emotions are managed in response to display rules for the job, namely rules about the appropriate display of emotion which may be stated explicitly in selection and training materials or learned by observation of coworker behavior. Many work roles have display rules regarding the emotions that employees should show in public.[24] Display rules have been conceptualized not only as role requirements of particular occupational groups but also as interpersonal job demands. In the service context, interpersonal job demands focus on effective interactions with customers and control of the interaction between the service provider and the customer.[35]

Organizational display rules are generally a function of societal, occupational or organizational norms.[34] Societal norms which are reflected in customer expectations provide general rules regarding the type of emotions that should be expressed during service encounters. Occupational communities and organizations provide more specific display rules which are often consistent with societal norms. Generally, the greater the power of the service provider, occupation, or organization *vis-à-vis* the customer, the greater the latitude to modify the degree of compliance with societal norms.[28] Moreover, due to the dynamic nature of many encounters, specific rules are dictated by the demands of each service interaction.[36,37]

Display rules are communicated through socialization processes. Service organizations for example, may provide training, use behavioral modification techniques, provide rewards and punishments, and teach display rules informally by means of role models.[32] These organizational socialization processes are effective, as employees tend to engage in emotional labor to meet the expectations of the organization.[25] Specifically, the perception of display rules about emotion was found to be related to emotional effort[38] as well as to surface acting and deep acting.[25,39] Moreover, the commitment to emotional display rules was found to moderate the relationships of emotional display rule perceptions with surface acting, deep acting, and positive affective delivery at work.[40]

Compliance with display rules can be seen as role internalization, namely the extent to which employees incorporate organizational demands in their identity. Jobs requiring emotional labor may be characterized by pressure to internalize the role demands.[28] In such jobs, failure to internalize organizational display rules may lead to poor performance and even job loss.[41]

In analyzing the effect of display rules on displayed emotions, control theory has been applied to the area of emotional labor.[42] In terms of control theory, a display rule is the standard against which emotional displays are compared. Should there be a discrepancy between the perception of a display rule and an emotional display, the discrepancy can be reduced by either behavioral change or cognitive change. In the case of behavioral change, people use emotion regulation strategies to align their emotional displays with display rules; cognitive change is reflected in replacing the display standard with a different standard for emotional expression, one that is consistent with the displayed emotion. After each attempt to reduce the discrepancy, the individual re-evaluates his/her emotional display. Because individuals have a great deal of experience with managing their emotional displays, the process may become automatic, operating with little conscious awareness. Diefendorff and Gosserand (2003)[42] review research which shows that display rule perceptions may be influenced by many factors, including occupational norms, task demands, social information at work, individual differences in personality, and 'transaction-defining cues' of particular situations. They maintain that considering the many potential sources of influence, organizations should clearly specify the desired emotional displays in order to have the employees express particular emotions at work. If display rules are vague, many different emotional displays may be judged as appropriate, resulting in a great deal of variability in emotional expression. Specific display rules clarify the standard and increase the likelihood that employees will display what the organization wants.

Autonomy. Having the organization control one's emotional state is unpleasant.[24] Therefore, several studies have examined whether job autonomy minimizes the stress involved in emotion regulation.[25,26,41] Employees with high job control were found to have the option of deciding whether or not to follow a display rule in a given situation, and to adapt the emotional display to their personality. Furthermore, employees with more autonomy might refuse to comply with organizational display rules when those rules conflict with their own genuinely felt emotions.[29] This same research shows that job autonomy was negatively related to emotional dissonance and emotional exhaustion and positively related to job satisfaction. In a similar vein, employees who reported high autonomy also expressed lower emotional exhaustion regardless of required emotional labor.[43] A qualitative study on supermarket clerks' performance found that the presence or absence of control over one's emotional display was a significant aspect of emotional labor.[44] In a study simulating service interactions,[45] display rules asking service providers to hide frustration were found to be related to emotional exhaustion and reduced performance. This was related to surface acting but not to deep acting. On the other hand, display autonomy, that is allowing employees to 'be themselves' while maintaining basic rules of courtesy, was not accompanied by such negative results.

Social support.   Social support has a direct positive effect on health; an indirect effect on health through the reduction of job stressors; and a moderating effect on the relationship between stressors and strains. Employees may need less surface acting to display positive emotions if they feel positive about the social environment at work. When the interpersonal relationships are positive, the employee may genuinely feel the emotions that are expected in a service environment.[25] Social support in service jobs was found to buffer the effect of job stressors.[46,47]

Role demands.   The frequency, attentiveness and variety of displayed emotions are viewed as role demands relating to the tasks assigned by the organization[48] and are therefore presented here as antecedents of emotional labor[49] (see Figure 1.2.).

The frequency of emotional display is determined by the organization's demands for regulated displays of emotion, which in turn is determined by the extent to which the job requires socially appropriate emotional displays in order to establish affective bonds of affinity, trust, and respect with customers.[29,50] Hochschild (1983)[24] warned that too frequent emotional displays may overtax the employees and lead to alienation and exhaustion.

Attentiveness to display rules requires psychological energy and physical effort and hence more 'labor'. Attentiveness to display rules consists of both the duration and the intensity of emotional display.

The longer the duration of an interaction with customers, the greater the emotional labor which will be required.[41] This is so because longer interactions may become less scripted and require greater attention, effort and emotional stamina.[24] Furthermore, as the interaction unfolds, more personal information about the customer becomes available. This may make it harder for employees to avoid showing 'real' feelings which violate organizational norms, especially since in longer inter-actions more intense emotions must be displayed.[29,41] By contrast, if an interaction is brief, it is likely to be highly scripted and the emotions usually of low intensity. Emotion work is thus more effortful in inter-actions of long duration.[25]

Emotional intensity refers to how strongly an emotion is expressed. It may be difficult to fake intensity, and therefore jobs that require dis-playing intense emotions involve more effort. Furthermore, the intensity of emotional display was found to be positively related to its duration. Short displays of emotion are more likely to be scripted and require little emotional intensity, while longer displays are more likely to be unscripted and require the display of more intense emotions.[29]

Emotional variety is another role demand. The greater the variety of emotions to be displayed, the greater the emotional labor required on the part of the service provider. The need to alter the kinds of emotions displayed to fit specific situational contexts requires psychological energy because service providers must employ active planning and conscious monitoring of their behavior.[29]

Given the dynamic nature of many service encounters, different sets of occupational and organizational display rules are sometimes utilized in response to changing demands in a given transaction.[37] Emotional variety may be reflected in emotional displays that may range from pos-itive to neutral to negative. Positive emotional displays aim to generate a relationship of empathy between service providers and customers; emo-tional neutrality is used to convey dispassionate authority and status; and negative emotions such as anger or hostility may be displayed to intimidate or subdue customers.[50] Some jobs require frequent changes of displayed emotions. Teachers for example, may convey positive emo-tions to build enthusiasm, negative emotions to reinforce discipline, and neutral emotions to demonstrate fairness and professionalism.[29]

Another categorization of emotions refers to emotional work require-ments that are integrative, differentiating or masking.[50] Most often service providers are expected to display integrative emotions such as cheerfulness and sympathy. In some types of jobs, however, such as bill collectors or bouncers, they are expected to portray differentiating emo-tions such as fear or anger.[37] The masking type of emotion describes jobs in which controlled emotions are called for, such as therapists or judges.[25]

The variety of emotional display is determined not only by organiza-tional display rules but also by the service provider's sensitivity and

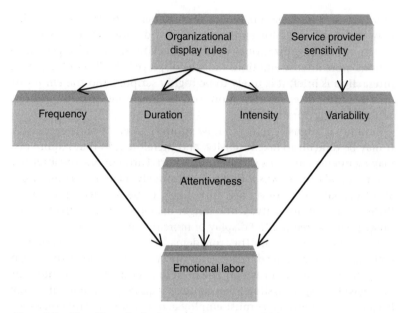

Figure 1.2   The effect of role demands on emotional labor

social perceptions. In interacting with customers, service providers may use the information provided by the emotional display of the customer to guide their own response.[51] Sensitivity requirements, which add to the effort invested in emotional labor, are high when knowledge of the customer's emotions is a prerequisite for the employee's own emotional reaction and low when the interactions are scripted and enable the service provider to display organizationally designated emotions independent from customers' emotions.[30]

Situational variables.   Time pressure, emotional events and emotional transactions are occupational factors that affect service providers' display of emotions. Time pressure is a job factor that results from having an insufficient amount of time to complete a job and is often accompanied by negative emotions such as fear of not meeting the organizational standards or anger at the lacking of organizational support. Such emotions may prevent the display by service providers of positive emotions to customers. Additionally, service employees under time pressure must focus on completing the task of serving the customer (e.g., offering different options), leaving limited resources for the task of conveying positive emotions.[52,53]

Time pressure in service is often related to busyness which is consistently found to be negatively related to the display of positive emotion by service employees.[54,55,56,57] Busy and crowded environments may cause stress in service providers, which might then be communicated to customers through verbal and nonverbal channels. A study conducted in convenience stores (Sutton and Rafaeli, 1988)[57] found clear organizational norms during busy times that encourage service providers to view customers as 'inputs for rapid processing' (p. 474). As a result of busyness, employees were less likely to offer greetings, eye contact, smiles and thanks to customers. Moreover, customers too were less likely to display positive emotions in busy stores.[57] Sutton and Rafaeli[57] suggested two explanations for the function of such behavioral norms during busy times. First, such norms help maintain efficiency, for although behaviors like greeting and smiling, etc. take only a small amount of extra time from the service provider, displaying these behaviors can encourage customers to prolong the interaction. Second, courteous service providers appear to customers to be slower, even if they are not, thereby reducing perceived efficiency. The fact that service providers' interpersonal behaviors were indeed affected by busyness was reflected in their completely different behaviors during slow times: service providers were more likely to greet, smile, and establish eye contact with customers when there were not many customers in the store.[57]

Emotional organizational events are acute events at work which affect employees' emotions. The source of the affective events may be the customer, co-workers, a supervisor, or personal situations. Research suggests[25] that an event which results in emotions that deviate from the organizational display rules, may generate emotional regulation. When an event interferes with the employees' goals, including the goal to express and induce positive emotions, it is appraised by the worker negatively and seen as stressful, and emotional regulation is applied to comply with the organizational display rules. The source of the event may influence the amount of self-regulation. Display rules for example, may be more explicit for interactions with customers than with colleagues, and therefore when the event is related to a customer, more emotional regulation is needed. However, all negative emotional events demand some effort to regulate emotions, and may have a cumulative effect on stress and well-being.[25]

Inevitably, emotions expressed by service employees are affected by the emotions customers express through both verbal and nonverbal cues.[32]

Service providers and customers are involved in continuous emotional transactions during the service interaction and both parties use each other's reactions to reach agreement about which display rules are appropriate to the interaction. Thus, the emotions displayed by the service provider may be modified during the interaction, because the reactions of the customer serve as a feedback that influences subsequent displayed emotions. These cycles of displayed emotions, reaction and readjustment may reinforce or weaken the effects of organizational display rules.

While negative encounters with customers are discussed prominently in the literature on emotional labor, many service jobs consist of positive encounters.[38] When customers display positive emotions, service providers express what they feel naturally and therefore experience less emotive dissonance and effort. Kruml and Geddes (2000)[38] found that the more attached service providers feel to customers, the more likely they are to express their true feelings and/or attempt to truly feel the positive emotions they display.

Yet, other research[56] showed that service providers expressed positive emotions toward demanding customers, namely customers who required a prolonged and complex response. These authors suggested that conveying positive emotions helps service providers control the interaction with customers. Such control is especially important with demanding customers as the price of loss of control is high in terms of further demands. Similarly, Morris and Feldman (1997)[41] suggested that in dealing with more powerful customers, service providers restrict the range of emotions they display to positive emotions.

Individual variables: service providers' characteristics and inner feelings on the job

Gender.   The majority of service jobs are performed by women, and as such gender becomes an issue in emotional labor. Social norms dictate that women are expected to focus on feeling more than men.[24] Even in the same occupation, women often are expected to perform more emotional labor than men.[29] Consequently, women engage in more emotion management situations in their everyday lives;[24,50] are more responsive than men to display rules that call on them to manage emotions at work;[38] and are more likely to be better at managing their emotions.[58]

Age.   Hochschild (1983)[24] suggested that age may be expected to be positively related to the management of emotions. Older employees have broader emotional memories from which to draw than younger employees, and are therefore better able to perform deep acting. Similarly, older workers are more skilled at controlling their emotions and 'putting on a face' even when they are unable to invoke the appropriate feelings, and are therefore better at surface acting than younger workers. Hochschild (1983)[24] also found that older workers speak more openly about their emotional labor. With this older service providers have reported more effort and emotional dissonance than younger workers.[38]

Emotional competence.   Emotional expressivity and emotional intelligence have been positively related to emotional work in that people with a high level of expressivity and emotional intelligence are better able to comply with display rules and require less emotion regulation.[25] This prediction is supported in a study[33] showing that emotional intelligence is related to some aspects of regulation.

Emotional competence – indicated by perspective taking, regulation of others' affect, and affective self-regulation, is an important personal resource in service work.[53] Perspective taking, which reflects a person's ability to understand the psychological state of others, is an important skill for service providers because they have to understand the feelings of customers in order to choose the optimal strategy for dealing with them. Once the customer's affective state is understood, the service provider can develop a strategy to regulate customer affect in the desired direction and act upon it. Self-regulation is another important skill for service providers because it helps them to deal with their own affective state, for example when they are confronted by angry or irritated customers. Employees with high emotional competence have the ability to process emotional information quickly and accurately and respond efficiently by adapting their own emotional state to what is required in the situation, thus reducing their chances of experiencing emotional dissonance. Furthermore, service providers with high emotional competence elicit more positive reactions from customers, which in turn generate true positive emotions.[32,59]

Emotional competence functions as a psychological resource in that it supports employees in their efforts to cope with the emotional demands of their work as well as with situations of emotional dissonance. Such coping involves the simultaneous processes of regulating customers' emotions and their own emotions. When confronted with heightened emotional demands, service providers with a high level of emotional competence have been found to experience less emotional dissonance than employees low in emotional competence.[53] Emotional competence also moderates the relationship between time pressure and emotional dissonance. Emotionally competent service providers deal effectively with negative emotions resulting from time pressure by saving resources to be used for the appropriate emotional display and by regulating customers' emotions, thereby making the service interaction smoother and facilitating the fulfillment of customer requests.[53]

Emphatic ability in the context of emotional labor may be conveyed in different ways by service providers. Some service providers respond with emotional contagion, displaying emotional response parallel to that of the customer and 'feeling with' the customer.[60] Such service providers perceive themselves as expressing their true feelings or as trying to feel the appropriate emotions. Other service providers respond to customers with empathic concern: their feelings are not parallel to those of the customer, but they 'feel for' the customer, as in active deep acting. This response is consistent with a strong concern for one's customers.[38]

The outcomes of emotional labor

Negative outcomes

The requirement to perform emotional labor can be viewed as an occupational stressor which involves lack of employee control over their emotional displays and a denial of their true selves.[61] Consequently, emotional labor may lead to familiar stress reactions such as burnout, as well as to more unique outcomes such as emotional dissonance and alienation from self.

Burnout.   Emotional labor is related to burnout and job stress because of the unpleasantness and the effort it often involves.[24] Emotional exhaustion, which is considered the major indicator of burnout, has been found to be related to emotional dissonance[41,46] as well as to surface acting.[25,39] A comparison of service providers and employees in other occupations[48] was made in the context of two perspectives of emotional labor as predictors of burnout: job-focused emotional labor, namely work demands regarding emotional expression (e.g., frequency of interactions with customers, or job expectations to express certain emotions), and employee-focused emotional labor, namely regulation of feelings and emotional expression (e.g., emotional dissonance). The findings were that service providers face higher emotional demands than employees in other jobs and that the requirement to hide negative feelings was related to emotional exhaustion. With this, emotional requirements were positively related to a sense of accomplishment.

Various explanations have been offered for the relationship of emotional labor with stress and burnout as follows:

(1) Emotional labor may require the suppression of negative emotions, an effort that is related to the sympathetic activation of the cardiovascular system. This physiological activity results in a weakening of the immune system (see Grandey, 2000[25] and Zapf & Holtz, 2006[30] for reviews).

(2) Emotion regulation requires cognitive resources and energy.[25,45,62] Surface acting or response-focused emotion regulation in particular may drain cognitive and motivational resources as it requires continual monitoring and modification of expression.[63]

(3) The threat to one's authenticity and the feelings of estrangement from the self that may be caused by emotional labor may lead to psychological strain.[24,61,62]

(4) Emotional dissonance may be related to emotional exhaustion because it is an indicator of unpleasant and stressful interactions with customers. Service providers are often expected to respond with positive emotions to customers who are aggressive, behave in an uncivil manner or present unrealistic expectations. Such customer behaviors were found to be related to service providers' stress.[64] Emotional dissonance may also lead to detachment from other people's feelings, which may be related to depersonalization.[30]

(5) Emotional labor in response to specific display rules may be highly related to stress because discrepancies are more likely with regard to specified display rules than with general rules. Conforming to specific display rules is more effortful, requires closer monitoring of one's emotional displays, and may result in higher levels of stress and burnout. In addition, in the case of a discrepancy between true internal emotions and display rules, the external control of emotional expression may lead to decreased intrinsic motivation for the job.

Notably, the effect of emotional labor on the service providers' well-being may be determined by their identification with the service role.[28] If a service provider's expectations do not conform to the expectations involved in the service role, then emotional labor will have a negative impact on his/her well-being because it is an 'identity-threatening' behavior. In contrast, when service providers identify with their professional role, fulfilling role expectations by performing emotional labor will have a positive effect on their psychological well-being. For these employees emotional labor provides an opportunity to 'act out' their role identification, that is, to express their loyalty to the identity. Perceived affective delivery among service providers has been found to be negatively related to surface acting but positively related to deep acting. Furthermore, surface acting, but not deep acting, was found to be related to stress.[31]

Since emotion regulation requires the expenditure of a limited pool of cognitive and energy resources, a sense of control may provide affective, motivational and cognitive resources and have a buffering effect against threatening or draining situations as suggested by Grandey, Fisk and Steiner (2005).[63] They found that high job autonomy buffered the relationship of emotion regulation with emotional exhaustion. In addition, in examining the effect of cross-cultural differences in attitudes toward emotional regulation on burnout and satisfaction, assuming that cultural differences would affect employee control over emotional expression, the authors found that the relationship was stronger when the culture has strong norms about regulating emotions to fulfill institutional roles and standards.

Emotional dissonance.[65]   Emotional dissonance is caused by a discrepancy or clash between the emotions expressed by employees in response to organizational display rules and their inner or 'real' emotions.[24] Such a discrepancy exists when service providers do not feel the emotion they are required to display, or when they are required to suppress the negative emotions they experience and to display a neutral or a positive emotion. Emotional dissonance may originate from 'faking in good faith' when the employee accepts the underlying display rule, or from 'faking in bad faith' when the display rule is not accepted.[32]

The display of organizationally desired emotions becomes more demanding when it requires the control of one's true emotions. Situations that generate a conflict between genuinely felt emotions and organizationally desired emotions require control, skill and attentive action,[41] as well as effort invested in the active stimulation of thoughts, images, and memories.[28] Emotional dissonance creates an unstable psychological state and may lead to negative outcomes such as estrangement between self and one's true feelings, job-related stress, and emotional exhaustion.[27]

The degree of experienced emotional dissonance may depend on the type of service provider-customer interaction. Service roles involving face-to-face interaction with customers require greater control of emotional expression than roles involving telephone contact, since both vocal and facial expressions must be regulated.[29] Service providers who are out of sight of their customers have more ways of expressing felt emotion without violating organizational display rules and therefore experience less emotional dissonance.

Alienation from self and inauthenticity.   The necessity to perform emotional labor is thought to cause alienation or estrangement from one's genuine feelings.[24] This is so because the more aspects of the self that are involved in emotional work, the more difficult it becomes to identify which aspects are truly one's own. Underlying this claim is the assumption that individuals are motivated to maintain and enhance an authentic sense of self. The experience of inauthenticity on the job was found to mediate the relationship between interactive service work conditions and depressed mood.[61] Deep acting in particular may distort emotional reactions; result in losing of touch with the authentic self as one's ability to recognize or even experience genuine emotions is impaired; and consequently damage service providers' well-being.[28]

Positive outcomes

Although emotional labor was originally viewed as a negative phenomenon,[24] later researchers,[25,28] suggested that the organizational requirement to display positive emotions may also have certain positive consequences for both customers and employees, namely mutually rewarding interpersonal interactions, high quality job performance and positive self-evaluation.

Pleasant interpersonal interaction.   The positive consequences of emotional labor result primarily from its effect on the service provider-customer interaction. The social expectations that guide the service providers' emotional display contribute to interactions by making them more predictable and avoiding embarrassing interpersonal problems.[28] The display of positive emotions by service providers increases the probability that customers will show reciprocal positive emotions in return. In addition, positive emotions expressed by a service provider can result in financial well-being (e.g., increased tipping).[32] The display of positive emotions by service providers may thus lead to an interaction which is rewarding for both parties.[30,54]

High quality job performance.   As a means of presenting a positive image of the organization and inducing the appropriate feelings in customers, managing emotions may result in good customer service performance.[25] Such performance can have an immediate impact on organizationally desirable outcomes such as in sales jobs, as well as long-term positive effects on the organization in terms of maintaining customer loyalty.[32]

Positive self-evaluation of service providers. Emotional labor provides a critical means of regulating interaction with customers and thus may increase self-efficacy, that is, the belief that one can successfully fulfill task requirements.[28] Positive feedback elicited from customers may contribute to the employee's satisfaction and self-esteem.[30,54] In addition, emotional labor may facilitate self-expression because of a degree of latitude in how display rules are enacted which enables service providers to project at least some of their 'authentic self' in the role. Display rules allow service providers to distance themselves cognitively from the implicated emotion and maintain their objectivity and emotional equilibrium.[28]

Conclusion

The literature discussed in this chapter suggests that the job of service providers, regardless of their specific role, has much in common with the role of theatrical players. The dramaturgical framework has been used to analyze the similarities between the two contexts, although the meaning of acting for service providers can be also understood as well by analyzing the differences between acting as the essence of the job and acting as a marginal part of the job.

The significance of acting in a specific context is primarily reflected in the degree of the centrality of the actors. In theater the focus is on the actors, who are literally in the limelight, while the audience is invisible, sitting in the dark, watching. Theater actors perform their job best when they lose their consciousness of the audience. By contrast, in the service context it is the customers who are in the limelight: they are the *raison d'être* of the encounter, while the service providers are often unnoticed. Customers expect the service provider to focus on them, and in fact part of the acting component in the service provider's work is feigning interest in the customer.

Furthermore, theatrical actors are usually physically remote from their audience, who are quiet most of the time and usually provide feedback only when the play is over. In service encounters the audience is often physically close to the service providers and audience reactions are palpable. Service providers are actually constantly exposed to customer reactions to their performance. This ongoing feedback is likely to generate stress, requiring them to immediately adapt and fine-tune their behavior in response to customer feedback. Improvisation therefore is a major part of acting in the service field, in contrast to theatrical actors who generally follow the exact words in the script.

This difference applies to other aspects of theater and service as well. In the theater, the play, the script, roles and the set are stable for the length of the production but change entirely when a new play is mounted. In service, there is somewhat greater flexibility of script, roles and setting, but no major change over time, as basically the same play is being produced over and over again. Furthermore, in the field of service the 'play' is often viewed repeatedly by the same audience, namely regular customers who have experienced such service in other places. The service audience expects each production to be similar either to the previous production by the same provider or to that of other service providers. Theater audiences in sharp contrast, would have a negative opinion of an actor who plays Hamlet exactly like his colleague in a previous production. Innovation and creativity are the sought-after criteria in the theater, whereas uniformity is the criterion in evaluating service.

Consequently, unlike actors, service providers usually do not get recognition for good acting. Bad acting, however, namely a failure to comply with display rules or a lapse in the service script, is noticed by customers as well as management. Customer satisfaction surveys, which might be considered equivalent to published reviews by theater critics, reflect mainly failures in acting, because a display of the expected emotions and behaviors is taken for granted and does not get noticed.

In sum, while theatrical acting can be seen as an exciting and creative job, the acting component of service is performed not to express creativity but to comply with rules, promote the purposes of service, and prevent trouble. More often than not, it is also performed from a position of inferiority.

Notes

1   Grove, S. J. & Fisk, R. P. (1983). Impression management in service marketing: A dramaturgical perspective. In R. A. Giacalone and P. Rosenfeld (eds), *Impression Management in the Organization*. Hillsdale, NJ: Earlabum.

2   Grove, S. J., Fisk, R. P. & Bitner, M. J. (1992). Dramatizing the service experience: A management approach. *Advances in Services Marketing and Management*, 1, 91–121.

3   Williams, A. & Anderson, H. H. (2005). Engaging customers in service creation: a theater perspective. *Journal of Services Marketing*, 19, 13–23.

4   Grayson, K. & Shulman, D. (2000). Impression management in service marketing. In T. A. Swartz & D. Iacobucci (eds), *Handbook of Service Marketing and Management* (pp. 51–68). Thousand Oaks: Sage.

5   Mohr, L. A. & Henson, S. W. (1996). Impact of employee gender and job congruency on customer satisfaction. *Journal of Consumer Psychology*, 6, 161–188.

6   Goodwin, C. (1996). Moving the drama into the factory: The contribution of metaphors to services research. *European Journal of Marketing*, 30, 13–36.

7   Solomon, M. R., Surprenant, C., Czepiel, J. A. & Gutman, E. G. (1985). A role theory perspective on dyadic interactions: The service encounter. *Journal of Marketing*, 49, 99–111.

8   Vilnai-Yavetz, I. and Rafaeli, A. (2003). Introduction note 13.

9   Shamir, B. (1980). Between service and servility: Role conflict in subordinate service roles. *Human Relations*, 33, 741–756.

10 Grove, S. J., Fisk, R. P. & Dorsch, M. J. (1998). Assessing the theatrical components of the service encounter: A cluster analysis examination. *The Service Industries Journal*, 18, 116–144.

11 Grove, S. J., Fisk, R. P. & John, J. (2000). Service as theater: Guidelines and implications. In T. A. Swartz & D. Iacobucci (eds), *Handbook of Service Marketing and Management* (pp. 21–36). Thousand Oaks: Sage.

12 Grove, S. J. & Fisk, R. P. (1992). Observational data collection methods for services marketing: An overview. *Academy of Marketing Science Journal*, 20, 217–224.

13 Deighton, J. (1992). The consumption of performance. *Journal of Consumer Research*, 19, 362–371.

14 Clark, T. & Salaman, G. (1998). Creating the 'right' impression: Towards a dramaturgy of management consultancy. *Services Industries Journal*, 18, 18–38.

15 Bitner, M. J. (1992). Servicescapes: The impact of physical surroundings on customers and employees. *Journal of Marketing*, 56, 57–71.

16 Baron, S., Harris, K. & Harris, R. (2001). Retail theater: The 'intended effect' of the performance. *Journal of Service Research*, 4, 102–117.

17 Moisio, R. & Arnould, E. J. (2005). Extending the dramaturgical framework in marketing: Drama structure, drama interaction and drama content in shopping experiences. *Journal of Consumer Behavior*, 4, 246–256.

18 Service providers in these organizations view themselves as providing memories rather than goods, and adopt the role of an 'experience stager'.

19 Goffman, E. (1959). *The Presentation of Self in Everyday Life*. New York: Doubleday and Anchor Books.

20 Broderick, A. J. (1998). Role theory, role management, and service performance. *Journal of Services Marketing*, 12, 348–361.

21 Stiles, J. L. (1985). Servicing alternatives. *Mortgage Banking*, 45, 81–82.

22 Bitner, M. J., Booms, B. H. & Mohr, L. A. (1994). Critical service encounters: The employee's viewpoint. *Journal of Marketing*, 58, 95–106.

23 Chebat, J. C. & Kollias, P. (2000). The impact of empowerment on customer contact employees' role in service organizations. *Journal of Service Research*, 3, 66–81.

24 Hochschild, A. R. (1983). *The Managed Heart: Commercialization of Human Feeling*. Berkeley: University of California Press.

25 Grandey, A. A. (2000). Emotion regulation in the workplace: A new way to conceptualize emotional labor. *Journal of Occupational Health Psychology*, 5, 95–110.

26 Zapf, D. (2002). Emotion work and psychological well-being. A review of the literature and some conceptual considerations. *Human Resource Management Review*, 12, 237–268.

27 Glomb, T. M. & Tews, M. J. (2004). Emotional labor: A conceptualization and scale development. *Journal of Vocational Behavior*, 64, 1–23.

28 Ashforth, B. E. & Humphrey, R. H. (1993). Emotional labor in service roles: The influence of identity. *The Academy of Management Review*, 18, 88–115.

29 Morris, J. A. & Feldman, D. C. (1996). The dimensions, antecedents, and consequences of emotional labor. *The Academy of Management Review*, 21, 1986–2010.

30 Zapf, D. & Holz, M. (2006). On the positive and negative effects of emotion work in organizations. *European Journal of Work and Organizational Psychology*, 15, 1–28.

31 Grandey, A. A. (2003). Managing emotions in the workplace. *Personnel Psychology*, 56, 563–566.

32 Rafaeli, A. & Sutton, R. I. (1987). Expression of emotion as part of the work role. *The Academy of Management Review*, 12, 23–37.

33 Totterdell, P. & Holman, D. (2003). Emotion regulation in customer service roles: testing a model of emotional labor. *Journal of Occupational Health Psychology*, 8, 55–73.

34 Rafaeli, A. & Sutton, R. I. (1989). The expression of emotion in organizational life. In L. L. Cummings & B. M. Staw (eds), *Research in Organizational Behavior*, Vol. 11: 1–42. Greenwich, CT: JAI Press.

35 Wilk, S. L. & Moynihan, L. M. (2005). Display rule 'regulators': The relationship between supervisors and worker emotional exhaustion. *Journal of Applied Psychology*, 90, 917–927.

36 Clark, R. E. & LaBeff, E. E. (1982). Death telling: Managing the delivery of bad news. *Journal of Health and Sociological Behavior*, 23, 366–380.

37 Sutton, R. I. (1991). Maintaining norms about expressed emotions: The case of bill collectors. *Administrative Science Quarterly*, 36, 245–268.

38 Kruml, S. M. & Geddes, D. (2000). Exploring the dimensions of emotional labor. *Management Communication Quarterly*, 14, 8–49.

39 Brotheridge, C. M. & Lee, R. T. (1988). On the dimensionality of emotional labour: Development and validation of the emotional labour scale. *Paper presented at the First Conference on Emotions in Organizational Life*, San Diego.

40 Gosserand, R. H. & Diefendorff, J. M. (2005). Emotional display rules and emotional labor: The moderating role of commitment. *Journal of Applied Psychology*, 90, 1256–1264.

41 Morris, J. A. & Feldman, D. C. (1997). Managing emotions in the workplace. *Journal of Managerial Issues*, 9, 257–274.

42 Diefendorff, J. M. & Gosserand, R. H. (2003). Understanding the emotional labor process: A control theory perspective. *Journal of Organizational Behavior*, 24, 945–959.

43 Wharton, A. S. (1993). The affective consequences of service work: Managing emotions on the job. *Work and Occupation, 20,* 205–232.

44 Tolich, M. B. (1993). Alienating and liberating emotions at work: Supermarket clerks' performance of customer service. *Journal of Contemporary Ethnography, 22,* 361–381.

45 Goldberg, L. & Grandey, A. (in press). Display rules versus display autonomy: Emotion regulation, emotional exhaustion, and task performance in a call center simulation. *Journal of Occupational Health Psychology.*

46 Abraham, R. (1998). Emotional dissonance in organizations: Antecedents, consequences, and moderators. *Genetic, Social, and General Psychology Monographs, 124,* 229–246.

47 Goolsby, J. R. (1992). A theory of role stress in boundary spanning positions of marketing organizations. *Academy of Marketing Science Journal, 20,* 155–164.

48 Brotheridge, C. M. & Grandey, A. A. (2002). Emotional labor and burnout: Comparing two perspectives of 'people work'. *Journal of Vocational Behavior, 60,* 17–39.

49 Notably, these attributes may also be viewed as dimensions of emotion work rather than antecedents (Morris & Feldman, 1996).

50 Wharton, A. S. & Erickson, R. J. (1993). Managing emotions on the job and at home: Understanding the consequences of multiple emotional roles. *Academy of Management Review, 18,* 457–486.

51 Zapf, D., Vogt, C., Seifert, C., Mertini, H. & Isic, A. (1999). Emotion work as a source of stress. The concept and development of an instrument. *European Journal of Work and Organizational Psychology, 8,* 371–400.

52 Grandey, A. A., Tam, A. P. & Brauberger, A. L. (2002). Affective states and traits in the workplace: Diary and survey data from young workers. *Motivation and Emotion, 26,* 31–55.

53 Giardini, A. & Frese, M. (2006). Reducing the negative effects of emotion work in service occupations: Emotional competence as a psychological resource. *Journal of Occupational Health and Psychology, 11,* 63–75.

54 Pugh, S. D. (2001). Service with a smile: Emotional contagion in the service encounter. *Academy of Management Journal, 44,* 1018–1027.

55 Rafaeli, A. (1989). When clerks meet customers: A test of variables related to emotional expressions on the job. *Journal of Applied Psychology, 74,* 385–393.

56 Rafaeli, A. & Sutton, R. I. (1990). Busy stores and demanding customers: How do they affect the display of positive emotion? *Academy of Management Journal, 33,* 623–637.

57 Sutton, R. I. & Rafaeli, A. (1988). Untangling the relationship between displayed emotions and organizational sales: The case of convenience stores. *Academy of Management Journal, 31,* 461–487.

58 Women are often socialized to act in a warmer and friendlier manner than men; they may have a greater ability to encode and present their emotions; and may show more positive emotions because of a greater need for social approval (Rafaeli, 1989).

59 Côté, S. (2005). A social interaction model of the effects of emotion regulation on work strain. *The Academy of Management Review, 30,* 509–530.

60 This reaction is similar to the concept of passive deep acting.

61 Erickson, R. J. & Wharton, A. S. (1997). Inauthenticity and depression: Assessing the consequences of interactive service work. *Work and Occupations*, 24, 188–213.

62 Brotheridge, C. M. & Lee, R. T. (2003). Development and validation of the emotional labour scale. *Journal of Occupational and Organizational Psychology*, 76, 365–379.

63 Grandey, A. A., Fisk, G. M. & Steiner, D. D. (2005). Must 'service with a smile' be stressful? The moderating role of personal control for American and French Employees. *Journal of Applied Psychology*, 90, 893–904.

64 In this explanation, both emotional labor and stress result from customer behaviors, although they are not necessarily interrelated.

65 Emotional dissonance is sometimes conceptualized as a component rather than an outcome of emotional labor (Morris & Feldman, 1996).

2
Influence and Control in the Service Interaction

The need for personal control is a universal human motivation, yet the service provider's need for control is challenged by both the organization and the customer. The organization seeks to control the encounter through its policies, procedures and supervision, while customers use the opportunity to satisfy their control needs through their participation in the service process.[1] The service encounter is described as 'a three-cornered fight', with the customer, the service provider and the service organization struggling for control.[2] Thus, it has been argued that in interactive service work, issues of power and control must be analyzed with simultaneous regard to all three parties.[3] Such an analysis is based on the assumption that the parties have interests that sometimes bring them into alliance and sometimes into opposition *vis-à-vis* the other two parties. Each party's success in achieving control depends in part on the balance of interests of all three parties.[3]

The chapter discusses three aspects of the issue of control: the managerial control of service providers; service provider-customer power relations; and the analysis of the power relationships of all three parties based on the alignment of their interests.

Organizational management of service providers: control and empowerment

Controlling service providers

The organizational control of service providers consists of general management procedures such as performance evaluation, as well as distinctive forms of control such as supervision of tone of voice and content of verbal interaction.[3] Organizations exert two distinct forms of control over service providers: bureaucratic control, reflected in standardization and technological surveillance; and normative control, reflected in managerial attempts to influence service providers' customer-related behaviors and attitudes.[4,5,6,7]

The discussion of organizational control revolves around two major issues: should service providers be strictly controlled, and are they in fact strictly controlled by organizations. Some researchers have argued that the strict principles of production-line control can and should be applied to the field of service, while others hold that service employees should be less controlled and more empowered than production-line employees, as empowerment has positive consequences for both the service providers and the organization. The notion presented by critical management researchers that organizations ruthlessly control and manipulate service providers via a combination of bureaucratic and normative methods has been challenged by other researchers who suggest that organizational control is generally not overly powerful and may even have advantages for service providers.

Despite the recognition that service is different from production, Levitt (1972)[8] recommended a production-line approach to service, and the industrialization of service, suggesting that service operations can be made more efficient with the application of manufacturing logic and tactics. A production-line approach to service implies a simplification of service roles, clarification of the service script, intensification of supervision, and the imposition of stronger punishment for poor performance.[9] Such an approach has the considerable advantage of producing efficient service operations and satisfied customers.[10] Indeed, many service organizations have applied production-line models of routinization[6] with little individual discretion,[11] often with great success.[9,11]

However, organizational control has been extensively criticized by critical management researchers who view conflict as inherent in the management – service provider relationship.[12] The results of systematic discipline are seen as negative, reflected in employees' cynicism, moral degradation, stifled resistance emotional pressure, work dissatisfaction,[13] and mental, physical and emotional exhaustion.[14] Furthermore, in addition to explicit forms of control, management in service organizations operates 'control from within', namely it attempts to produce workers who discipline and control themselves.[7] Following a review of contemporary perspectives on control, Rosenthal (2004)[7] concluded that service providers are portrayed as 'amongst the most controlled of creatures' (p. 601), described as either burned-out as the result of excessive emotional demands or powerless and helpless, perceived as passive recipients of control and manipulated by their organization.[15]

Other researchers, however, have suggested that the criticism of organizational control is too extreme.[7] Employees have been shown to be aware of organizational control[4] and to express a range of positive and negative responses, rather than uniformly negative reactions.[4,9]

Furthermore, organizational control may actually have various advantages for service providers and operate in their interests, for example in defining the requirements of their task explicitly.[6,7] Service employees, in this view, should not be seen as victims of customer or managerial demands, but as using the resources available to them to perform their work, protect their self-evaluation and achieve a more pleasurable work experience.[7] Rosenthal proposed the following ways by which organizational control might serve the interests of service providers:

(1) The managerial approach of normative control often emphasizes respect for employees as well as for customers because of the assumption that employee satisfaction is positively related to customer satisfaction.

(2) Human resource principles often include enhanced work discretion as well as customer service training designed to enhance the interpersonal skills of service providers.

(3) Control reduces the likelihood that employees will face sanctions and demands for extra effort to correct management failures.

(4) Formal appraisal systems as part of organizational control provide a defense against biased informal evaluations.

(5) Employees can manipulate the information available to management to their advantage. Service providers in call centers for example, know when they are subject to taping and may use this electronic surveillance to demonstrate their proficiency and/or regulate their effort.

(6) Technological control and documentation may protect service providers against customer complaints.

Additionally, organizational control may serve the interest of service providers in exercising control over the other parties involved in the service act. Organizational controls enhance the capacity of service providers to control customers or to protect themselves psychologically from treatment they consider demeaning (see the section on influence tactics in this chapter). The service script[16] for example, is sometimes used by service workers to control, influence and distance themselves from customers.[3] A service script makes the encounter predictable so that even if the service provider has little behavioral control over the encounter, the element of predictability may give him/her a sense of control.[2]

Empowering of service providers

Because of the intangibility of service, organizational empowerment is widely considered to be a more appropriate managerial approach in service organizations than a production-line-control approach.[17] Empowerment has been conceptualized in many different ways,[9] yet there seems to be agreement regarding its core characteristics. Empowerment is described as a motivational construct meaning to enable;[18] as increasing intrinsic task motivation;[19] as a self-generated exercise of judgment;[20] and as providing authority to make everyday decisions.[21] These definitions reflect a differentiation between management practices, or the objective facts of what a person is empowered to do, and employees' cognitions about those practices, namely psychological empowerment.[11,19] Empowerment conveyed in managerial practices is described as sharing information with service providers about the organization's performance, providing rewards based on the organization's performance, providing knowledge that enables employees to understand and contribute to organizational performance, and granting power to make decisions that influence organizational direction and performance.[22] Psychological empowerment from the employee's point of view has been described as consisting of a sense of being able to influence organizational outcomes, feelings of self-efficacy and self-determination, and finding meaningfulness in one's work.[11,19,23,24,25]

Empowerment ensures appropriate behaviors of service providers in accordance with customers' needs and their expectations regarding quality service.[9] Notably, what is considered quality service varies greatly on the part of customers.[26] Moreover, individual customers may frequently change the definition of their needs. Accordingly, service quality is evaluated by customers not just by efficiency but also in regard to service providers' flexibility and concern for their needs.[9] Furthermore, since customers' needs often cannot be predicted in advance, service providers must react quickly in real time, rely on interpersonal skills, and exercise initiative and discretion.[11,27,28,29] Therefore, the organization must reduce its reliance on standardized rules, procedures and a formal hierarchy of decision making which slows employees' responses to customers,[10,29] especially in complex service relationships which require more adaptability than a service involving a simple transaction.[10]

The amount of flexibility reflected in various levels of empowerment is relevant to the process of recovery of service failures and therefore to customer satisfaction.[30] The highest level – full or flexible empowerment – involves granting considerable latitude to the service provider in making decisions. This approach enables service providers to solve customer problems in a flexible manner without delay. Consequently, the customers' sense of procedural justice is enhanced, they feel respected and experience control over the likely resolution of the complaint. A more limited level of empowerment permits the service provider to make some decisions but under tight control. Service providers may for example, deal with customers' problems by selecting a solution from a predetermined list of alternatives prescribed by the organization. This strategy promises relatively speedy responses but it might result in lesser perception of control by the customer. Lastly, with no empowerment, the employee is required to refer the matter to a supervisor for advice or instructions before dealing with the customer's complaints. This approach limits the customer's sense of control in terms of interaction with the service provider, but offers other opportunities for customer control *vis-à-vis* the supervisor.[30]

Empowerment contributes to flexibility not only in the interaction with customers but also in regard to the service providers' willingness to learn and adapt. Empowered employees are more likely to modify their own behaviors and attitudes towards customers in order to attain both personal and organizational goals, and are willing to internalize customer feedback in their personal conduct.[27] Empowerment was found to be related to service orientation[9] and to the tendency to respond more quickly to customer needs, complaints and changes of taste.[31] Furthermore, empowerment contributes to well-being: empowered service providers feel better about their jobs and themselves, identify with the job, find the work meaningful, show lower turnover, less absenteeism and less resistance,[22] experience less role conflict and role ambiguity, and report higher levels of self-efficacy, job satisfaction, loyalty and morale.[27,32] At the same time, the effect of empowerment seems to interact with the service provider's personality characteristics: empowerment was found to interact with trait control to affect job-related sense of control[33] and with power motivation to affect burnout.[34]

Notably, empowerment also evokes certain disadvantages for the organization: greater costs involved in selection and training of service providers, slower and inconsistent service, and errors in decisions made by service providers.[22] Thus, empowerment is inappropriate or even counterproductive in situations of low service heterogeneity because flexible behaviors will disrupt the quasi-industrialized service delivery operations.[27] In addition, empowerment has been criticized as being managerial control in disguise.[28] Since direct control is unsuitable to service, and customer interaction requires flexibility from workers, management adopts an empowerment approach which achieves control through the transformation of workers' personalities and thoughts so that their reactions to various situations are predictable. Paradoxically, while the empowerment method seems unobtrusive, it frequently invades more areas of the employees' personal life than other modes of supervision. Instead of presenting employees with service scripts, management selects employees who are instinctively likely to follow the desirable organizational script, so that empowerment does not involve any risks. The use of customer feedback is but another indirect method of management control which ostensibly gives freedom to employees but in actuality enables management to work together with customers to control employees. This practice strengthens managerial power by providing an additional source of data to be used by management for evaluation and discipline.

Power and dependence in the service provider-customer interaction

The service providers' need for control in their interaction with customers is affected by the various characteristics of the situation and the interaction, such as the physical proximity of the customers, the immediate feedback they convey, the psychological as well as physical effort involved in meeting their demands, and the power of customers to affect rewards and sanctions.[7] Moreover, service providers seek control not only to satisfy a psychological need but also as a means to do their job well and to avoid errors.[3,35] Notably, service providers' sense of control as well as customers' sense of control were found to be positively related to customer satisfaction.[36] However, a struggle for control may develop as customers also seek control in order to demonstrate competence and mastery over the environment.[37] Service providers and customers often have different notions of who has the right of control in the service encounter, which may strain the service process[35] and create a rift between the parties.[37]

The power gap in the service interaction

The customer's tendency to control the interaction depends on the extent of the special expertise required in the service, the relative status of service provider and customer, and the dependence of the customer on the service provider or the service organization.[3,38] Consequently, it is mainly unskilled low-status workers who struggle with the need to control the service interaction, which in their case is characterized by a predetermined large power gap in favor of the customer. Referring to such interactions, Macdonald and Sirianni (1996)[38] observe that 'The idiom of servant and master is alive and well in many service workplaces' (p. 16). This policy holds that the customer is always right and that the role of the server is to be deferent, even if the customer presents unreasonable demands and behaves abusively.

Bolton and Houlihan (2005) however, challenge the blanket notion of customers as 'mythical sovereigns' (p. 686) who expect servitude from service providers, and suggest a view of customers as being interested to carry out their transaction in a simple manner, and as 'moral agents' (p. 686) who fully engage with service providers and who see customer interaction as a socially relevant activity. In this approach, both parties in the service encounter are active players exercising control[12] and relating to each other, socially and morally.[39]

The significance of the service provider's ability to control the interaction was demonstrated in a classic study by White (1949),[40] who examined the behavior of restaurant waitresses. White[40] found that the ability of waitresses to cope with the stress involved in their role was related to length of service, with longtime waitresses better able to handle stress. One of the reasons was that senior waitresses served steady customers, which enabled them to assume an active leadership role with the customer, take initiative and control the customer's behavior. Service providers were found to perceive the ideal customer as one who facilitates work by helping the delivery of service and allowing employees to control the interaction services, rather than interfering or seeking to influence the exchange.[41]

Two theories of power and control in the social relationship are highly relevant to the service context: interdependence theories (Kelley and Thibaut, 1978; Emerson, 1962)[42,43] and the model of bases of social power (French & Raven, 1959),[44] as will be discussed below.

Customer-service provider interdependence

The interdependence theory formulated by Kelley and Thibaut (1978)[42] provides an appropriate framework for analyzing the commonalities and differences in various service situations.[45] Interdependence in the service encounter is reflected in the effect each party's behavior has on the other's outcome, which is a function of the rewards each party receives minus the costs of enacting the behaviors. Typical rewards within service relationships are receiving the desired service, financial gain, or recognition. Costs may include the investment of effort, money or time. Each party evaluates the outcome as satisfying if it exceeds the comparison level, namely the quality of the expected outcome. In addition to this internal anchor the parties employ a second standard of evaluation of outcomes, defined as the comparison level of alternatives, or comparing the outcome in a relationship to alternative outcomes that may be available. The party with more attractive alternatives is less dependent on the other and thereby has more power.

A similar notion is presented in Emerson's (1962) power dependence theory of social relations,[43] which posits that dependence is produced by the availability or lack of alternatives. The more dependent an individual is on a social relationship, the less power that individual has. According to Emerson,[43] power develops in two ways. First, the more a person values resources controlled by another, the more dependent that person is. Second, the more available those valued resources are outside the relationship, the less dependent that person is.

Kelly and Thibaut[42] and Emerson's[43] theories were applied in analysis of customer dependence on the service provider (McCallum & Harrsion, 1985).[45] Accordingly a customer is considered to be dependent on a particular service provider to the extent that the outcomes the customer experiences in the encounter with the service provider exceed those perceived to be available elsewhere. Furthermore, the distinction between comparison level and comparison level of alternatives explains those situations in which customers remain in service relationships that are below their expectation: the outcomes they receive may be below their comparison level but still better that what they expected to receive in the alternatives.

Mills and Margulies (1980)[46] too, analyze the relative power of the parties in terms of customer dependence on the service provider. Specifically, the customer's dependence and, consequently, both parties' power, are determined by the information each party has about the goals of the service interaction and the means of achieving it. Customers who are knowledgeable about both the goals and the means are not dependent on the service provider, and the power balance is in their favor. Greater dependence exists when customers know what the goal is but not how to achieve it. The highest level of customer dependence on service providers exists when customers have no knowledge about either the goals or the means of achieving them.

Although they use different criteria of dependence, both Mills and Margulies (1980)[46] and McCallum and Harrsion (1985)[45] view the extent of customer dependence on service provider as a basis for classifying service encounters. Indeed, it would appear that interdependence theory, and especially the notion of comparison with alternatives, is more relevant to the customer's rather than the service provider's position. Service providers serve many customers and presumably their evaluation of the outcome of each interaction is not guided by comparing customers to each other and seeking the best alternative. While customers may switch to a service that is evaluated as a better alternative, service providers do not discharge customers for better ones. Still, the fact that a service provider has many customers gives him/her prestige and power in the perception of the customer and is likely to affect customer behavior in the interaction. Additionally, the service provider's knowledge about the goal of the service interaction and the means of achieving it increase customer dependence (see Figure 2.1).

A study of headhunters,[47] aptly demonstrates the association between alternatives, dependence and power. This research showed that the major problem facing headhunters was that their customers have available alternatives: regardless of the quality of the relationship and the quality of the service, customers could eventually seek the services of another headhunter who offered a more attractive candidate. The availability of alternatives for the customers was found to generate a dilemma for the headhunters regarding exclusivity. On the one hand, a guarantee of exclusivity from customers eliminated the customer's alternatives and therefore increased the headhunter's power. On the other hand, headhunters reciprocated the exclusivity granted them by customers by investing a great deal of effort in working for the customer and reducing the efforts they put into developing alternatives for themselves. This situation raised the price of losing the customer, making the customer more valuable and the service provider more dependent. Headhunters were found to cope with this dependence by evaluating various signs of potential customer loyalty. They tested the customer's responsiveness to questions as an indication of his/her willingness to cooperate, and adjusted their investment in the customer accordingly. In addition, they were prepared to behave opportunistically themselves, and believed that under certain circumstances it was acceptable to be disloyal and even dishonest in their dealings with the customer.

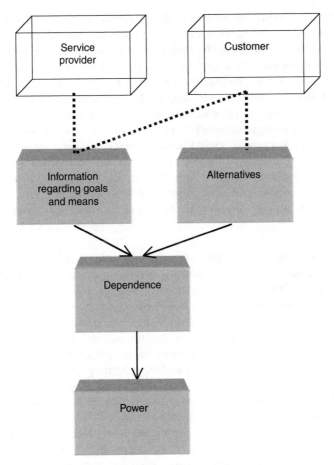

Figure 2.1   Interdependence in the service interaction

Social power bases in the service interaction

Interpersonal power is described as a person's potential ability to influence another person.[44] Behaviors designed to influence the other party's behavior in the service interaction range from routine acts that constitute a natural part of the service interaction to outstanding behaviors (see Table 2.1). The exercise of these behaviors and their effect on the other party's behavior are determined by the parties' bases of power.

French and Raven's (1959)[44] model of the bases of social power can serve as a useful framework for analyzing the factors that affect the leverage of service providers and customers in their encounter.[35] According to this model, social power bases underlie the evaluation by the influence target of the subjective probability that the influence agent will behave in a certain way. By way of example 'coercive power... stems from the expectation on the part of P (i.e., the influence target) that he will be punished by O (the influence agent) if he fails to conform to the influence attempt' (French & Raven, 1959, p. 157).[44] The original theory[44] consisted of five power bases: reward power, coercive power, expert power, referent power, and legitimate power. Another source of power, informational power, was described as being related to expert power. This model of power bases is useful in the analysis of the sources of leverage each party in the service encounter employs to influence the other's behavior as follows:

(1) *Reward power* results from control over resources and rewards. While service providers control mostly intangible resources and rewards, the customer's reward power is usually tangible, generally reflected in the money paid for the service. Rewards may be also provided by positive behaviors performed for the other party's sake, which are beyond the content of a routine interaction.[1] For example, customer satisfaction was found to be related to service providers' responses to service failures and the way they handled the service recovery; responses to customers' special needs; and spontaneity in delivering outstanding service (see review in Zeithaml & Bitner, 1996).[48] Similarly, the customer can provide a generous tip, give gifts, write letters of praise, and provide indirect rewards through positive word of mouth. Such 'beyond the duty' positive behaviors are especially rewarding because they are likely to be perceived as personal and as requiring a special effort.

(2) *Coercion power*, consisting of control over punishments, is sometimes used by customers who complain about the service provider to supervisors[35] or behave aggressively toward the service provider.[49,50] Service providers, however, are generally prevented from resorting to direct punishment of customers. However, they may sometimes exhibit indirect aversive behaviors such as forcing the customer to wait unnecessarily, concealing information or providing defected goods.[51]

(3) *Expert power*, or task expertise, is the service provider's main source of power in professional services. The service provider's influence is reflected in the customer's responsive behavior either within the

service process, e.g., following the instructions of a fitness trainer; or outside the service encounter, e.g., taking medication, or following legal advice. The service provider's expert power may be the basis of his/her reward power, and like reward power, it may influence the customer's behavior in terms of willingness to invest time, effort and money in the service. Notably, the extent of the service provider's expert power is inversely related to that of the customer. Customers who have expert power and possess the same skills and knowledge as the service provider may become competitors and decide to produce the service for themselves.[48]

(4) *Information power* consists of the control of information, and is often used to promote the service process, e.g., a travel agent in describing possible travel routes, or a patient in providing details about his/her physical condition to a doctor. However, since service providers usually know more about the service than the customer, they may manipulate the information in various ways to affect customer behavior and gain control. For example, experienced waitresses suggested dishes they could easily get from the kitchen.[40] Customers too may manipulate information they are required to give about themselves, such as medical or financial details, by hiding or exaggerating details in order to gain advantages such as special attention or discounts.

Furthermore, both parties can access information that is beyond the basic information required to promote the service process and can be shared as a special favor for the other party. The service provider may provide valuable knowledge reflected in 'inside' information (e.g., a pending sale); information that supports the customer's interests while contradicting the interests of the organization (e.g., dishes that are not recommended); or gossip about other customers or service providers. Customers can provide valuable information about competitors, other customers' attitudes or feedback about the service.

(5) *Referent power* which results from friendship and loyalty, is likely to be a source of power mainly in service relationships where the customer and the service provider have repeated interactions.[52] However, even in one-time service encounters the parties may develop a certain level of affinity for one another. Service providers who display courteous service behaviors create a warm and positive climate, an immediate bond with customers, and a sense of rapport and ease.[53] Moreover, both parties sometimes use ingratiation to affect the other party's behavior.[54]

(6) *Legitimate power* is the ability to influence another because of a socially prescribed role giving legitimacy to one's influence[44] and is reflected in a predetermined entitlement of one party to make demands and an obligation of the other party to accede to those demands.[55] While in most service contexts there is no formal definition of one party as an authority, an inherent characteristic of many services is the entitlement of the customer to make demands, as the primary purpose of the interaction is to satisfy the customer's needs.[38] This entitlement is explicitly reflected in the notion of the customer being always right. Customer may make that power source explicit if they feel that they do not get what they are entitled to receive and mention the fact that this is a service situation and it is the service provider's duty to do what they request.

Service providers are usually entitled to make demands of customers in regard to highly specified behaviors such as paying for the service, performing the activities that are vital for the performance of the service (e.g., be present, fill in forms, provide information), or refrain from disturbing the other customers. Thus, to some extent, the customer must give up some control and obey the procedures and the service provider.[2] Service providers' legitimate power in especially prominent in jobs which include formal components of authority, such as teachers or police officers. Furthermore, in certain service contexts there is a suspension of the parties' status and the service provider gets the authority within the situation like in nurse-patient interaction.[45,55]

In summary, power bases may be used as an inherent part of the service process to promote the process or as outstanding activities which are beyond the basic requirement of the encounter. The following table summarizes examples of routine and outstanding expressions of power bases in doctor-patient relationships.

Influence tactics in the service encounter

The literature on the tactics service providers and customers use in their attempts to influence each other shows an impressive repertoire of tactics, most of them informal. An extensive qualitative study on the social interactions of supermarket cashiers[35] reveals the struggle for control between cashiers and customers and the strategy each party uses. Customers attempted to undermine the cashiers' power by criticizing things outside their responsibility, such as prices; discouraging them from interacting with other service providers or with management in order to avoid waste of time; commenting about waiting time;

Table 2.1 Examples of service provider and the customer power bases

Bases of power	Service provider		Customer	
	Routine activities, within the role	Outstanding activities	Routine activities within the role	Outstanding activities
Reward	Prescribe a medicine	Call several times Patient home for follow-up	Pay for the service	Bring a gift
Coercion (not used routinely in most services)	Talk severely	Refuse to treat	Complain informally	File a formal complaint
Expert	Perform a medical examination	Perform a complicated treatment	Describe medical history of family	Present medical information obtained from internet
Information	Describe possible outcomes of an operation	Present recent research findings regarding treatment	Provide details about illness	Tell about equipment purchased by a competitor
Referent	Smile	Behave in a warm and caring manner	Express gratitude	Use ingratiation
Legitimate	Order a simple laboratory test	Order an expensive laboratory test	Sign agreement for an operation	Lawsuit

offering suggestions about how to save time; and doing things instead of letting the cashier do them. Excessive involvement by the customer in the service process created resistance among cashiers, who were unwilling to relinquish their control of the service encounter. To maintain this control, cashiers employed passive as well as more active strategies: ignoring customers (e.g., avoiding eye contact, ignoring customers' comments or attempts to take charge), rejecting customers' right to control (e.g., saying negative things about customers who try to control), reacting to customers' attempts to control (e.g., verbally confronting customers who attempted to control, attempting to convince customers that they were wrong, expressing agreement in an attempt to calm the customer), and engaging customers in activities and conversation so that they were too busy to try to seek control (e.g., telling jokes, making small talk, asking customers to do certain things).

In another study in hotels and public transport,[56] service providers were found to use several tactics to gain control in their interaction with customers, such as ignoring customers, educating customers by providing information about organizational procedures, withdrawing psychologically from the interaction to cope with stress, and overacting the role to keep a distance between their true identity and the service role.

Salespeople were found to use two subsets of ingratiatory tactics in their efforts to influence customers: assertive and defensive.[54] Assertive ingratiatory tactics (self-enhancement, self-promotion and favor-rendering) consist of attempts to manipulate the customer's attributions, requiring salespeople to present themselves in ways that will attract the target. Such tactics involve overtly political efforts to manipulate customer attributions and therefore are riskier and more likely to harm interpersonal relationships and credibility than are defensive ingratiation tactics. Such tactics were found to be used more often by males[54] and to be negatively related with the level of customers' trust in salespeople.[57]

Defensive tactics (other enhancement, behavioral conformity, opinion conformity, court and counsel) describe ingratiatory efforts intended to make it difficult for a target to respond negatively. The behavioral conformity construct suggests salesperson ingratiators may purposefully agree with a target to enhance the degree of interpersonal attraction between the two. In opinion conformity and court and counsel the salesperson directly and indirectly reflects the expression of favorable opinions and evaluations of the target customer.[54] The use of court and counsel and other enhancement was found to be positively related to customers' trust.[57] Additionally, most dimensions of ingratiation were found to have a positive effect on the relationships within salespeople work groups.[58]

A study of dyads of service providers and customers in terms of the use of ingratiation and assertiveness in the service encounter,[59] found that the influence tactics used by service providers to affect customers were influenced by the organization as well as by customers: service providers reciprocated the influence tactics used by customers toward them and were also affected by the organizational service climate (i.e., a strong service climate was related to the use of ingratiation, while a weak climate was related to the use of assertiveness).

Additionally, the latitude given to service providers by the organization largely determines the intensity and explicitness of tactics they use to control customers. A study on MacDonald's[3] found that service providers had few resources for exercising control over customers or even for defending their dignity in the face of insult or abuse, since organizational policy about proper treatment of customers ruled out most countermeasures by which workers might respond to aversive customer behaviors. As a result, the service providers in this study tried to guide customer behaviors in minor ways such as conveying by their manner that the customer should make decisions quickly, prompting customers with questions, or trying to preempt a display of impatience or anger by being especially cordial.

However, service providers were found to use tactics to influence management as well as customers,[1] as follows:

(1) *Investing effort* tactics which seek to satisfy the demands placed on the service provider by attempting to perform the task efficiently.
(2) *Negotiating* tactics which attempt to alter the demands placed on the service provider by getting the other party to perform some aspects of service (i.e., delegating); giving reasons why it is impossible to meet certain expectations (i.e., explaining); doing extra favors or providing an unusually good service (i.e., rewarding); punishing the other party for adding to the service provider's role conflict (i.e., punishing).
(3) *Pre-empting* tactics which attempt to prevent the other party from placing demands on the service provider by: putting the other party in a good mood (i.e. ingratiating); engaging the other party in order to block any opportunity to express expectations (i.e., distracting).
(4) *Avoiding* tactics which allow the service provider to manipulate and alter demands from customer or management by pretending to interpret the other party's expectations in a way that minimizes role stress (i.e., reinterpreting); not paying attention to the other party (i.e., ignoring).[60]

The three-way dynamics of control

Rather than a struggle between two parties whose interests are assumed to be directly contradictory, another approach views interactive service work as a more variable three-way pattern. To analyze this complex dynamic, the alignment of interests of all three parties must be taken into consideration.[3,7] When customers share an interest with management in maximizing both the speed and quality of service, service providers may face conflicting job requirements and find that the presence of customers weakens their position. In McDonald's,[3] for example, customers and management were found to share an interest in having service providers comply with their prescribed routine. Customers joined management in pressuring service providers to perform speedily, politely and accurately.[3] Yet, management also shared an interest with service providers in controlling and shaping customer behavior and demands. When the interests of management and employees were aligned, routines were designed to increase the service providers' control over customers, and service providers welcomed rather than resisted routinization. In McDonald's,[3] routinization offered certain benefits for workers by limiting the intensity and duration of exchanges with customers, thus allowing workers to distance themselves from unwanted emotional involvement with customers. Similarly, a study of insurance salespeople,[6] found that the interests of management and employees were often aligned in the effort to persuade potential customers to buy policies. The sales routines to which the service providers were expected to conform, such as scripting of the sales presentation and standardization of body language, were perceived by them to 'work' and there were viewed as beneficial rather than aversive.

The complex dynamic of three-way control is demonstrated in the notion of customer management, namely the use of customer evaluation to control service providers.[28] The centrality of customer evaluations leads to a situation in which it is the customer who best knows how the work should be done, not the manager. Customers rather than managers are designated as the authority who must be satisfied, whose orders and desires dictate how the work is performed. Service providers are judged on their interaction with customers by customers themselves. It would appear that managers, in using customer data to control service providers, are acting as customer agents, but in fact service providers acquire an additional boss. In this situation, the authors maintain, managers have formal accomplices in controlling workers insofar as they exploit customers for their observations about how service is delivered. Thus, customer reports broaden management power augmenting it with customer power. In addition, customer management gives organizational power a constant presence. The fact that customers can potentially evaluate the service interaction at any time can serve as a continuous control on service providers' interaction with customers. The knowledge that any interaction can turn into a failure if the service providers does not comply with the customer's demands may affect the employee's behavior.

Conclusion

The literature about control and power justifiably creates the impression that service providers are in a position of weakness. Service providers inevitably have two bosses who strive to control them – the organization and the customers. If the interests of both these bosses are aligned, they form a coalition against service providers; if their interests do not align, they present contradictory demands, resulting in role conflict. The best that can happen in the latter case is that service providers can achieve certain minor advantages from each party's desire to control the other. The boundary position of service providers results in their being in a state of invisibility to the other two parties, who perceive them as a conduit or as mediators to the other party. While arguably all employees are perceived by management to some extent as a means to achieve organizational goals, this is more acute in the case of service providers because the resources that the organization invests in its human capital in almost entirely for the benefit of customers. Customers overshadow service providers in the sense that it is their needs, well-being and motivation that are the true concern of service organizations. As the literature demonstrates, service providers are also often invisible to customers, who view them only as a means to provide the organizational service. Being invisible between two parties who see only each other clearly diminishes the service providers' ability to exert power and control.

The service providers' weakness is best demonstrated by the tactics they use to maintain some level of control, which share the traits of tactics used by the weaker party in a social relationship: subtle, indirect and fearful behaviors. Service providers do not try to gain respect in the eyes of customers by hiding the fact that they are strictly controlled by the organization, but sometimes actually emphasize their weakness and use it in their encounter with customers to avoid coping with customer demands. They might sometimes take risks, confront customers or sabotage the organization, but research shows that most of the time they use covert and indirect means to maintain control.

Most studies of control and power focus on blue-collar service providers who work in highly routinized environments. While it might seem that the professional status of these workers determines their power, it is also possible that the amount of relative power *vis-à-vis* customers and the organization is inherent in the service role regardless of professional expertise, social status or supply and demand trends in a specific service. In other words, the relative power of service providers might be constant, with the status of these employees determining only the subtlety of the means of control used towards them by the organization and the customers. While high-status workers are not subjected to electronic surveillance, they are often appraised by formal and informal customer evaluation and are pressured to comply with customers' wishes, sometimes compromising their professional integrity in doing so. This also applies to external appearance: although they may wear designer clothes rather than same-color uniforms, there are often strict dress codes for high-status service providers. Furthermore, these high-status employees too, are expected to engage in emotional labor, although the emphasis might be different – instead of the pleasant expression uniformly expected of low-status service providers, high-status service employees may be expected to demonstrate more subtle behaviors that would emphasize their expertise. Yet, they too are usually expected to show good manners in interacting with customers, and while a temperamental chef might be overbearing in the kitchen, he/she will be all smiles with customers. A 'star' service provider may have greater latitude to resist organizational control, but only to the point that such resistance damages the service provided to customers.

The service provider's status is probably reflected in the influence tactics used in his/her relationship with customers. Unlike the indirect tactics used by low-status employees, high-status service providers may use their expert power, legitimate power and sometimes even coercive power to influence customers. Yet, in accordance with dependence theory, high-status service providers inevitably have less power than their customers because basically they have fewer alternatives than the customers, they need them more, and it is almost always service providers who compete for customers and not the other way around. A world-famous surgeon who has a long waiting list of patients is still dependent on having customers so long as his/her customers can go to the second best surgeon. Monopolies which would give service providers more power than their customers are very rare in this age of competition.

Notes

1 Weatherly and Tansik (1993). Introduction note 17.
2 Bateson, J. E. G. (1985). Perceived control and the service encounter. In A. Czepiel, M. R. Solomon & C. F. Suprenant (eds), *The Service Encounter: Managing Employee/Customer Interaction in Service Business* (pp. 67–82). Massachusetts: Lexington Books.
3 Leidner, R. (1996). Rethinking questions of control: Lessons from McDonald's. In C. L. Macdonald & C. Sirianni (eds), *Working in the Service Society* (pp. 29–49). Philadelphia: Temple University Press.
4 Frenkel, Korczynski, Shire & Tarn (1999). Introduction note 18.
5 Korczynski, M. (2001). The contradictions of service work: call centre as customer-oriented bureaucracy. In A. Sturdy, I. Grugulis & H. Wilmott (eds), *Customer Service: Empowerment and Entrapment* (pp. 79–102). Basingstoke: Palgrave.
6 Leidner, R. (1993). *Fast Food, Fast Talk: Service Work and the Routinization of Everyday Life*. Berkeley: University of California Press.
7 Rosenthal, P. (2004). Management control as an employee resource: The case of front-line service workers. *Journal of Management Studies*, 41, 601–622.
8 Levitt, T. (1972). Production-line approach to service. *Harvard Business Review*, 50, 41–52.
9 Peccei, R. & Rosenthal, P. (2001). Delivering customer-oriented behaviour through empowerment: An empirical test of HRM assumptions. *The Journal of Management Studies*, 38, 831–857.
10 Bowen, D. E. & Lawler, E. E. III (1992). The empowerment of service workers: What, why, how, and when. *Human Resource Management and Industrial Relations*, 33, 31–39.
11 Lashley, C. (1999). Employee empowerment in services: A framework for analysis. *Personnel Review*, 28, 169–191.
12 Bolton, S. C. & Houlihan, M. (2005). The (mis)representation of customer service. *Work, Employment and Society*, 19, 685–703.
13 Rose, E. & Wright, G. (2005). Satisfaction and dimensions of control among call centre customer service representatives. *International Journal of Human Resource Management*, 16, 136–160.
14 Taylor, P. & Bain, P. (1999). 'An assembly line in the head': Work and employee relations in the call centre. *Industrial Relations Journal*, 30, 101–117.
15 Bain, P. & Taylor, P. (2004). Call centres and human resource management: A cross-national perspective. *Employee Relations*, 26, 569–571.
16 See Chapter 1.
17 Schneider, B. & Bowen, D. E. (1985). Employee and customer perceptions of service in banks: Replication and extension. *Journal of Applied Psychology*, 70, 423–433.

18 Conger, J. A. & Rabindra, N. (1988). The empowerment process: Integrating theory and practice. *The Academy of Management Review*, 13, 471–482.

19 Thomas, K. & Velthouse, B. (1990). Cognitive elements of empowerment: An 'interpretive' model of intrinsic task motivation. *Academy of Management Review*, 15, 666–681.

20 Bell, C. & Zemke, R. (1988). Do service procedures tie employees' hands? *Personnel Journal*, 67, 76–83.

21 Sternberg, L. E. (1992). Empowerment: Trust vs. control. *Cornell Hotel and Restaurant Administration Quarterly*, 33, 68–72.

22 Bowen, D. E. & Lawler, E. E. III (1995). Empowering service employees. *Sloan Management Review*, 36, 73–84.

23 Spreitzer, G. M. (1995). Psychological empowerment in the workplace: Dimensions, measurement, and validation. *Academy of Management Journal*, 38, 1442–1465.

24 Curson, D. L. & Enz, C. A. (1999). Predicting psychological empowerment among service workers: The effect of support-based relationships. *Human Relations*, 52, 205–224.

25 Notably, psychological empowerment among service providers is determined not only by management practices but also by customer behaviors. When customers respect and dignify the service provider, the likelihood that the service provider will experience empowerment is enhanced (Curson & Enz, 1999).

26 Rust, R. T. & Oliver, R. L. (2000). Should we delight the customer? *Academy of Marketing Science Journal*, 28, 86–94.

27 Chebat and Kollias (2000). Chapter 1 note 23.

28 Fuller, L. & Smith, V. (1996). Consumers' reports: management by customers in a changing society. In C. L. Macdonald & C. Sirianni (eds) *Working in the Service Society* (pp. 74–90). Philadelphia: Temple University Press.

29 Gronroos, C. (2001). *Service Management and Marketing: A Customer Relationship Management Approach* (Second Edition). Chichester: Wiley.

30 Sparks, B. A., Bradley, G. L. & Callan, V. J. (1997). The impact of staff empowerment and communication style on customer evaluations: The special case of service failure. *Psychology & Marketing*, 14, 475–493.

31 Barbee, C. & Bott, V. (1991). Customer treatment as a mirror of employee treatment. *S.A.M. Advanced Management Journal*, 56, 27–32.

32 Fulford, M. D. & Enz, C. A. (1995). The impact of empowerment on service employees. *Journal of Managerial Issues*, 7, 161–175.

33 Yagil, D. (2002). The relationship of customer satisfaction and service workers' perceived control: examination of three models. *International Journal of Service Industry Management*, 13, 382–398.

34 Yagil, D. (2006). The relationship of service provider power motivation, empowerment and burnout to customer satisfaction. *International Journal of Service Industry Management*, 17, 258–270.

35 Rafaeli, A. (1989). When cashier meet customers: An analysis of the role of supermarket cashiers. *Academy of Management Journal*, 32, 245–273.

36 Yagil, D. & Gal, I. (2002). The role of organizational service climate in generating control and empowerment among workers and customers. *Journal of Retailing and Consumer Services*, 9, 215–226.

37 Bateson, P. & Martin, P. (2000). Why all work and no play can be bad for business: Organisations with problems should look to where people have stopped having fun, advise Patric Bateson and Paul Martin. *Financial Times*, 8 April, 9.
38 Macdonald and Sirianni (1996). Introduction note 8.
39 Sayer, A. (2005). Class, moral worth and recognition. *Sociology: The Journal of the British Sociological Association*, 39, 947–963.
40 White, W. (1949). *Men at Work*, Irvin-Dorsey series in Behavioral Sciences. Homewood, III: The Dorsey Press and Richard Irwin.
41 Rosenthal, P. & Peccei, R. (2006). The social construction of clients by service agents in reformed welfare administration. *Human Relations*, 59, 1633–1658.
42 Kelley, H. H. & Thibaut, J. (1978). *Interpersonal Relations: A Theory of Interdependence*. New York: Wiley.
43 Emerson, R. M. (1962). Power-dependence relations. *American Sociological Review*, 27, 31–41.
44 French, J. R. P. & Raven, B. (1959). The bases of social power. In D. Cartwright (ed.), *Studies in Social Power* (pp. 150–167). Ann Arbor, MI: University of Michigan.
45 McCallum, J. R. & Harrsion, W. (1985). Interdependence in the service encounter. In J. A. Czepiel, M. R. Solomon & C. F. Surprenant (eds) *The Service Encounter: Managing Employee/Customer Interaction in Service Business* (pp. 35–48). Massachusetts: Lexington Books.
46 Mills and Margulies, 1980. Introduction note 16.
47 Finlay, W. & Coverdill, J. E. (2000). Risk, opportunism, and structural holes: How headhunters manage clients and earn fees. *Work and Occupations*, 27, 377–407.
48 Zeithaml, V. A. & Bitner, M. J. (1996). *Service Marketing*. New York: McGraw-Hill.
49 Dormann, C. & Zapf, D. (2004). Customer-related social stressors and burnout. *Journal of Occupational Health Psychology*, 9, 61–82.
50 See Chapter 4.
51 See Chapter 5.
52 Gutek (1995). Introduction note 10.
53 Zabava Ford, W. (1995). Evaluation of the indirect influence of courteous service on customer discretionary behavior. *Human Communication Research*, 22, 65–89.
54 Strutton, D., Pelton, L. E. & Lumpkin, J. R. (1995). Sex differences in ingratiatory behavior: An investigation of influence tactics in the salesperson-customer dyad. *Journal of Business Research*, 34, 35–45.
55 Kelman, H. & Hamilton, V. L. (1989). *Crimes of Obedience: Toward a Social Psychology of Authority and Responsibility*. New Haven, CN.: Yale University Press.
56 Shamir (1980). Chapter 1 note 9.
57 Strutton, D., Pelton, L. E. & Tanner, J. F. (1996). Shall we gather in the garden: The effect of ingratiatory behaviors on buyer trust in salespeople. *Industrial Marketing Management*, 25, 151–162.
58 Strutton, D. & Pelton, L. E. (1998). Effects of ingratiation on lateral relationship quality within sales team settings. *Journal of Business Research*, 43, 1–12.

59 Yagil, D. (2001). Ingratiation and assertiveness in the service provider-customer dyad. *Journal of Service Research*, 3, 345–353.
60 The notion of a three-way dynamic consisting of organization, service providers and customers has been discussed in the literature mainly in relation to interests and control strategies, but it is also relevant to the concepts of power bases and power tactics. Service providers can manipulate the information they transfer from organization to customers and from customers to organization to serve their interests and gain control. They may reward customers in a way that conflicts with organizational interests, use organizational means to enhance their expert power in their relationship with customers or use customer complaints to improve their working conditions within the organization.

3
Social Exchange: Equity and Justice in Service

Social exchange relationships develop between two parties through a series of mutual, although not necessarily simultaneous, exchanges that yield a pattern of reciprocal obligation by each party[1] (Blau, 1964). One party makes a contribution or provides a service to the other, and in so doing develops an expectation of a return at a future time. The other party, having received something of value, develops a sense of obligation to reciprocate. Social exchange relationships are different from those based on a purely economic exchange, in that the obligations of the parties in a social exchange with one another are often unspecified and the standards for measuring contributions are often unclear.[2] The evaluation of the social exchange process is largely determined by perceived justice. A recent multifocal approach to this evaluation[3,4,5] posits that the source of perceived injustice, namely the perpetrator of the potentially fair/unfair treatment, might not be solely the employee's relationship with the organization, supervisor and colleagues, as most previous research has indicated. An additional source of perceived justice is the customer. Thus, in the context of service, service providers maintain two distinct systems of social exchange, one with the organization and the other with the customers.[6] The first part of this chapter presents studies that focus on the service provider-customer social exchange while the second part explores the exchange with the organization.

A central theme in studies of social exchange in the service context is related to the notion that people in social exchange relationships pursue a balance between what they invest in a particular relationship and what they receive from it in return. Equity theory (Adams, 1965;[7] Walster *et al.*, 1978)[8] outlines the conditions that cause individuals to perceive a situation as balanced. According to equity theory, people evaluate their relationships with others in terms of rewards, costs, investments and outcomes. Individuals perceive a situation as fair when their own ratio between outcomes and inputs equals that of a comparison other. Inputs are the contributions perceived by an individual as relevant to an exchange and can consist of factors such as time, attention, skills and effort. Outcomes are described as the perceived receipts from the exchange, including status, appreciation, gratitude and pay. When outcomes relative to inputs are lower than those of a comparison other, one feels deprived, and when outcomes relative to inputs are higher than those of a comparison other, one feels advantaged. Another analysis of equity (Pritchard, 1969)[9] maintains that it is determined by intrapersonal standards, namely that people use their own internal standard to determine the fairness of their investment/gains ratio in a relationship. This internal standard is based on past experience in comparable relationships and the person's perception of the value of his/her investments. Inequity thus results from a discrepancy between one's internal standard, on the one hand, and one's own investments and gains in a relationship, on the other. The outcome of this process is perceived intrapersonal inequity.

A central proposition of Adams' equity theory is that individuals have an evolutionary tendency to pursue reciprocity. Partners assume that when an investment is made, they will gain something in return. In interpersonal relations, reciprocity exists when a person's investments and outcomes in a relationship are proportional to the investments and outcomes of the other person in the relationship.[7,8] At work, perceived investments may consist of education, seniority, time, attention, skill, and efforts. Perceived gains may include status, appreciation and pay.[7] A second proposition in equity theory is that the greater the inequity that exists, the more distress individuals will experience and the harder they will try to restore equity.[8]

Social exchange in the relationship with customers

Expectations of equity

The relationship between a professional service provider and a customer may be viewed as an ongoing social exchange process that is governed by the principles of equity.[10,11,12] However, expectations of equity are often not fulfilled, because this relationship is asymmetrical by its very nature: the service provider provides care, assistance, and support, while the customer merely receives.[13] This type of exchange, which is especially typical of the helping professions, is described in the social exchange theory context as an exchange in which the actors' contributions are separately performed and not negotiated. Actors initiate exchanges individually by performing a beneficial act for another (such as giving assistance or advice) without knowing whether, when, or to what extent the other will reciprocate.[14]

Even within the exchange based on one party giving more than the other the assumption is that the service providers expect some rewards, such as gratitude or obedience, in return for the caring and attention they provide.[12] Service providers were found to categorize customers, among other things, according to the extent to which they were pleasant and amenable, their gratitude for services received and their capacity for aggression.[15] However, customers frequently take the service providers' effort for granted or are unwilling to follow their advice. Inequity is especially acute in the health professions, where patients may be worried or aggressive, and interacting with such individuals may often be unrewarding. Many health professionals are regularly confronted with patients who do not follow their advice, make impossible demands, resist change, and may lie to or manipulate the service provider. This situation may progress into chronic inequity, whereby health service providers feel that they constantly put more into relationships with their patients than they receive in return.[12] Since human service-professionals often consider their job a calling and perceive the responsibility for others' well-being as their primary concern, they may experience considerable stress as a result of inequitable relationships with customers. Studies on the relationship between outcomes/inputs ratio and service provider burnout[12,13] found, as predicted by equity theory, a curvilinear effect of inequity on service providers' emotional exhaustion, namely that feeling more deprived and feeling more advantaged resulted in higher emotional exhaustion levels.

Equity theory suggest that sense of equity is determined by the subjective evaluation of inputs and outcomes. A study of teachers' perceived investments and outcomes[16] which distinguished between the task-oriented aspects of the job, such as teaching and coaching of students, and the relationship-oriented aspects of the job, such as respect, support and appreciation, found that teachers reported significantly more investments than outcomes in regard to both aspects of the job.

The service provider's inputs are often influenced by the demands made by customers. A longitudinal study of general practitioners that examined the consequences of dealing with demanding patient behaviors from the perspective of equity theory[12] found that the more demanding the patient, the stronger the physician's perception of a lack of reciprocity in the relationship with the patient. The underlying reasoning is that higher patient demands increase the chance of imbalance in the relationship: higher demands by patients require higher investments by physicians, which may be evaluated as lower outcomes for the physicians. The perceived lack of reciprocity in the study above resulted in feelings of emotional exhaustion which evoke negative attitudes towards patients (i.e., depersonalization), with the physicians attempting to gain emotional distance from their patients as a way of coping with their exhaustion. This, in turn, elicited more negative patient behaviors.

In as much as the valuation of the ratio between inputs and outcomes is highly subjective, it is also affected by the standard used by the individual in comparing gains and investments. According to equity theory, the standard of reference is usually a person or group comparable in a number of attributes. A comparison with one's colleagues is a major way of evaluating one's equity regarding relationships at work. A study among medical specialists, of the association between perceived inequity in work relationships and burnout, compared the effect of intrapersonal inequity involving an internal standard of reference with the effect of interpersonal equity, based on a comparison with others.[17] The finding was that intrapersonal equity affected all burnout dimensions: emotional exhaustion in all relationships at work, depersonalization in the relationship with patients, and reduced personal accomplishment in relationships with colleagues and the organization. Moreover, intrapersonal inequity explained more variance in burnout than did interpersonal inequity. The authors suggest that because medical specialists' work is, to a large extent, individual work, medical specialists may not be aware of the investments and rewards of their colleagues.

Several studies have examined service providers' reactions to perceived inequity and unfairness in their relations with customers. In studies simulating unfair treatment by customers[3,4] participants who were unfairly treated by customers or who observed co-workers being unfairly treated, were found to engage in higher levels of emotional labor and to have more difficulty complying with display rules than did participants who were fairly treated. In a study on the effect of lack of reciprocity on police officer burnout and attitudes towards the use of violence,[18] inequity was found to be positively related to burnout, which was positively related to attitudes towards use of violence. However, the negative effect of a sense of inequity was found to be buffered by the police officers' interpersonal orientation. A study examining the role of communal orientation – the willingness to give stemming from concern for others rather than exchange considerations – among nurses who worked with mentally retarded patients on perceived inequity and responses to the inequity,[19],[20] found that communal orientation buffers the negative effects of inequity on burnout. However, the buffering effect of communal orientation might depend on the service providers' helping model or expectations regarding the customer's role: communal orientation had a buffering effect on inequity only when the service provider expected the customer to be passive in the relationship.[21]

People tend to be active in attempting to restore a sense of equity. According to equity theory the stress resulting from a disturbed balance between investments and outcomes leads people to attempt to restore this balance. Such attempts may be reflected in attempts to decrease one's investments in the relationship (e.g., through behavioral withdrawal by leaving the organization, or through psychological withdrawal in the form of reduced commitment to the organization or depersonalization regarding customers), or directed to increasing the benefits gained from the exchange relationship (e.g., employee theft). Depersonalization may be a psychological strategy employed by service providers to restore equity reflected in developing negative attitudes towards customers. By responding to customers, or to their colleagues, in a depersonalized way instead of expressing empathy and concern, service providers lower their investments in these exchange relationships. In this sense, depersonalization towards customers or colleagues can be considered as motivational outcomes aimed at restoring a disturbed exchange relationship with colleagues or customers, that is, as coping behavior.[16] Yet, withdrawal behaviors were found to adversely affect the relationship with customers, because a reduction in the service provider's investment generates a similar behavior from the customer who also seeks to maintain equity.[5]

The possibility of externally buffering the negative effects of inequity was explored with a group-based burnout intervention program for health-care professionals working with mentally disabled individuals using equity theory as the theoretical framework.[11] The main objective of the program was to reduce perceptions of inequity in the relationship with the organization and with the customers by increasing the fit between the professionals' goals and expectations and the actual work situation. Results showed that burnout, absence and feelings of deprivation diminished in the group that experienced the intervention. A review of research on social exchange and burnout[5] demonstrates that lack of reciprocity at the interpersonal level is related to burnout even after controlling for situational and personal characteristics.

Closeness and self-disclosure

Since the service interaction involves many social elements, the exchange in service interactions consists not only of task-related inputs but also of social inputs, which are determined by the relationship in each specific service provider-customer dyad. Customer-service provider relationships may be described as ranging from more professional to less professional.[22,23,24] In highly professional relationships which are instrumental in nature, the customer and the service provider are focused on the functional aspects of the service. However, as the parties become closer, the social exchange becomes more intimate, reflected in the customer's willingness to provide personal information and the employee's willingness to provide personal advice.

Another perspective of social exchange views it as a means to create trust and intimacy so that the service provider can obtain important information from customers.[25] Many service organizations seek to initiate and maintain long-term relationships with preferred customers and acquire information about them. This is especially important in service industries where the provider is expected to judge the needs and preferences of each individual customer and adapt the delivered service accordingly. Such personal information can most successfully be gathered by direct face-to-face interaction between individuals with some degree of self-disclosure often elicited from the customer if the organization wants to be able to obtain certain covert information.

Adhering to the norm of reciprocity, customers are likely to reveal personal information in response to a service provider's benevolence. If benevolent employees signal a caring attitude and a personal commitment to the interests of the customer, the norm of reciprocity will likely motivate the customer to reciprocate this perceived benevolence by seeking repeated interactions, including disclosure of information to the employee. In a similar vein, satisfaction with the relationship with the service provider is also likely to be related to a willingness to share personal information. Being satisfied with a relationship implies that it is associated with feelings of pleasure and liking. When a customer enjoys the interaction with the service employee, the propensity to reveal more intimate information increases.[25]

Another theory of social exchange – the affect theory[26] – is highly relevant to the area of service provider-customer relationships.[27] This theory views social exchange as a joint activity that can be performed by at least two parties, and therefore involves a shared responsibility in which both parties are somewhat accountable for the outcome. The outcomes of the exchange produce emotions and the theory predicts that the greater the shared responsibility, the stronger the emotions people will attach to the social units of the exchange.

In a service setting, the social units are the relationships between service providers and customers; jointness is the source of shared responsibility in a service exchange – namely, the perception that both the customer and service provider are needed for a successful exchange; and emotional reactions are the result of the service outcomes. In light of the high level of interdependence between service providers and customers in service transactions, a high degree of customer involvement is needed to make a successful exchange. Thus, service providers are encouraged to heighten shared responsibility by drawing customers into the process, making them feel part of the service transaction and thereby increasing the customer's perception of joint control over the outcomes. Joint tasks that generate perceptions of shared responsibility are likely to create a sense of self-efficacy among customers which can produce positive emotions. The greater the perception of shared responsibility for service exchange success, the stronger the positive emotions felt by the customer toward the service provider. Furthermore, according to the affect theory of social exchange, emotions are directed at the group context and are not limited to the service provider. Emotions that result from social exchanges thus affect social relations, and a successful service encounter or relationship with a service employee will positively impact a customer's view of the entire service organization and his/her loyalty to it.[27]

Social exchange with the organization

Both social exchange theory and equity theory indicate that perceived inequity in the employment relationship constitutes a potentially powerful factor in the employee's work attitudes. Social exchange models assume that individuals pursue equity in their exchange with the organization, namely service providers agree to make specific contributions to an organization (e.g., talents, experience, time, service-oriented behaviors), and they expect the organization to provide benefits in return (e.g., payment, fringe benefits, promotion prospects, a supportive climate) proportional to their contributions.[13,28] Social exchange theory contends, in the context of the employee relationship with the organization, that employee actions and attitudes toward the organization exist on a continuum anchored by contractual or economic exchange, on the one end, and social exchange on the other. Contractual exchange relationships rely on formal agreements that specify and reward role expectations. Social exchange relationships are characterized by diffuse and open-ended role expectations that rely on reciprocity and norms of justice as their foundation.[29]

Perceived organizational justice

The employees' evaluation of their exchange with the organization is determined by perceived organizational justice. In organizations, justice refers to the rules and norms that determine the distribution of outcomes, i.e., rewards and punishments; the procedures used for making decisions; and interpersonal treatment of employees. Organizational justice may be broken down into three major dimensions: (1) distributive justice – the perceived fairness of outcomes or rewards provided by the organization;[30] (2) procedural justice – the perceived fairness of the decision-making procedures used in an organization[31] with fair decision processes characterized by formal decision-making procedures that are representative, consistent, impartial, accurate and subject to appeal; and (3) interactional justice – the perceived fairness of interpersonal treatment by managers[32] with fair treatment characterized by managers who make decisions showing interpersonal sensitivity (e.g., considerate, respectful, without bias) with adequate explanation and justification.[30,32,33]

There is agreement in the literature, however, that the relationship between perceived justice and employees' attitudes and behaviors is mediated by norms of social exchange. Employees feel obligated to reciprocate just treatment received from the organization in order to ensure a balance in their exchange with the organization. Reciprocation is reflected in positive work attitudes and contributions.[2,29]

However, when the relationship with the organization is evaluated as inequitable, the need for reciprocation will result in negative behaviors by employees. The notion of a psychological contract between employer and employee[34] is useful in explaining the negative side of the employee-organization exchange relationship, namely an inequitable relationship.[6,28] The psychological contract in this context consists of a set of expectations that employees hold about the nature of their exchange relationship with their organization. More specifically, the psychological contract reflects the employees' subjective notion of equity and serves as a baseline against which their personal investments and benefits are evaluated. Expectations concern both concrete or explicit issues (e.g., payment, work load), and less tangible or implicit matters (e.g., esteem, dignity at work). Inequity, or a violation of the psychological contract, is experienced when the expectations of reciprocity remain unfulfilled because the costs of the exchange with the organization outweigh the benefits that one receives in return.

A violation of the psychological contract may result in negative work outcomes, demonstrated mostly by withdrawal behaviors. Decreasing one's commitment to the organization may be viewed as a possible strategy to restore equity. By reducing their commitment, employees decrease their psychological investment in the organization, which leads to a more equitable balance between investments in and benefits gained from this exchange relationship.[16] Another available means for reducing inequity is withdrawal through absenteeism. Employees may perceive time away from work as instrumental in decreasing their investments and attaining other, more valued, nonwork outcomes simultaneously.[28] Perceived inequity may also result in an intention to quit.[35] Viewed from the perspective of equity theory, therefore, the psychological process that underlies withdrawal reactions is a response to an inequitable employment relationship.[28] Human-service professionals are especially vulnerable to perceived violations of the psychological contract because they often make high emotional investments in their work, and are therefore relatively sensitive to the rewards the organization provides in return (e.g., salary, positive feedback, career advancement).[11]

Additionally, one of the characteristics of human-service roles is solitude. This work situation makes conveying organizational information to employees problematic, namely information about service levels, new equipment, new work procedures, organizational goals and policy issues, solutions for dealing with such work-related problems as working with customers from different cultural backgrounds, personality clashes or sexual harassment. The scarcity of vital information may produce feelings of inequity because employees feel that the organization is not committed enough to them or that their status is not important enough in the organization. Informal organizational support may prevent these emotions and to a certain degree compensate for the insufficiency of other rewards.[36]

Much of the research that examined service providers' exchange relationships with customers has also explored the exchange with the organization. Perceptions of inequity in the relationship with the organization were consistently found to lead to negative results such as burnout, dissatisfaction and turnover intentions.[6,11,13,16,17,18,28,37,38] The relationship between perceived inequity and these negative behavioral reactions was found to be mediated by the emotional state of resentment which motivates the employee to reduce inequity and its associated negative feelings. When expectations of reciprocity remain unfulfilled, or a violation of one's psychological contract is experienced, employees develop feelings of resentment, grievance, betrayal and mistrust that, in turn, trigger various behavioral withdrawal reactions (see Geurts, Schaufeli & Rutte, 1999, for a review).[35] In a study of mental health care professionals, for example, feelings of resentment mediated the relationship of perceived inequity in the employment situation with turnover intentions.[35]

Fairness and the triple social exchange: customer-service provider-organization

Fairness is salient in service industries because of the specific characteristics of the industry: the intangibility of services heightens the customers' sensitivity to fairness and they are most likely to form enduring relationships with organizations who they believe 'play fair'. During service delivery, customers view fairness as a measure of whether the service organization has fulfilled its obligation to provide the results and benefits it promised. Fairness is not a separate dimension of service but, rather, touches on all dimensions of customer expectations of service quality:[39] delivering of the promised service dependably and consistently, attractive facilities, prompt service, competence and courtesy. Moreover, how the service provider responds in situations of service failure will strongly influence whether customers feel they have been treated fairly. The customer may be justly viewed as a victim who has been harmed by the service organization and now seeks reparation in the form of caring, individualized attention.[40]

At the same time, the organizational treatment of customers may affect the service providers' perception of fairness. Treating customers unfairly can reduce employee motivation. When employees see management charging inflated prices, or applying customer-insensitive procedures, they find it difficult to take service quality seriously.[40]

More importantly, the critical role of service providers as the principal focus of the customers' perception of fairness highlights the importance of the organization treating them fairly.[40] The exchange relationship of service providers with the organization may affect their behavior toward customers. Unfair acts within organizations affect service quality by decreasing employees' motivation to provide high-quality customer service.[39] Put another way, employees treat customers fairly to the extent that they themselves feel fairly treated,[41] thereby creating a triple social exchange.

A model describing the relationship between perceived fairness and behavior towards customers[2] shows that employees' perceptions of distributive and procedural fairness influence their organizational commitment. Commitment as a result of perceived fairness leads to a sense of obligation to reciprocate by providing the organization with something of value in return. In a service context, this reciprocation is likely to be through extra effort or helpful behaviors toward customers. Service employees who feel committed to the organization are likely to exert increased effort towards customers, such as persistence in trying to fulfill customer needs or extra time spent in working with them. In addition, committed employees are more likely to display pro-social behaviors towards customers, such as helping customers identify their needs. Effort and helpful behaviors heighten the customers' perception of the organization as fair.

Employees' evaluation of fair organizational treatment is often determined by human resource decisions.[40,42] Employees thus judge the fairness of their performance evaluation, the consistency and appropriateness of the evaluation process, the explanations and feedback that accompany the communication of performance evaluation and the rewards associated with those evaluations. In service organizations, if employees are treated fairly, they will, in turn, treat their customers more fairly. Fair human resource management can be expected to lead to satisfied, committed service providers willing to exert extra effort and display organizational citizenship behaviors, namely behaviors that are beyond the formal duty of the job. Such employees will deliver fair service reflected in fair outcomes, procedures and interpersonal treatment that customers expect. Thus, the indirect results of fair human resources are satisfied and committed customers and bottom-line returns.[40]

More specifically, the willingness of service providers to perform extra-role behaviors is likely to be related to perceived organizational support, namely the extent to which the organization is perceived by its workers as valuing its employees' contributions and caring about their well being. A perception that an organization supports its employees will lead to reciprocal contributions from employees in the form of extra-role behaviors. In addition, service providers who identify with the organization and perceive that a high quality service is important to the organization are more likely to subscribe to this objective. As a consequence, these service providers are more likely to engage in extra-role behaviors that help facilitate the goal of superior service quality. Such behaviors, in turn, result in positive customer evaluation of service quality.[43,44]

In addition, in a fair relationship with the organization, the employee may have confidence that extra effort will produce additional personal benefits. These may go beyond mere economic obligations as social exchange develops. A study that examined the relationships between perceptions of organizational fairness and pro-social service behaviors found that these behaviors were related to fairness of job supervision, pay and promotion rules, and the supervisory administration of these rules.[45]

The triple social exchange was manifested in a study on perceived organizational justice[29] that found service providers' customer-oriented behaviors to be related to their perceptions of organizational justice through the mediation of job satisfaction and organizational commitment. The authors hold that more discretionary forms of customer-oriented service behaviors are more likely to be viewed as social exchange gestures and, therefore, as more appropriate forms of reciprocation.

Conclusion

The service role consists essentially of giving, as implied by the adjective 'providers' widely used to describe the job, and reflected as well in the expectations of both the customers and the employing organization. The relationship with customers, therefore, is exceptional in terms of reciprocity primarily because service providers constantly maintain relationships in which they mainly give but do not receive. Furthermore, the intangible nature of service makes it difficult to define or acknowledge everything the service provider gives to the customer. Unlike in other social relations, the content of the exchange is very different for each party and customers rarely reciprocate for what they receive.

The service providers' need to receive something from customers in return is often frustrated, not only because customers may behave negatively, but also because of the nature of the role played by the organization in the customer-service provider exchange: the customer pays the organization, the organization pays the service provider, and the service provider provides the service to the customer. Thus, while service providers are generally cast in the role of mediators between the organization and the customers, when it comes to the exchange of rewards, it is the organization which mediates between customers and service providers, receiving from one and giving to the other. This is yet another reason why the service provider receives such little reward from the customer in return for the service.

Most research on the dynamics of the exchange relationships between the three parties has studied the effect of service providers' outcomes in their relationship with the organization on their input in the relationship with customers. Yet, as with the dynamics of power described in Chapter 2, it may be assumed that in these triadic relationships the exchange within each set of relationship affects the other two dyadic sets of exchange. According to equity theory, parties engaged in inequitable exchange relationships may restore equity by either reducing the investment or by attempting to improve the outcomes. This may be achieved either directly within the relationship itself, or indirectly in regard to another relationship set. For example, a service provider who experiences inequity in the relationship with customers may resort to depersonalization and decrease his/her investment in customers, but may also request a higher pay from the organization as compensation for the difficulties in the job. This in turn may affect not only the organization-service provider relationship, but also the organization-customer relationship (e.g., the need to raise service providers' salaries may result in less investment in service to customers). Service providers may reciprocate negative customer behaviors by counterproductive behaviors directed towards the organization if they perceive that the organization is 'on the customers' side' and does not protect them or if they see themselves as being 'on the customer's side' and feel that they are paying the price of insufficient organizational investment in service.

In a similar vein, customers' attempts to maintain equity may be directed either at the party who is directly involved in the exchange or at the third party of the triad. For example, customers might reciprocate good service from a certain service provider by positive word or mouth, which often serves the interests of the organization rather than the interests of the specific employee who provided the service. When service is bad, customers may attempt to restore equity by expecting the organization to provide compensation for the service provider's unsatisfactory behavior. Customers may reciprocate an organizational service failure by behaving aggressively towards a service provider even when he/she is clearly not responsible for the failure. Whether the customers' reaction is directed at the organization or the service provider, in either case it will affect both parties.

Notes

1 Blau, P. M. (1964). *Exchange and Power in Social Life*. New York: Wiley.
2 Masterson, S. S. (2001). Trickle-down model of organizational justice: Relating employees' and customers' perceptions of and reactions to fairness. *Journal of Applied Psychology*, 86, 594–604.

 3 Rupp, D. E. & Spencer, S. (2006). When customers lash out: The effects of perceived customer interactional injustice on emotional labor and the mediating role of discrete emotions. *Journal of Applied Psychology*, 91, 971–978.

 4 Rupp, D. E., Holub, A. S. & Grandey, A. (2007). A cognitive-emotional theory of customer injustice and emotional labor. In D. DeCremer (ed.), *Advances in the Psychology of Justice and Affect*, pp. 199–226. Greenwich: Information Age Publishing.

 5 Schaufeli, W. B. (2006). The balance of give and take: Toward a social exchange model of burnout. *The International Review of Social Psychology*, 19, 87–131.

 6 Schaufeli, W. B., van Dierendonck, D. & van Gorp, K. (1996). Burnout and reciprocity: Towards a dual-level social exchange model. *Work and Stress*, 10, 225–237.

 7 Adams, J. S. (1965). Inequity in social exchange. In L. Berkowitz (ed.), *Advances in Experimental Social Psychology*, Vol. 2, 267–299.

 8 Walster, E., Walster, G. W. & Berscheid, E. (1978). *Equity: Theory and Research*. Boston: Allyn & Bacon.

 9 Pritchard, R. D. (1969). Equity theory: A review and critique. *Organizational Behavior and Human Performance*, 4, 176–211.

10 Buunk, B. P. & Schaufeli, W. B. (1993). Professional burnout: A perspective from social comparison theory. In W. B. Schaufeli, C. Maslach, C. & T. Marck (eds), *Professional Burnout: Recent Developments in Theory and Research*, pp. 53–69. New York: Taylor & Francis.

11 Van Dierendonck, D., Schaufeli, W. B. & Buunk, B. P. (1998). The evaluation of an individual burnout intervention program: The role of inequity and social support. *Journal of Applied Psychology*, 83, 392–407.

12 Bakker, A. B., Schaufeli, W. B., Sixma, H. J., Bosveld, W. & van Dierendonck, D. (2000). Patient demands, lack of reciprocity, and burnout: A five-year longitudinal study among general practitioners. *Journal of Organizational Behavior*, 21, 425–441.

13 van Dierendonck, D., Schaufeli, W. B. & Buunk, B. P. (1996). Inequity among human service professionals: Measurement and relation to burnout. *Basic and Applied Social Psychology*, 18, 429–451.

14 Other types of service relationships, mainly services that include the provision of goods to customers, may be described as exchanges in which benefits are exchanged bilaterally and neither actor can profit without making an agreement that benefits both [Molm, L. D., Takahashi, N. & Peterson, G. (2003). In the eye of the beholder: Procedural justice in social exchange. *Sociological Review*, 68, 128–152].

15 Rosenthal and Pecci (2006). Chapter 2 note 41.

16 Van Horn, J. E., Taris, T. W., Schaufeli, W. B. & Schreurs, P. J. G. (2004). The structure of occupational well-being: A study among Dutch teachers. *Journal of Occupational and Organizational Psychology*, 77, 365–375.

17 Smets, E. M. A., Visser, M. R. M., Oort, F. J., Schaufeli, W. B., Hanneke, J. C. & de Haes, J. M. (2004). Perceived inequity: Does it explain burnout among medical specialists? *Journal of Applied Social Psychology*, 34, 1900–1918.

18 Kop, N., Euwema, M. C. & Schaufeli, W. B. (1999). Burnout, job stress and violent behavior among Dutch police officers. *Work & Stress*, 13, 326–340.

19 Van Yperen, N. W., Buunk, B. P. & Schaufeli, W. B. (1992). Communal orientation and the burnout syndrome among nurses. *Journal of Applied Social Psychology*, 22, 173–189.

20 Van Yperen, N. W. (1996). Communal orientation and the burnout syndrome among nurses: A replication and extension. *Journal of Applied Social Psychology*, 26, 338–354.

21 Truchot, D. & Deregard, M. (2001). Perceived inequity, communal orientation and burnout: The role of helping models. *Work and Stress*, 15, 347–356.

22 See Introduction.

23 Coulter, R. A. & Ligas, M. (2000). The long good-bye: The dissolution of customer-service provider relationships. *Psychology & Marketing*, 17, 669–695.

24 Coulter and Ligas (2004). Introduction note 15.

25 Hansen, H., Sandvik, K. & Selnes, F. (2003). Direct and indirect effects of commitment to a service employee on the intention to stay. *Journal of Service Research*, 5, 356–368.

26 Lawler, E. J. (2001). An affect theory of social exchange. *The American Journal of Sociology*, 107, 321–353.

27 Sierra, J. J. & McQuitty, S. (2005). Service providers and customers: Social exchange theory and service loyalty. *The Journal of Services Marketing*, 19, 392–400.

28 Geurts, S., Schaufeli, W. & de Jong, J. (1998). Burnout and intention to leave among mental health-care professionals: A social psychological approach. *Journal of Social and Clinical Psychology*, 17, 341–362.

29 Bettencourt, L. A., Brown, S. W. & MacKenzie, S. B. (2005). Customer-oriented boundary-spanning behaviors: Test of a social exchange model of antecedents. *Journal of Retailing*, 81, 141–157.

30 Folger, R. & Cropanzano, R. (1998). Organizational justice and human resource management. *Foundations for Organizational Science*. Thousand Oaks, CA: Sage Publications, Inc.

31 Lind, E. A. & Tyler, T. R. (1988). *The Social Psychology of Procedural Justice. Critical Issues in Social Justice*. New York, NY: Plenum Press.

32 Bies, R. J. & Moag, J. S. (1986). Interactional justice: Communication criteria of fairness. In R. J. Lewecki, B. H. Sheppard & M. H. Blazerman (eds), *Research in Negotiation in Organizations*, Vol. 1, 43–55. Greenwich, CT: JAI Press.

33 The dimensionality of organizational justice is not clear. Cropanzano and Ambrose (2001) pointed to the difficulties in distinguishing between procedural justice and distributive justice, since the evaluation of procedural justice is based on outcomes. Colquitt (2001) in a comprehensive empirical test of the dimensionality of the organizational justice construct, found that organizational justice consists of four distinct dimensions: procedural justice, distributive justice, interpersonal justice, and informational justice.

34 Robinson, S. L. & Rousseau, D. M. (1994). Violating the psychological contract: Not the exception but the norm. *Journal of Organizational Behavior*, 15, 245–259.

35 Guerts, S. A., Schaufeli, W. B. & Rutte, C. G. (1999). Absenteeism, turnover intention and inequity in the employment relationship. *Work and Stress*, 13, 253–267.

36   Van Yperen, N. W. (1998). Informational support, equity and burnout: The moderating effect of self-efficacy. *Journal of Occupational and Organizational Psychology*, 71, 29–33.

37   Taris, T. W., Peeters, M. C. W., Le Blanc, P. M., Schreurs, P. J. G. & Schaufeli, W. B. (2001). From inequity to burnout: The role of job stress. *Journal of Occupational Health Psychology*, 6, 303–323.

38   Van-Horn, J. E., Schaufeli, W. B. & Enzmann, D. (1999). Teacher burnout and lack of reciprocity. *Journal of Applied Social Psychology*, 29, 91–108.

39   Berry, L. L. (1995). Relationship marketing of services – Growing interest, emerging perspectives. *Academy of Marketing Science Journal*, 23, 236–245.

40   Bowen, D. E., Gilliland, S. W. & Folger, R. (1999). HRM and service fairness: How being fair with employees spills over to customers. *Organizational Dynamics*, 27, 7–23.

41   Schneider, B. & Bowen, D. E. (1993). The service organization: Human resources management is crucial. *Organizational Dynamics*, 21, 39–52.

42   Perceived fairness is one of the only ways that employees can evaluate human resources management practices because most employees do not have the information relating to various concerns (i.e., technical, financial, legal, and strategic) that guide human resources management (Bowen, Gilliland & Folger, 1999).

43   Bell, S. J. & Menguc, B. (2002). The employee-organization relationship, organizational citizenship behaviors, and superior service quality. *Journal of Retailing*, 78, 131–146.

44   The issue of extra-role or organizational citizenship behaviors is elaborated in Chapter 5.

45   Bettencourt, L. A. & Brown, S. W. (1997). Contact employees: Relationships among workplace fairness, job satisfaction and prosocial service behaviors. *Journal of Retailing*, 73, 39–61.

Part II

Customer and Service Providers' Attitudes and Behaviors

4
Being Always Right: Customer Behavior Towards Service Providers

Customer influence on service providers is much more immediate than management influence. This is due to the physical proximity that often exists between service provider and customer, the great amount of time they spend together, and the significant amount of positive and negative feedback along with varied information that customers provide.[1] Moreover, customers and service providers influence each other mutually, as reflected in findings showing that customer satisfaction with service affects service providers' attitudes and well-being (reviewed by Homburg & Stock, 2005).[2] For example, customer satisfaction is negatively related to service providers' job dissatisfaction and health complaints,[3] while customer perceptions of service quality affect employee morale and service climate.[4]

As described in Chapter 3, customer interpersonal behaviors may be perceived by service providers in terms of social exchange, affecting their perception of equity in the relationship. However, since customer behavior is often perceived as reflecting an attitude towards the organization rather than towards a specific service provider, such behavior is generally discussed in the literature from an instrumental perspective in terms of feedback. Thus, it has been argued[5] that customer complaints should be defined as negative customer feedback. Without customer feedback, unrecognized organizational problems cannot be fixed, and opportunities to develop and extend customer relationships are lost. Therefore, customer communications, whether in the form of complaints or compliments, must be heard and given attention.[6,7] This is especially important because the majority of customers do not provide feedback and the overall incidence of both complaining and complimenting behavior is low,[8] making it all the more valuable.

As feedback received from inside the organization, customer behaviors might be expected to affect service providers' performance. Yet, customers often display emotional behaviors which are far from conveying the objective and impartial message that characterizes formal organizational feedback. Therefore, customer behaviors cannot be seen simply as a desirable feedback, but must also be considered as interpersonal behaviors often motivated by emotions and eliciting emotions in the other party as well.

The first part of the chapter describes customer complaints and compliments. Customers' motives for both are presented, followed by a description of variables that affect service providers' perception and interpretation of, and reactions to, these behaviors. While organizations and service researchers generally view customer complaints and compliments in a positive light, customer reactions in the form of misbehaviors are almost unanimously condemned. Misbehavior is often displayed in the form of interpersonal aggression, yet it may also be impersonal and directed towards the organization's property or its reputation. Nevertheless, all forms of customer misbehavior are likely to have some impact on service providers who must face them and internalize their implications. The second part of the chapter presents explanations for customer misbehavior, its various manifestations, and its effects on service providers.

Customer complaints

While the literature on customers generally discusses complaining as a behavioral outcome of a perceived discrepancy between expectations and performance, not all complaints stem from unfavorable attitudes or feelings of dissatisfaction. People complain even when they are not subjectively dissatisfied, in an attempt to elicit interpersonal reactions from others, such as sympathy or approval. Kowalski (1996)[9] conceptualizes a complaint as 'an expression of dissatisfaction, whether subjectively experienced or not, for the purpose of venting emotions or achieving intrapsychic goals, interpersonal goals, or both' (p. 181). Accordingly, complaints are seen as a form of reciprocal interpersonal communication between the complainer and his/her audience. Like other forms of interpersonal behavior, complaints involve a pattern of mutual influence in which the complainer influences the behavior of the listener, and the listener's response to the complaint subsequently affects the complainer.

There is agreement among researchers of organizations that customer complaining is good for the service organization (see Reynolds and

Harris, 2005, for review).[10] Customer complaining behavior and its management are considered to be areas of great importance for businesses, especially since organizations increasingly recognize the value of pursuing long-term relationships with customers. A widespread assumption is that for every complaining customer, there may be as many as 20 others with the same problem who remain silent. This is particularly significant considering the powerful impact of word of mouth on an organization's reputation and its subsequent ability to retain customers.[6] In recognizing the importance of complaints, organizations have also focused their attention on complaint resolution in the realization that when customers complain, organizations get a chance to solve the specific problem and save the relationship with the customer. Furthermore, complaints can reveal areas that need improvement and thus contribute to organizational learning processes.[11]

Motives for complaining

Given the importance of complaining, and the fact that many unsatisfied customers do not complain, a large part of the literature focuses on analyzing customers' motives for complaining or not complaining, as well as on various differences between complaining customers and those who remain silent. Major factors that were found to lead to customer complaints are[10,12]:

(1) Product/service type; severity of the problem; customer's assessment of the justifiability of the cause of complaint; perceived injustice; the intensity of dissatisfaction experienced; discourtesy of service providers.
(2) Evaluation of the process and anticipated outcome: perceived costs of complaining; perceived probability of a successful complaint outcome.
(3) Customer-organization relationship: customer loyalty; prior relationship between the organization and customer.
(4) Customer characteristics: assertiveness; attitude towards complaining; level of sophistication.

In addition, cultural characteristics affect customers' tendency to complain. Customers in individualistic cultures who believe in self-responsibility for example, expect others to be efficient; therefore, they are more demanding and more likely to complain than customers in more collectivist cultures who believe in shared responsibility.[13]

Customer complaints are essentially derived from dissatisfaction, but customers may sometimes complain without experiencing any service failure or genuine dissatisfaction. Customers have been found to make illegitimate or fake complaints in order to obtain free goods and services, evade responsibility for their own errors, enhance their feelings of self-worth, receive a positive evaluation from other customers, or simply cause some form of disruption and, ultimately, a service failure.[10]

Service provider reactions to complaints

Kowalski (1996)[9] provided a broad theoretical framework which can be applied to the service context in order to understand the variables that affect reactions to complaints. According to the model, the reaction to a complaint depends on the focus of the complaint, namely whether the complaint was directed at an individual service provider or at some other person or event. People frequently react defensively when complaints are directed towards them. Thus, complaints directed at the individual service provider are more likely to engender negative reactions than are complaints directed at another source. In addition, the reaction depends on the intensity accompanying the complaint. Complaints that are accompanied by intense negative affect are less likely to be met with agreement than complaints presented in a mild manner. Responses to a complaint also depend on the perceived content of the complaint. Complaints are accepted more readily when they are perceived as authentic and stemming from a genuine source of dissatisfaction rather than as stemming from ulterior motives. In addition, complaints that can be supported by objective evidence, and that are perceived as made to bring about change rather than to make the complainer feel better, are accepted more readily. Lastly, complaints addressed directly to the source of dissatisfaction (at least as long as that individual is not the service provider him/herself), and not to a third party, are accepted easily.

Service researchers believe that a large quantity of customer complaints may be a source of stress for service providers.[5,6] Customer complaints have an effect similar to negative feedback which was found to have a negative influence on employee performance and job attitudes. Negative feedback tends to elicit a negative mood in the recipient which inhibits cognitive flexibility and consequently lowers performance mainly in complex tasks (see Bell & Luddington, 2006, for review).[6] In a study on retail chain service providers, customer complaints were found to be negatively associated with employees' commitment to customer service.[6] A similar negative effect was found in a study of passengers' behavior towards tram drivers: customer complaints were found to be negatively related to drivers' professional efficacy.[14]

Stress may be also generated by the role conflict experienced by service providers when they perform according to organizational expectations but are confronted with consumer complaints that demand a different set of behaviors from the organizational norms. In addition, employees begin to see that reciprocating organizational support with customer-oriented behaviors is futile as customers continually 'let them down'. Consequently, employees may lose confidence in organizational support, or may doubt that commitment to customer service is warranted by organizational support.[5]

Service providers often react to customer complaints with prescribed organizational responses. Yet, employees' underlying attitudinal and emotional reactions to complaints have been rarely studied. People's reactions to complaints generally have been found to range from very supportive, to complete dismissal of the complainant's expressed dissatisfaction. Classifications of responses to complaints include agreement/disagreement with the expressed dissatisfaction, justifications or excuses for the criticized behavior, denial of the legitimacy of the complaint, expressing sorrow and empathy with another's dissatisfaction, attempts to help another resolve the problem, complaining in response to the complaint, a neutral response, or ignoring the complaint (see Kowalski, 1996, for review).[9] Service providers' reactions to complaints were described in a study[15] comparing customer attributions with employee perceptions of incidents of customer dissatisfaction. Employees rarely attributed the causes of customer dissatisfaction to their own attitudes or behaviors; rather, they blamed external factors and customer behaviors. Conversely, customers tended to attribute problems to the employee. These tendencies were explained in terms of self-serving attribution bias, i.e., both employees and customers are unlikely to attribute failings to themselves.

Customer compliments

Customer compliments have received far less attention in the literature than customer complaints. However, like complaints, compliments, too, represent an important form of feedback to organizations. In fact, their potential to influence both organizational and individual behaviors is considered greater than that of complaints, as people are more willing to listen to and accept praise than criticism.[7] In addition, like complaints, compliments provide employees with information that is both explicit and concrete.[16] However, compliments may be difficult to recognize because they are often subtle, may not occur immediately at the time of the service, and are not necessarily directed to the service provider responsible for the performance. Although compliments may address various levels of the organization, service providers will be the object of the compliment only when the contact is non-routine in nature, or when the product is largely intangible. Therefore, organizations should devise ways to encourage customers to provide compliments, devote effort to recognizing and understanding compliments, and make sure to act on compliments.[7]

Customers were found to compliment service providers for the following motives: delight or exceptional satisfaction, reciprocity/social norms, wishing to improve relationship with a service provider, high involvement with product or service, wishing to continue special services or products, buffering complaints to increase their effectiveness (i.e., improve receptivity of an accompanying complaint), and flattery to get a reward.[7] Furthermore, customers' motives determine the target of their compliments as well as their content. Compliments motivated by the desire to improve the relationship with the service provider are given directly to the service provider – mostly to men, while compliments offered as sociable behaviors address some special effort and/or added service and are more often given to women. Apparently, compliments are instrumental and are mostly designed to achieve a certain purpose.[17]

The effect of compliments on service providers is likely to be determined by their trust that the compliment is sincere, although there are contradictory approaches to the question of belief in the sincerity of compliments. Because service providers are aware of possible motives of customers in complimenting them, some compliments may be perceived as insincere, have no impact, or are not even considered as a compliment.[7] Yet, other literature on flattery suggests otherwise,[18] showing that people generally tend to like those who flatter them and tend to believe the flattery. The assumption is that this effect is caused by the motivation of the recipient to be flattered: when people are the target of ingratiation, their self-esteem is served by accepting the flattery uncritically. Since psychologically healthy people have reasonably high self-esteem, a flattering message is usually consistent with the self-concept of the target and is therefore accepted at face value. This approach is supported by the finding that the most frequent response by service providers to customers' compliments was acceptance of the compliment (which is also the most common reaction between strangers) followed by making a comment about the appreciated aspect, in addition to acceptance. Other reactions were offering an impersonal comment on the object of the compliment, upgrading the compliment – namely accepting it and indicating that its extent is insufficient, returning the compliment to the customer, disagreeing with the compliment, or transferring the compliment to a third party or to the object itself.[19]

In addition to compliments, customers display various friendly behaviors towards service providers, such as seeking personal advice or socializing outside the service setting.[20] Informal friendly and positive customer behaviors improve both parties' experience of the interaction[21] as well as the service providers' professional efficacy, and reduces cynicism.[14]

Customer misbehavior

Service providers are highly vulnerable to workplace victimization. Statistics show a strong relationship between workplace violence and the routine job of face-to-face contact with large numbers of people involving the handling of money which typifies many service provider occupations.[22,23] In a frequent type of violent incidents, the perpetrator is a customer who commits an act of violence towards the service provider. Health care providers and social service employees are particularly vulnerable to this type of violence.[24]

While not all misbehaviors amount to violence, deviant customer behaviors are displayed by the majority rather than the minority of consumers.[25] Since misbehavior by customers is under-reported by business sources and in official crime statistics (it usually fails to lead to a criminal charge), misbehavior is more common than usually thought.[26] The assumption underlying many studies on customer orientation – that customers behave in a manner that is both rational and functional – conflicts with findings demonstrating that norm-breaking deviant behaviors are frequent and accepted.[25]

Customer misbehavior is described by such terms as deviant, aberrant, dysfunctional, problem customers, and 'jaycustomer' behavior.[25] These terms are used to describe behavior such as shoplifting, vandalism, aggression and illegitimate complaining, or behaving in a deliberately thoughtless or abusive manner, causing problems for the organization, employees or other customers.[27]

While not all misbehaviors are directed towards service providers, most are likely to have some effect on service providers as they represent a blunt violation of the service script, and disturb the customers' relationship with the organization and the service providers. Misbehavior represents the dark side of customers, expressed in violations of generally accepted norms of conduct in service situations and disruption of the service process. Although customer misbehaviors have negative consequences for everyone involved, including other customers, much of the misbehavior is tolerated as it has become an accepted part of the customer experience.[26]

Reasons for misbehavior[28]

Organizations do not wish to draw attention to customer misbehaviors, and legal prosecution, therefore, is extremely rare.[26] A study on violence in employment services found that although service providers experienced much of customer behavior as violent, this high level of violence was systematically denied by the organization and construed by management in such a way as to make it invisible.[29]

According to another view, customer misbehavior is the result of the evolution of a customer-focus policy and the notion of the customer as 'king', which leads to customers behaving like dictators.[25] Customers perceive a low level of danger from verbal abuse toward service providers because customers are often anonymous which allows them to act in socially undesirable ways without the constraints of shame and perceived consequences. Even if without anonymity, the customer is better able to avoid future interactions and reduce the risk of retaliation. Furthermore, customers are aware of the strong constraints on employees' behavior toward them, namely that they are inhibited from retaliating overtly.[30]

The notion of the customer as being always right communicates the unequal power relationship in the customer-employee transaction. This results in customer aggression,[31] is used as a rationalization for consumer misbehavior, and leads to a situation in which organizations ignore such misbehavior.[26] Not only are organizations generally tolerant of consumer misbehavior directed at their employees, but employees are expected to smile through customer discourtesies and outbursts, while the service reality may result in customer anger, abuse and even violence.[32]

From an instrumental perspective, the manifestation of dissatisfaction in the form of misbehavior may depend on the customer's behavioral intentions. A dissatisfied customer who intends to remain in a relationship with the service provider for a long term is likely to be committed to maintaining and building the relationship. However, a dissatisfied customer whose intention is to remain in the relationship for a short term might be critical towards the service provider and make suggestions for improving the next encounter. Customers who focus exclusively on their dissatisfaction are committed to dissolving the relationship as quickly as possible. Such customers are antagonistic towards the service provider, express their disagreement with how the service provider conducts business, and might become physically aggressive.[33]

While most researchers agree that customer aggression towards service providers is a negative phenomenon, an opposite view is also presented[34] in considering whether customers should be encouraged to behave aggressively in order to attain catharsis, namely vent their negative emotions via an acute expression of aggression. Because suppressing hostility may lead to a dislike of the cause of the tension and harboring a grudge in the long run, retaliation against a perceived wrong, and aggressive words and/or behavior which provide a catharsis and prevent the repression of the grievance, may be preferable to passive acceptance. Organizations should actively encourage customers to explode when making complaints, as this may induce them to feel good after the incident and hence maintain more positive attitudes towards the organization. These ideas seem to represent an extreme form of the notion, adopted by many service organizations, that the customer is always right.

Types of customer misbehavior

Customer misbehaviors are expressed in the violation of transactional role expectations and generally prevailing norms of behavior as well as a challenge to the organization's legitimacy and authority to set boundaries. Of these behaviors, customer abuse concerns service providers most as it is directed towards them rather than the organization. The intention of abusive behaviors is usually intimidation or defiance. Such behaviors enable the customer to vent frustration and anger at the service provider.[26]

Verbal aggression (e.g., shouting, insults, cursing) is a common source of stress for service providers.[31] In a study comparing the frequency of customer verbal abuse with supervisors and colleagues verbal abuse[30] customer abuse was found to be more frequent. Physical violence, manifested in harm to the service providers themselves and sometimes to their property, is less common but even more stressful.[35]

In addition to abuse, the most common customer misbehavior is theft or shoplifting. Vandalism is also common, especially among teenage customers. Additional frequent behaviors are tag-switching, passing bad checks, and willful disobedience of rules.[26] These behaviors are often the result of the customers' wish to retaliate against the organization. Customer retaliation was found to take the following forms: spoiling products or placing false orders in order to cost the organization money by creating extra work; vandalism reflected in destruction or damage of property; trashing, making a mess; stealing in order to get back at the organization; negative word of mouth with the intent to hurt the organization; and personal attacks against service providers not only through abuse but also through negative feedback to supervisors.[36]

While these overt misbehaviors are clearly aversive, less extreme types of customer behaviors may also be experienced as stressful by service providers.[37] Such behaviors include taxing the service that customers need to receive from the service provider by demanding service which might be legitimate but seems disproportionate, unjustified and unfair from the service provider's point of view. A customer's behavior may antagonize other customers who are forced to wait for an excessively long time as a consequence; it may be disproportionate compared with what the organization receives from the customer in exchange; or customers may be requesting things they could do themselves. Service providers view such situations as one-sided and lacking reciprocity. Additionally, service providers experience stress as a result of interactions with hostile, humorless and unpleasant customers. These customers may display behavior that is not explicitly perceived as aggressive because there is no obvious intention to harm, but it may come close to behaviors described as uncivil, disrespectful and damaging to the service provider's self-esteem.[15,37]

Another type of distressing customer misbehavior is grudge-holding, which stems from a strong negative emotional reaction experienced by the customer during the service process. The customer's emotional response leads to the formation of a negative attitude, followed by an appraisal of the coping alternatives, and ending in the behavioral manifestation of a grudge-holding attitude. A grudge-holding response may occur over a longtime and may include complaining, avoidance behavior, negative word of mouth, or the enlistment of an outsider to bring about a desired result. While the customer engages in grudge-holding behavior, interaction between the customer and the service provider may continue and may involve vengeance that takes the form of threats, lawsuits or participation in an online hate community. These types of behaviors may be designed to achieve equity is response to an unsatisfying transaction, but they may also be punitive, motivated by the desire to harm the offending organization or service provider.[38]

Some types of service contexts, such as police, prison or psychiatric services, inherently involve contact with misbehaving clients. Misbehavior, in other, more mundane service contexts, however, have been the subject of several more relevant studies. Airlines and railway service providers are at an especially high risk of customer violence because they spend more time with customers, cannot walk away from a violent customer, and cannot request external help. An added source of violent behavior in airlines is attributable to the stress of the flying experience for some passengers, who consequently become aggressive. Service providers in this field were often found to experience verbal abuse in the form of sarcasm, condescending remarks and swearing while physical abuse could take the form of pushing, kicking, punching, slapping, scratching, striking with an object, spitting, pointing, poking and maintaining inappropriate contact.[39]

Human services employees who provide social services often experience threatening episodes in their interaction with customers, both in the workplace and during home visits. Specifically, the interview situation, when clients are asked to describe their familial and personal lives, was found to increase the risk of personal injury.[40] Health care professionals who work inside their client's home sometimes experience sexually harassing behaviors by customers. The unique features of this work environment have two important consequences for understanding the potential impact of customer misbehavior: the relative isolation of in-home workers, which reduces the organizational protections afforded to employees within traditional organizational contexts and leads to a greater co-occurrence of such abusive behaviors; and the necessity for workers to continue visiting clients' homes (i.e., to provide health care) despite the occurrence of abusive behavior, which leads to an increased sense of vulnerability on the part of the worker. Customer misbehavior was found to be related to fear of the recurrence of such behavior in the workplace, which in turn predicted negative mood (anxiety and anger) and perceptions of injustice. In turn, fear, negative mood, and perceived injustice predicted lower affective commitment and enhanced withdrawal intentions, poor interpersonal job performance, greater neglect and cognitive difficulties.[41]

Misbehaving customers in libraries[42] were identified as alcohol and drug users, young people, vandals, irate customers and psychiatric patients, who, due to a variety of motives, including lengthy queues, unavailability of new titles, and perceived negative staff attitude, may act in a violent or aggressive manner towards staff.

Restaurant employees sometimes encounter what has been described as the customer from hell, namely a paying guest whose behavior is 'beyond rude'.[43] Service providers describe the behavior of such customers as insensitive and arrogant and believe that 'customers from hell' enjoy making someone else's life miserable by their behavior. Different behaviors were described for men and women: men use foul language, call service providers by a pet name, want to deal only with the manager, and scream at employees, while their female counterparts demand special orders at no extra charge, act as if they are the only guest in the restaurant, and throw tantrums if anything goes wrong.

Customer behaviors in the bar, hotel and restaurant sectors were analyzed in one study[44] from two perspectives: covertness and primary motivation. In terms of covertness, behaviors range from public displays to concealed vandalism, with motivation ranging from customer ego needs to financial gain. Within this framework eight categories of misbehaving customers emerge:

1. Letter writers claiming compensation – customers who attempt to gain monetary compensation without justification by appealing in writing to centralized customer service departments. This type of customer requests unspecified compensation for perceived service failures that were not drawn to the attention of the service providers at the time of the service. This is a covert type of behavior because such behaviors are characteristically hidden from the service providers. Furthermore, these customers typically contact head or regional offices rather than the branch or outlet where service was claimed to have been inappropriate.

2. Undesirable customers – consumers or users of services who are viewed as unattractive, unwanted or objectionable by customer-contact personnel, the management of the organization, or fellow service users. Behavior by undesirable customers is typically covert and intentional in nature, and performed as a means of obtaining monetary gain. Such 'rule breaking' behavior fails to conform with the unwritten norms of service encounters, and ranges from comparatively mild varieties of customer misbehavior, such as distasteful behavior by 'family feuders' who quarrel obtrusively with each other and other customers, to extreme forms of criminal behavior (also see Lovelock, 1994[27], 2001[45]).

3. Property abusers (also see Lovelock, 2001)[45] – customers who intentionally vandalize, destroy or remove items from the organizational environment. Such behavior is often performed in a deliberate and covert manner, as a means of obtaining non-financial gain. The behavior is usually motivated by peer-induced fun-seeking and other psychological motives for causing disruption.

4. Ex-service providers – customers who, due to experience as a service provider, behave in a dysfunctional manner when in the role of customer. Such behavior is preplanned and overt in manner. In the

majority of incidents, such customers intentionally disrupt service encounters as means of obtaining financial gain. The behavior is motivated by the service provider's superior knowledge over non-service employee customers, and therefore an acute understanding of how things should be done, or know-how about how to obtain financial compensation during service encounters. Furthermore, heightened confidence gained from their role as service providers increases their self-assurance and belief in their ability to gain financial reward.

5. Vindictive customers – those who perform premeditated and pre-dominantly overt acts of malicious behaviors for either personal or financial gain. This category can be subdivided into three main forms of behavior: customers who deliberately and maliciously spread neg-ative messages by word of mouth concerning an organization; phy-sical acts of perceived retaliation or revenge by customers towards either the organization or the front-line staff; and customers who attempt to evade responsibility for their own behaviors by blaming employees.

6. Verbal abusers – customers who, principally for financial but often subsequently for non-financial gain, verbally disrupt the service encounter by abusing other customers or service providers. Find-ings reveal that verbal abuser behaviors range from professional com-plainers to customers who abuse service providers, often through condescension, in order to enhance perceptions of self-worth. A differ-entiation has been made[46] between aggressive customers who interact with service providers in an aggressive style, and resort to aggression customers who use a combination of assertive and aggressive strategies in dealing with service providers, resorting to aggressive behaviors such as rudeness or threats when their demands are not granted.

7. Physical abusers – customers who intentionally and overtly act in an aggressive and violent manner, physically harming service employ-ees in order to satisfy non-financial motives. Behaviors in this cate-gory range from mildly harmful and degrading to severely harmful acts. All behaviors in this category are illegal.

8. Sexual predators – customers who overtly express their sexual desires to service providers. This category consists of such behaviors as offensive body language, sexual comments and physical sexual harassment. The fact that service providers often work for long periods without supervision distances them from the support and advice they need if they are faced with a possible sexual harassment situation.[47]

Outcomes of customer misbehavior

In the short term, customer aggression results in heightened emotional regulation by service providers. In a study of managers and customers in hotels, customer aggression was found to be related to feigned emotional displays by the service provider, most often to pacify disruptive customers.[35] Similarly, customer verbal aggression towards call center employees was found to be related to emotion-regulation strategies: employees who felt more threatened by customer aggression resorted to surface acting in an effort to mask negative emotions when interacting with customers.[31] Another study conducted in call centers[48] found the number of incidents involving abusive customers to be related to employees' emotional labor and to absence levels.

Paradoxically, by complying with management's customer-relations policies, and the consequent necessity for engaging in emotional regulation, service employees contribute to management's indifference to customer violence. Service employee exposure to increasing levels of customer violence may be viewed as the result of minimal investment by management in violence reduction strategies. However, to some degree workers are forced to collaborate in their own exploitation by deploying their emotional labor as a palliative for management's failure to address and remove the stimuli or sources of customer abuse. The greater the success achieved by service providers in managing customer dissatisfaction, especially when it takes the form of verbal abuse, the less management will be motivated or required to address the source of customer violence.[39]

Long-term effects of customer misbehavior are reflected in sustained feelings of degradation, namely feelings of worthlessness and humiliation, as well as stress disorders reflected in memory flashbacks, anxiety and sleeplessness.[35] Another long-term effect of customer misbehavior is burnout, which was found to be related to various types of stressful interactions with customers,[37] and specifically to customer aggression.[49,31,14,30] Moreover, incidents of public violence and aggression were found to be related to service employees' fear of violence as well as to turnover intentions.[24] Additionally, customer verbal abuse results in exhaustion because service providers are expected to suppress the negative emotions that results from the abuse, and this demand for emotional regulation leads exhaustion.

Service provider coping with customer misbehavior

Service providers were found to use several forms of tactics designed to cope with misbehaving customers, most of which were informal and often performed without managerial consent.[25] These coping tactics were employed before, during and after acts of customer misbehavior. Tactics adopted in preparation for a stressful work environment were mental and emotional preparatory work to help the service provider enter the workplace; consuming alcohol, and cigarettes, and to a lesser extent drugs; wearing modest clothing to prevent aggressive customer behaviors; and observing customers to identify those who may be potentially deviant.

Tactics adopted by service providers during encounters with misbehaving customers were ignoring difficult customers; making efforts to discount or overlook acts of deviant behaviors; bribing customers, namely offering free goods or services (without formal managerial consent) to calm deviant customers or induce them to exit the site; faking an emotional display; exploiting sexual attractiveness in order to diffuse acts of customer deviance; eliciting physical and emotional support from regular customers when dealing with acts of deviant customer behaviors; altering personal speech patterns to socially align themselves closer to the deviant customer; and manipulating the service environment by modifying or removing objects within the service setting.

Most tactics used after stressful incidents were designed to restore the service providers' balance, namely by isolating themselves both from their colleagues and the customers to enable themselves to regain their composure in private; conversely, by engaging coworkers in conversation and coping in a collaborative manner; and releasing tension by physical exercise. Some service providers, however, reacted by performing acts of revenge either after incidents of deviant customer behavior or over extended time periods.[25]

Other tactics employed by service providers to cope with potential or actual customer violence include blaming other service providers' skills; avoiding violent incidents; bending the rules rather than confronting the customer and risking violence; displacing anger, namely venting anger in ways other than retaliating to the customer; and putting on a brave face to minimize the incident.[32]

A more combative coping pattern was found in a study on resistance among waitresses.[50] When customer aggression was encountered, waitresses adopted a waitress as soldier persona, with customer hostility matched and even surpassed by that of the waitress. In doing so, the waitresses were able to maintain a sense of self-worth and deflected assaults on their dignity.

More broadly, a study that examined the effectiveness of coping strategies and resources used by service providers in coping with customer aggression[49] found that service providers tend to use emotion-focused coping strategies in response to aggression, namely they deal with the emotional and psychological outcomes of the problem by behaviors such as denial or disengagement. Such coping was found to be ineffective in terms of its effects on burnout, as it was shown to be related to a higher level of depersonalization and a lower sense of accomplishment. Problem-focused coping strategies, reflected in dealing with the problem itself, were not used consistently in response to customer aggression, but when used, they were found to be related to high levels of sense of accomplishment. Conceivably, functioning under the organizational notion of the customer being right, service providers are highly restricted in their ability to apply direct problem-focused coping in response to customers' aggression.

Moreover, while organizations believe that adopting a customer orientation is universally beneficial, it may result in potentially harmful, unintended consequences not only for the service providers but also for management and customers. Because service providers are subjected to direct control, they adopt a customer orientation pretense for the benefit of managers and customers. However, once free of such control, service providers use a wide range of tactics to cope with the stress involved in customer misbehavior. While some of the coping tactics can be viewed as consistent with managerial prescriptions (e.g., calming angry customers), other tactics (e.g., bribing customers) may be physically harmful, emotionally taxing, illegal, immoral and even degrading, and cause damage to the organization.[25]

Figure 4.1 summarizes types of misbehavior and their effects on service providers.

Conclusion

Several authors maintain that the notion of the customer being always right is the source of customer misbehavior. The phrase, of course, should not be taken literally, but as conveying a message regarding the infinite entitlement of customers that deems questions of objective right and wrong as irrelevant. This message, which is addressed primarily to customers, is likely to have several effects. The customers' level of expectation for perfect service is heightened, while their tolerance of service failures is likely to decrease. Every small problem or imperfection is magnified, creating a sense of deprivation and violation of the customer's rights, as the entitlement to perfection is unfulfilled. Furthermore, the sense of entitlement affects the way customers choose to react to such

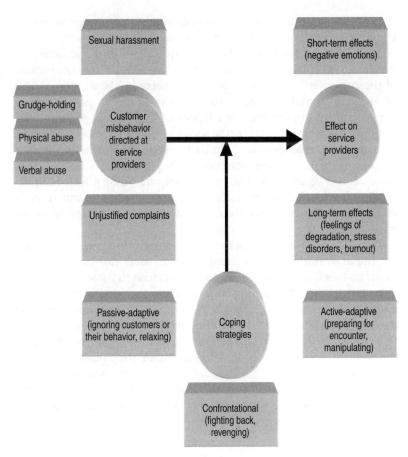

Figure 4.1   Customer misbehavior, its outcomes, and service providers' coping strategies

failures. Being always right conveys an implicit message that customers can get away with practically anything. Thus, the service encounter becomes a venue in which customers sometimes behave in ways they would not behave ordinarily. Conceivably, even non aggressive people become more aggressive and demanding when they are under the impression that every service problem is a violation of their rights and that they are almost expected to demand amendments. In a similar vein, service providers are expected to put up with behaviors they would not accept in any other situation. They are expected to put aside their self-esteem, dignity and basic rights and accept behaviors that are sometimes intolerable.

Both parties' behavior in the case of customer abuse is explainable by the concept of depersonalization. Customers do not view the service provider as an individual with an identity, needs and emotions, but rather as a role player or an organizational representative who, because of the customers' total entitlement, is expected to be a willing target of abuse if something goes wrong. Notably, the abusive behavior may be almost impersonal and adopted to some extent without truly noticing the service provider: the scenario would have been the same with another service provider. Similarly, service providers may be able to contend with abusive behaviors because they too do not view the customer as an individual but as someone filling a role. Still, the service provider's task in accepting such behavior is much more difficult than the customer's role, as abuse cannot be perceived totally impersonally.

Customer misbehavior violates basic norms of interpersonal behavior, the organizational service script, and, in some cases such as fraud, moral and legal standards. Yet, organizations tend to ignore these inevitable consequences of granting customers infinite rights, since the competition for customers outweighs the prospect of restricting customer behavior. In the context of the employee-organization relationship, this implies that organizations do not protect their employees. The literature shows that service providers sometimes reciprocate the organization's disloyalty by being disloyal themselves and evading customer aggression by sacrificing organizational interests. Thus, unrestricted customer misbehavior eventually results in mutual disloyalty by both the organization and the service provider.

Notes

1   Rafaeli (1989). Chapter 1 note 55.
2   Homburg, C. & Stock, R. M. (2005). Exploring the conditions under which salesperson work satisfaction can lead to customer satisfaction. *Psychology & Marketing*, 22, 393–420.
3   Dormann, C. & Kaiser, D. (2002). Job conditions and customer satisfaction. *European Journal of Work and Organizational Psychology*, 11, 257–283.
4   Schneider, B., White, S. S. & Paul, M. C. (1998). Linking service climate and customer perceptions of service quality: Test of a causal model. *Journal of Applied Psychology*, 83, 150–163.
5   Bell, S. J., Menguc, B. & Stefani, S. L. (2004). When customers disappoint: A model of relational internal marketing and customer complaints. *Academy of Marketing Science Journal*, 32, 112–126.
6   Bell, S. J. & Luddington, J. A. (2006). Coping with customer complaints. *Journal of Service Research*, 8, 221–233.

7 Kraft, F. B. & Martin, C. L. (2001). Customer compliments as more than complementary feedback. *Journal of Consumer Satisfaction, Dissatisfaction and Complaining Behavior*, 14, 1–12.

8 Oliver, R. L. (1997). *Satisfaction: A Behavioral Perspective on the Consumer.* New York: McGraw Hill.

9 Kowalski, R. (1996). Complaints and complaining: Functions, antecedents and consequences. *Psychological Bulletin*, 119, 179–196.

10 Reynolds, K. L. & Harris, L. C. (2005). When service failure is not service failure: An exploration of the forms and motives of 'illegitimate' customer complaining. *The Journal of Services Marketing*, 19, 321–335.

11 Stephens, N. (2000). Complaining. In T. A. Swartz & D. Iacobucci (eds) *Handbook of Service Marketing and Management*. Thousand Oaks: Sage.

12 Marquis, M. & Filiatrault, P. (2002). Understanding complaining responses through consumer's self-consciousness disposition. *Psychology & Marketing*, 19, 267–292.

13 Liu, B. S. C., Furrer, O. & Sudharshan, D. (2001). The relationships between culture and behavioral intentions toward services. *Journal of Service Research*, 4, 118–129.

14 Van Dierendonck, D. & Mevissen, N. (2002). Aggressive behavior of passengers, conflict management behavior and burnout among trolley car drivers. *International Journal of Stress Management*, 9, 345–355.

15 Bitnter, Booms and Mohr (1994). Chapter 1 note 22.

16 Goetzinger, L., Park, J. K. & Widdows, R. (2006). E-customers' third party complaining and complimenting behavior. *International Journal of Service Industry Management*, 17, 193–206.

17 Otto, S. D., Payne, C. R., Parry, B. L. & Hunt, H. K. (2005). Complimenting behavior – The complimenter's perspective. *Journal of Consumer Satisfaction, Dissatisfaction and Complaining Behavior*, 18, 1–30.

18 Vonk, R. (2002). Self-serving interpretations of flattery: Why ingratiation works. *Journal of Personality and Social Psychology*, 82, 515–526.

19 Payne, C. R., Parry, B. L., Huff, S. C., Otto, S. D. & Hunt, H. K. (2002). Consumer complimenting behavior: Exploration and elaboration. *Journal of Consumer Satisfaction, Dissatisfaction and Complaining Behavior*, 15, 128–147.

20 Coulter and Ligas (2004). Introduction note 15.

21 Vilnai-Yavetz and Rafaeli (2003). Introduction note 13.

22 Scalora, M. J., Washington, D. O., Casady, T. & Newell, S. P. (2003). Nonfatal workplace violence risk factors: Data from a police contact sample. *Journal of Interpersonal Violence*, 18, 310–327.

23 In many violent incidents the perpetrator of the violence has no legitimate business relationship with the targeted workplace but enters the work environment in order to commit a criminal act (e.g., robbery). Individuals at particular risk to such acts include taxi drivers, convenience store employees and gas station attendants (Scalora *et al.*, 2003).

24 LeBlanc, M. M. & Kelloway, E. K. (2002). Predictors and outcomes of workplace violence and aggression. *Journal of Applied Psychology*, 87, 444–453.

25 Reynolds, K. L. & Harris, L. C. (2006). Deviant customer behavior: An exploration of frontline employee tactics. *Journal of Marketing Theory and Practice*, 14, 95–111.

26 Fullerton, R. A. & Punj, G. (2004). Repercussions of promoting an ideology of consumption: consumer misbehavior. *Journal of Business Research*, 57, 1239–1249.

27 Lovelock, C. H. (1994). *Product Plus: How Product + Service = Competitive Advantage*. New York: McGraw-Hill.

28 Specific explanations of customer misbehaviors, which are beyond the scope of this review, refer to interactions between customer-related variables (i.e., psychological, demographic and social/group influences) and contextual variables (i.e., physical environment, types of products/services offered, level of deterrence and public image of the organization) (Fullerton & Punj, 2004).

29 Godwin, B. F., Patterson, R. G. & Johnson, L. W. (1995). Emotion, coping and complaining propensity following a dissatisfactory service encounter. *Journal of Consumer Satisfaction, Dissatisfaction and Complaining Behavior*, 8, 155–163.

30 Grandey, A. A., Kern, J. H. & Frone, M. R. (2007). Verbal abuse from outsiders versus insiders: Comparing frequency, impact on emotional exhaustion, and the role of emotional labor. *Journal of Occupational Health Psychology*, 12, 63–79.

31 Grandey, A. A., Dickter, D. N. & Sin, H. P. (2004). The customer is not always right: Customer aggression and emotion regulation of service employees. *Journal of Organizational Behavior*, 25, 397–418.

32 Bishop, V., Korczynski, M. & Cohen, L. (2005). The invisibility of violence: Constructing violence out of the job centre workplace in the UK. *Work, Employment & Society*, 19, 583–602.

33 Ligas, M. & Coulter, R. A. (2000). Understanding signals of customer dissatisfaction: Customer goals, emotions, and behaviors in negative service encounters. *American Marketing Association, Conference Proceedings*, 11, 256–262.

34 Bennet, R. (1997). Anger, catharsis, and purchasing behavior following aggressive customer complaints. *Journal of Consumer Marketing*, 14, 156–172.

35 Harris, L. C. & Reynolds, K. L. (2003). The consequences of dysfunctional customer behavior. *Journal of Service Research*, 6, 144–161.

36 Huefner, J. C. & Hunt, H. K. (1994). Extending the Hirschman model: When voice and exit don't tell the whole story. *Journal of Consumer Satisfaction, Dissatisfaction and Complaining Behavior*, 7, 267–270.

37 Dormann and Zapf (2004). Chapter 2 note 49.

38 Aron, D. (2001). Consumer grudgeholding: Toward a conceptual model and research agenda. *Journal of Consumer Satisfaction, Dissatisfaction and Complaining Behavior*, 14, 108–119.

39 Boyd, C. (2002). Customer violence and employee health and safety. *Work, Employment and Society*, 16, 151–169.

40 Shields, G. & Kiser, J. (2003). Violence and aggression directed toward human service workers: An exploratory study. *Families in Society*, 84, 13–20.

41 Barling, J., Rogers, K. A. & Kelloway, E. K. (1995). Some effects of teenagers' part-time employment: The quantity and quality of work make the difference. *Journal of Organizational Behavior*, 16, 143–154.

42 McGrath, H. & Goulding, A. (1996). Part of the job: Violence in public libraries. *New Library World*, 97, 4–13.

43 Withiam, G. (1998). Customers from hell. *Cornell Hotel and Restaurant Administration Quarterly*, 39, 11.

44 Harris, L. C. & Reynolds, K. L. (2004). Jaycustomer behavior: An exploration of types and motives in the hospitality industry. *The Journal of Services Marketing*, 18, 339–357.

45 Lovelock, C. (2001). *Services Marketing: People, Technology, Strategy*, 4th ed. Sydney: Prentice-Hall.

46 Richins, M. L. (1983). An analysis of consumer interaction styles in the marketplace. *Journal of Consumer Research*, 10, 73–82.

47 Fine, L. M., Shepherd, C. D. & Josephs, S. L. (1994). Sexual harassment in the sales force: The customer is NOT always right. *The Journal of Personal Selling & Sales Management*, 14, 15–30.

48 Deery, S., Iverson, R. & Walsh, J. (2002). Work relationships in telephone call centers: Understanding emotional exhaustion and employee withdrawal. *Journal of Management Studies*, 39, 471–496.

49 Ben-Zur, H. & Yagil, D. (2005). The relationship between empowerment, aggressive behaviours of customers, coping, and burnout. *European Journal of Work and Organizational Psychology*, 14, 81–99.

50 Paules, G. F. (1996). Resisting the symbolism of service among waitresses. In C. L. Macdonald & C. Sirianni (eds) *Working in the Service Society* (pp. 264–290). Philadelphia: Temple University Press.

5
Being Only Human: Service Providers' Behavior Towards Customers

A large part of service provider behavior towards customers is determined by the formal and informal requirements of the roles as dictated by the organization. These behaviors include not only the technical aspects of service provision, but also specified interpersonal behaviors designed to enhance the positive experience of the customer within the encounter. Other behaviors, however, which are discretionary may be either constructive or destructive. These behaviors are affected by the service provider's predispositions and attitudes towards the organization and customers. In addition, since service is a social interaction, some behaviors emerge as a reaction to customer behavior toward service providers.

The behaviors discussed in this chapter represent various aspects of the service interaction, as follows: personalization which is a comprehensive concept consisting of various behaviors designed to put the customer in the center and provide personal in contrast to customized service; organizational citizenship, which also consists of several dimensions considered to reflect extra-role behaviors relating to the service provider's attitudes towards the organization; and courtesy, a specific and basic behavior required of service providers in all services.

These are constructive service-provider behaviors that may be categorized as 'in-role'/'extra-role' behaviors. By contrast, the following destructive behaviors may be categorized as intentional/unintentional behaviors: Discrimination, which is often unintentional, stemming from deep-rooted stereotypes and prejudices; and other destructive behaviors, namely dishonesty and service sabotage, which are intentional and may reflect either a temporary reaction to a specific situation or a permanent negative attitude.

Personalization

Personalization is reflected in individualized service.[1,2] Service organizations often face the challenge of providing efficient standardized service at an acceptable level of quality while simultaneously treating each customer as a unique person. In a broad sense, personalized service refers to any behavior occurring in the interaction intended to contribute to the individualization of the customer. That is, the customer role is established in the service encounter through specific recognition of the customer's uniqueness as an individual over and above his/her status as an anonymous service recipient.[2] It is 'tailored service', or service that attempts to address the unique needs of individual customers. Such service is welcomed by customers in flexible service contexts but may not be viewed positively in routinized or customized service encounters.[2]

Another conceptualization views personalization as the service employee's manner of relating to the customer on a human level. As such, it includes such aspects as employee politeness and courtesy, an attempt to get to know the customer as a person and to engage in friendly conversations, and exhibiting personal warmth. 'Personalization' in this sense concerns the manner in which service employees relate to customers as people – cold and impersonal at the one end to warm and personal at the other. Personalization involves behaviors (conversation) which move the interaction from a more formal realm to a more personal one.[3]

Personalization was found to have a significant influence on customer experience in organizations that deliver service in interactive encounters with customers, such as health clinics.[4]

Customers' as well as service providers' expectations regarding the degree of personalization in a specific encounter depend on the structural dimensions of the service. In high-contact services, where the customer is paying for individualized attention (e.g., legal, medical, hair care), both parties expect the service to be uniquely tailored to the needs of the customer. In other situations (e.g., fast food services), both parties realize that in order to receive service promptly and efficiently, the customer must agree to temporarily relinquish the right to be treated as an individual with specialized needs. In these situations, the service is highly formalized and the customer has learned appropriate role behaviors. Increased personalization would be contrary to expectations and to the need to focus concentration on the routine service encounter, and might thereby disrupt the smooth progress of the service process.[2]

Outcome-directed and process-directed personalization

Personalization may be directed toward personalizing the outcome of the service (option personalization) or towards personalizing the inter-active process of obtaining the service (programmed personalization or customized personalization). Option personalization is the most common mode of personalization, allowing a customer to choose the option best suited to his/her needs from a set of service possibilities. Yet, many service organizations implement personalization by focusing on the way service providers interact with customers. Programmed personalization is reflected in giving the impression of personalized service by such behaviors as encouraging small talk and using customers' names. Customized personalization is based on the desire to assist the customer in obtaining the best possible form of the service offered for his or her needs. This strategy enhances individuation by attending to the unique needs of the customer and providing helpful advice.[2]

Interaction involvement

Communication behaviors associated with all forms of personalized service involving interaction, such as asking questions to identify customers' specific needs, offering options and advice to help customers make decisions, actively listening to customers, voluntarily providing information on topics of interest to customers, and providing informal counseling.[1] Service providers demonstrate their attentiveness by nonverbal cues (e.g., maintaining eye contact, leaning forward, head nods) that indicate interest in what the customer has to say. Additionally, when sharing information with a customer, involved service providers are attentive to the customer's reactions to that information and try to correctly interpret what the customer is trying to communicate, or ask clarification questions.[1,5]

Information sharing

Service providers may also employ strategies for communicating specialized, complex information to customers. Effective information sharing requires, at a minimum, spending sufficient time conveying information and making suggestions, particularly if the information is new and important to the customer, if it enhances the customer's ability to make sound decisions, or if it directly addresses the customer's questions or concerns. Service providers may heighten the clarity of information by limiting their use of technical language, simplifying explanations, translating technical explanations into simpler language, or otherwise framing information in a form that facilitates customer understanding.[1]

Social support

Social support occurs when service providers' verbal or nonverbal communication increases clients' sense of control by reducing their uncertainty, improves clients' self-esteem, or enhances the clients' sense of social connection to others.[6] Social support in the service context is reflected in help extended by service providers to customers to meet their personal needs. It consists of practical guidance, nondirective support (e.g., informal counseling), positive social interaction and tangible assistance (e.g., providing transportation).[7] Social support is also reflected in interpersonal interaction, in that service providers communicate interest in a customer's well-being, show sensitivity to a customer's feelings and needs, and provide encouragement. Customer expectations regarding social support in a service encounter were found to be related to the type of the interaction: customers in a service relationship, namely repeated encounters, expect more support than customers in a one-time interaction.[5] Additionally, it was found that anxious customers receive more supportive responses from service providers and evaluate them more positively than angry customers do.[8]

Service adaptiveness

Another concept related to personalization is service adaptiveness, which is the ability of service providers to adjust their interpersonal behavior to the demands of the service encounter and the customer's needs.[3,9,10] It can be described as a continuum, ranging from conformity to an established script, in which employees approach each customer the same way, to service personalization, in which employees must adapt to serve customers individually.[11]

Interpersonal adaptiveness differs from service personalization demonstrated in such behaviors as using the customer's name (programmed personalization) in that truly adaptive behavior is not always 'personal', but rather is contingent on each customer's preferences. Thus, interpersonal adaptation entails being 'personal' if the customer desires a personal interaction and being 'nonpersonal' when the customer prefers that type of interaction (see Figure 5.1). Because services are devised and received during the encounter, service providers have the opportunity to customize the level of personalization in 'real time'.[9]

The successful adaptation by the service provider of either the service offering or of one's interpersonal behavior can be a difficult task. The service provider must infer the customers' preferences from subtle, often nonverbal cues, then react with appropriate interpersonal behaviors and service solutions. Several factors, however, make this task

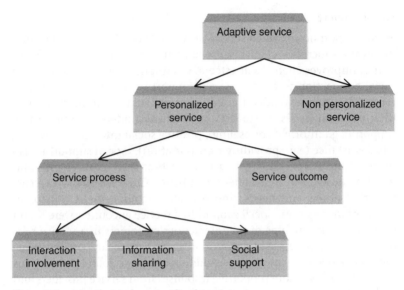

Figure 5.1 Adaptive and personalized service

easier. First, based on their experience, service providers who are able to accurately categorize customers can identify their common needs and desires, and are more likely subsequently to alter their interpersonal behavior and modify the service offering to provide the best match with customer preferences. In addition, such predispositions as self-monitoring (the ability to modify self-presentation from one situation to another), tolerance for ambiguity, customer orientation, and intrinsic motivation to adapt, increase the service providers' adaptiveness. Lastly, the task of adaptiveness becomes easier under high levels of interpersonal contact, which allow for more information sharing regarding customer expectations and service provider capacity. Service providers gather relevant information in 'real time', which provides them with the insight necessary to adapt the service offering needs.[3,9]

Organizational citizenship behaviors

Discretionary behaviors that employees display for both customers and organizations can significantly influence customers' perceptions of service quality. These behaviors, termed organizational citizenship behavior (OCB), are not formally rewarded, yet they promote the effective functioning of the organization.[12] Service-oriented OCB is emerging as an important element of the service provider job[13] since service providers are expected to delight customers by providing exceptional service. These behaviors are differentiated from role-prescribed customer service behaviors which derive from implicit organizational norms or from explicit rules that require such basic behaviors as demonstrating accurate knowledge of policies and products or greeting customers.[14]

Organ (1988)[12] has identified five categories of OCB: (a) altruism – the helping a coworker with a task; (b) conscientiousness – carrying out one's duties beyond the minimum requirements; (c) coworker courtesy – alerting others in the organization about changes that may affect their work; (d) sportsmanship – refraining from complaining about trivial matters; and (e) civic virtue – participating in the governance of the organization. Another dimension relevant to service-oriented OCB is loyalty OCB which reflects allegiance to the organization through the promotion of its interests and image to outsiders.

Several reasons explain the relevance of service providers' OCB to service quality and to customer perceptions of service. First, discretionary behavior is critical in service encounters because of the unpredictability of customer requests and the range of service-provider required activities.[15] Second, successful encounters and exchanges with customers often require effective internal exchanges among employees.[16] Third, employee OCB spills over to service quality. Therefore, employees who exhibit OCB towards coworkers or the organization will be an asset in fulfilling customer needs.[16] Lastly, high levels of OCB lead to a more efficiently functioning organization and assist in the acquisition of new resources by the organization.[12] Such acquisitions refer not only to attracting new personnel or raw materials, but also to such intangible factors as enhancing company goodwill or the public reputation of the organization. OCB therefore is associated with customer perceptions of service quality.[17]

Altruism

Of the components of OCB, only altruism is directly associated with service quality. Altruism, or prosocial behaviors, may be directed at customers as well as at colleagues.[14,18] Notably, customer-directed prosocial behaviors can involve the provision of services either in organizationally consistent or inconsistent ways. A service provider might for instance resolve a customer's complaint by following organization policy or by deviating from that policy. In both instances, if the employee is acting in the customer's best interest, he/she is displaying customer-directed prosocial behaviors. Such behaviors were found to be positively related to positive employee affect.[18,19]

The relationship between altruism and service quality may also be indirect. Altruism directed towards coworkers encourages teamwork and cooperation, which allows service providers to increase the pool of available resources.[17] Employees who are committed to a high level of service quality realize that for successful exchanges with customers to occur, effective internal exchanges must occur first. These service providers will go beyond the call of duty to assist coworkers as a means of ultimately satisfying customers.[20] An example of this is seen when a service provider helps a colleague who is temporarily overburdened or absent to ensure that customers will receive quality service without an undue wait. Similarly, when an experienced service provider helps less skilled or new employees solve service-related problems and devise more efficient ways of performing their service, this is likely to improve customers' perception of service quality. In addition, altruism has been shown to create a positive, group-cohesive climate among employees, which in turn spills over into their interactions with customers.[16]

Consciousness and coworker courtesy

Conscientious role performance is another critical attribute for service providers, especially in the context of behaviors that directly affect customers. Research on service quality reveals the importance of consistently reliable, responsive and courteous behaviors by service providers.[21] Conscientious employees keep themselves informed about up-to-date knowledge regarding products or services as well as pass on the information to their colleagues. Such behaviors ensure that service providers will not act on outdated information or provide customers with erroneous information. Conscientious employees who maintain predictable work schedules also increase the reliability of service.[17] Moreover, service providers act as representatives of the organization to customers and can enhance or damage the organizational image. Loyal OCB behavior by these employees, therefore, is important for the organization, as they act as advocates of the organization's products, services and image.[21]

Sportsmanship

Sportsmanship may also contribute to service quality in that it creates a positive climate among employees that is likely to be transferred to their interactions with customers. If employees are cooperative with each other, they are likely to be more cooperative in their contact with customers. Service providers who often complain about the organization cannot be expected to provide qualitative service to customers. Ultimately, a positive work climate among service providers creates an overall pleasant environment for customers.[16]

Civic virtue

Civic virtue (e.g., taking part in unit meetings, providing ideas that enhance customer service) can also affect service quality in several indirect ways. Service employees constitute a strategic link between the external environment and internal operations by providing information about customer needs and suggested improvements in service delivery. Thus, service provider suggestions to improve service quality are fundamental to the organization's ability to meet customers' needs[21] and form the basis for controlling services, improving service quality, and developing new services.[17,16] Civic virtue in the form of attending and actively participating in meetings may also provide opportunities for employees to hear about other employees' experiences during service encounters, identify their own problems in providing service, and learn how to improve service.[16]

The different subsets of OCB were found to be predicted by different antecedents: Job attitudes were found to predict loyalty OCB,[21,13] personality characteristics were found to predict prosocial OCB, and customer knowledge and personality jointly were the best predictors of civic virtue OCB.[21]

Courtesy and friendliness

Employee courtesy appears to be an important service variable, in that when evaluating a service organization, consumers are likely to give more weight to attributes they can easily assess, such as courtesy, than attributes more difficult to assess, such as the professional level of the employee.[22] Service provider courtesy was found to heighten customers' positive evaluation of the service, willingness to recommend the service to friends, and willingness to use the service again.[23]

However, the influence of customer evaluations of employee courtesy on their overall evaluation of service quality is controversial. When the outcomes of a particular service are viewed as paramount, such behaviors as friendliness or courtesy are not likely to affect consumers' evaluations.[24] Furthermore, when the line between courtesy and over-friendliness is crossed, friendly behavior prompted by goodwill might actually diminish customer satisfaction.[25]

There is no agreement among researchers regarding the ideal proportion of friendliness in courteous service. Courtesy is conceptualized as any behavior that conveys immediacy, sociability or a positive emotion. In the service context it has been described as a friendly type of behavior used to break the ice, form a quick bond with the customer, and create the necessary rapport for a positive encounter.[23] It involves exchanges of pleasantries to build goodwill between people, greeting and thanking behaviors, small talk, and nonverbal behaviors such as eye contact and smiling.[23] According to another conceptualization, however, courtesy is reflected in an employee approach marked by respect for and consideration of the consumer.[22] Friendliness suggests a warm familiarity, whereas courtesy reflects a respectful reserve.[25] Friendliness might enhance the customers' perception of service quality, yet it might also leave customers alienated rather than loyal. A service provider who attempts to induce friendliness by addressing a customer by his/her first name may cause alienation if the customer expects to be addressed more respectfully by his/her last name.[25]

While personalization and courtesy may be considered positive generally, the optimal mix or repertoire of service provider behaviors must be determined by the specific service context. In a situation of a low degree of personal interaction (e.g., remote services), the important aspects of a service provider's behavior are such attributes as reliability, concern for quality and conforming behavior. In services that focus on offering something unique to customers, service providers should demonstrate behaviors such as creativity and innovation, a high tolerance for unpredictability, a high degree of risk-taking, and a propensity to obtain satisfactory results even if this means disregarding formal procedures. Service providers operating in high-reliability environments where customers expect to receive error-free outcomes (e.g., banking services) must demonstrate reliable and predictable behaviors, show a high concern for quality of the outcome, be willing to invest time to achieve perfection, display a low risk-taking approach and focus on satisfying customer needs.[26]

While the contingency approach depicts positive service-provider behaviors, the behaviors described below are clearly destructive to the service process. Service providers may intentionally or unintentionally adopt a variety of behaviors that negatively affect customers, who are often unaware of the flaws in the service they receive.

Discrimination

Service providers sort customers into categories and then act on the basis of these judgments.[27] A potential behavioral expression of this categorization process is discrimination. Contemporary research on discrimination contends that although the incidence of major discriminatory acts (i.e., negative actions towards members of a group) and overt prejudices (i.e., negative attitudes about a group) have decreased considerably, these actions and attitudes have been replaced by pre-judice manifested in subtle, indirect discriminatory behaviors (see review in King *et al.*, 2006).[28] Accordingly, discrimination in organizations may be conceptualized in terms of both formal discrimination (biases prevented by laws or by organizational policies) and interpersonal discrimination (biases that tend to be nonverbal and are more covert).[29] In organizational interactions, formal discrimination (traditional, overt manifestation of discrimination), such as refusing to greet, help, hire, or train stigmatized employees and customers, is uncommon because this form of discrimination is often prohibited by law. However, inter-personal discrimination is not subject to legal regulations. Although service providers are not legally permitted to refuse to serve a customer on the basis of a stigmatized attribute such as race or age, discrimina-tion may persist in implicit forms such as less eye contact, less smiling, and greater rudeness.[28]

In addition to the social and personal origins of prejudice, organiza-tions may impose prejudice on employees by myths or questionable heuristics that have evolved as part of the organizational culture, training programs, and in some cases formal policies. Interviews with service providers revealed that they believe that children make a mess, women are gullible, poorly dressed customers go for the bargain rack, and older customers have a lot of time.[30] Additionally, discrimination is likely to be affected by the type of interaction with customers. In one-time encounters, the service provider does not have a prior basis for judging the customer and therefore stereotyping is easy. In longer relationships, the history of the interaction fosters a more accurate image of the customer.[31]

Customer characteristics that affect discrimination (see Figure 5.2)

Ethnicity

In a study of Afro-American customers' shopping experiences in both Afro-American and Caucasian neighborhoods, respondents reported that most service provider-customer interactions in Afro-American neighborhoods are positive rather than negative but that Afro-Americans are treated worse when they shop in predominantly Cau-casian neighborhoods.[32] The respondents reported that they are more frequently followed, treated rudely, accused of theft, or in contrast, ignored when they shop in department stores or boutiques located in predominantly Caucasian neighborhoods.[33]

Business owners in Caucasian neighborhoods may treat Afro-American customers poorly because they feel that Afro-Americans do not belong in certain social spaces. However, it appears that the customer's age is also an important factor in determining service provider behavior: Afro-American service providers too, were found to follow their younger Afro-American customers in low-income neighborhoods. Furthermore, customers in middle-class Afro-American neighborhoods reported better treatment from store owners compared with those who reside and shop in low-income Afro-American neighborhoods, regardless of age.

These cumulative negative personal experiences with discrimination are at the very least hurtful and take a heavy psychological toll on Afro-American customers, who react with a range of responses, from disbelief to anger to paranoia. Not only do Afro-Americans consistently receive negative treatment; they also witness Caucasian customers receiving preferential treatment. Service providers greet and approach Caucasian customers more promptly than they do Afro-American customers, sometimes even skipping over Afro-Americans to help Caucasian customers who are clearly behind them in line.[32,34]

A study conducted in restaurants found that service providers tended to stereotype and categorize Afro-American customers one-dimensionally based on the single characteristic of race. In using this stereotype to form cognitive expectations about future interactions with this group, the service providers revealed Caucasian supremacist attitudes and, furthermore, a feeling of their own social superiority. Their use of negative other-presentation when speaking about Afro-American customers was generally followed with positive self-presentation, demonstrating a strategy to separate themselves socially and psychologically from a stigmatized social group.[35]

Prejudice against Afro-Americans may occur in Afro-American neighborhoods as well. A study of the sale of cigarettes to children in California, where such sales are illegal, found that service providers sold more cigarettes to Afro-American children than to Caucasian children.[36] Another study, exploring racial attitudes among minorities by examining the attitudes of Korean immigrants in the United States who have established businesses in Afro-American communities, found that everyday personal contacts accounted for a large part of Korean merchants' attitudes towards Afro-American customers. While many encounters were routine exchanges, brief and casual, and even included an exchange of pleasantries, others were more conflictual, involving unilateral or mutual rudeness, miscommunication, and ignorance of the other group's cultural norms. Korean culture for example frowns on making eye contact, smiling, or touching strangers (including putting change in someone's hand) – inhibitions regarded by Afro-American customers as signs of discourtesy.[37]

Gender

Service providers were found to give service more promptly to male than to female customers. Men are less likely to have to wait for service than women customers:[30] when a man and a woman would approach a service provider simultaneously, the man received service priority most of the time.[38,39] A possible explanation is that shopping is not seen as part of the traditional male role, so that a man stands out when he does shop. The male may be regarded by the service provider as someone who needs help, but nonetheless, someone who is quick to make purchase decisions. In contrast, when a woman shops, she is one of many women. The stereotype of the female shopper is that of a browser: she is expected to 'shop around' and make extensive comparisons before purchasing. When questioned about the reasons for providing quicker service to men, service providers cited causes associated with these stereotypes, namely that women shop around more and therefore men need more help, while men are also more serious buyers.[39]

Weight

Recent research exploring sales-personnel prejudice towards obese customers used the concept of formal and interpersonal discrimination. Formal discrimination was examined by such behaviors as greeting the customer and recommending items upon request. Interpersonal discrimination was examined by behaviors such as smiling, being friendly, maintaining eye contact, being rude and ending the conversation prematurely. Interpersonal prejudice was found to be shown towards obese customers.[28,40] Similar results were found in a study conducted in shoe stores showing that overweight customers experienced significantly longer response times from salespersons than did customers of normal weight.[41]

A study focusing on physicians' responses to overweight and obese patients found that the patients' weight significantly affected the way physicians viewed and treated them. Physicians evaluated overweight patients as less healthy, worse in taking care of themselves, and less self-disciplined. Patient obesity was positively related to physicians' reports that seeing patients is a waste of their time, that they like their job less, that patients are annoying, and that they feel less patient. Most significantly, physicians indicated having significantly less personal desire to help overweight patients.[42]

Sexual orientation

Service providers were found to treat heterosexual and homosexual couples differently.[43] Heterosexual couples were assisted by store staff more quickly than were homosexual couples who often were not assisted at all and who were more likely to be denied. Lesbian and gay couples consistently experienced discourteous employee behavior, such as staff persons laughing and pointing at them in their presence. Such behavior was contrary to the organizations' formal policy. Managers consistently stated that sales associates are expected to greet, approach and help all customers promptly.

Attire

Service providers demonstrate less proactive behaviors towards casually dressed customers than towards those dressed more formally.[30] They provide prompter and friendlier service to well dressed as compared to poorly dressed customers,[38] and are more willing to refund or exchange in response to customer's request for reimbursement, depending on the customer's attire.[44]

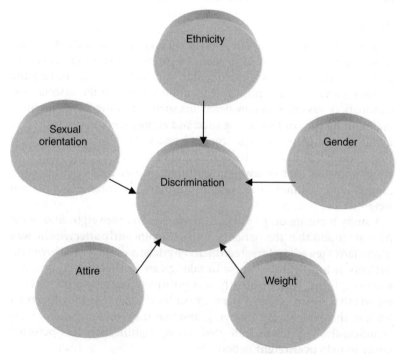

Figure 5.2   Customer-related factors affecting discrimination in service

Dishonesty

Ethical behavior in the service context is conceptualized as behavior that is both legal and morally acceptable to the larger community.[45] Service providers, however, often find themselves in a situation conducive to unethical behaviors. One reason is that they generally function on the boundary of the organization, often without close supervision. More importantly, they face multiple, conflicting demands presented by the customers and the organization, and generated by the nature of the service job itself. Consequently, service providers often cope with situations where they may compromise ethical standards in an effort to comply with all these demands at once. Service providers may also adopt unethical behaviors to cover their mistakes, promote the organization's business, or keep customers happy. The following categories of unethical behaviors adopted by service providers have been identified: (a) Misrepresenting the nature of the service or creating unrealistic expectations (e.g., exaggerating the benefits of a specific service offering, quoting only partial prices or prices for the least desirable service options, or creating a false need for the service); (b) Customer manipulation (e.g., hiding mistakes in service delivery, performing unnecessary services, or overcharging for services); and (c) Total dishonesty and lack of integrity (e.g., sharing customer information with third parties, failing to follow stated company policies and procedures regarding service delivery, or being unresponsive to customer requests).[45]

The type of unethical behaviors displayed by service providers is related to service context. In a study of flight attendants,[46] service providers reported that they sometimes engage in dishonest behavior, manifested most frequently in deceit. Deceit was reflected in both outright lying and concealing the truth. Although the employees indicated a reluctance to lie and cited reasons which they thought explained or justified their behavior, respondents in the study could cite instances when they had lied. The second form of deceit, concealment, was reflected mostly in concealing information from customers, especially information about their own emotions (i.e., emotional regulation), but also information about the safety of the flight. Service providers who concealed safety information thought that customers should not know 'too much' and expressing concern that passengers would overreact if they knew the truth. The service providers' chief motivation for dishonest behavior was to help themselves, mostly in terms of comfort (e.g., informing customers that there were no more drinks left in order to avoid the effort of serving a drink). Other motivations were to help the organization or the customers.

Service sabotage

Service sabotage is viewed as employee actions that are designed to negatively affect customer service.[47,48] Acts of service sabotage differ from other types of organizational sabotage in that they usually have an immediate impact (rather than a delayed impact as in other forms of sabotage); sabotage target is usually customers (rather than the organization itself or coworkers); and the act is often public (rather than being a hidden phenomenon).[48]

Deviant behaviors in the service context vary along two dimensions: customary-sporadic behaviors (behaviors that conform to behavioral norms dictated by the organizational culture vs. unique behaviors) and covert-overt behaviors (behaviors that are concealed from customers vs. behaviors that are displayed before an audience, mainly coworkers). Overt service sabotage is comparatively more common than covert, behind-the-scenes sabotage. Furthermore, coworkers and managers are sometimes involved in service sabotage actions.

Following this typology, four groups of sabotage behaviors may be identified:[47]

(a) Customary covert service sabotage, reflected in behaviors that are deliberately concealed but that are part of the organizational culture and have actually become behavioral norms. Such behaviors are reflected in the covert reduction of service provision. Behaviors calculated to influence the speed of service are common in this category, with staff paid by the hour often slowing the service encounter in order to gain overtime payments, and salaried staff frequently increasing the speed of service to reduce their work hours. Additionally, service providers may covertly bypass customer-oriented procedures, thereby acting in contrast to management conceptions of service quality. Service providers view instances of customary covert service sabotage as legitimate and reasonable reactions to unfair treatment or inequitable demands by either customers or managers.

(b) Customary overt service sabotage, often reflected in public behaviors designed to affect the speed of service in a manner opposite to that desired by customers. Additionally, service providers may act in a manner that is intended to condescend to customers without giving the customers the option to complain. Service providers may overtly adhere to bureaucratic annoying rules and procedures that have a negative effect on service delivery (e.g., time-consuming credit card verification). Overt service sabotage acts are always conducted in the presence of an audience. This form of service sabotage, too, is often routinized, considered normal, and passed on to employees via informal socialization and training. Adhering to overt service sabotage norms has been found to be a source of status among some service providers.

(c) Sporadic covert service sabotage, manifested in concealed behaviors not considered an everyday occurrence. This category includes sabotaging the service of particular customers without their knowledge, often for no apparent reason. These behaviors might be also aimed at colleagues, but disguised or framed as workplace humor. Sometimes covert sabotage behaviors is generated by feelings of frustration and is not targeted to any particular individual.

When sporadic covert service sabotage is discovered, it may result in severe punishment such as loss of job, criminal charges and claims by customers/workers for compensation. Service providers explain such behaviors as motivated by organizational and role alienation, claiming that they act antisocially as a demonstration against perceived suppression by both management and/or customers.

(d) Sporadic overt service sabotage, is often sophisticated and requires careful planning and execution. Service providers intentionally and publicly disrupt the service encounter, damage property, or even harm customers, and subsequently immediately apologize. Sometimes several employees cooperate to sabotage service. This form of sabotage is rare and requires the cooperation of a large number of employees. Similar to customary overt sabotage, the sporadic overt form of service sabotage is a demonstration to colleagues. The rationale for such activities is linked to group solidarity and socialization.

Service sabotage is affected by many individual, group, organizational and environmental variables. It was found to be positively related to employee risk-taking tendencies, need for social approval from colleagues and organizational commitment, and negatively related to organizational control and self-control.

The consequences of service sabotage for service providers are a negative relationship with customers and a low level of service delivery, but positive self-esteem among peers and perceived positive team spirit. Thus, from the service provider's perspective, acting in a manner that contradicts organizational regulations may actually have positive outcomes, while adhering to service guidelines may be physiologically and emotionally damaging. Nevertheless, many of the service sabotage behaviors are potentially hazardous to customers or the service providers themselves.[47,48]

Conclusion

Positive customer-related behaviors by service providers are reflected in a sustained focus on the customer. While the customer is always the center of the service interaction, such service seems to be defined as outstanding if the customer gets even more attention than usual. Although such attention and care ought to be universally positive for the customer, findings have shown that personalized service may not be suitable to all service contexts. Specifically, it might be counter-productive when it violates the equilibrium between the core service and the interpersonal aspect of the service. Too much attention given to one customer may come at the expense of other customers who are waiting to be served. Moreover it may also violate the basic service script and even evoke dissatisfaction by the customer who gets the specialized treatment if he/she prefers formal service relations.

Even the basic attribute of courtesy does not always have positive results, since it may violate another delicate balance in the service interaction – that between formality and familiarity. Service providers are required to be polite and to express 'measured friendliness'. However, discerning the exact measure of friendliness suitable for each customer is difficult. Moreover, it is not the service provider but the customer who should set the tone in the relationship. Service providers who are instructed to express interest in customers might be perceived by some customers as crossing the line between formal relationships appropriate to the service context and friendly personal relationships that are inappropriate. Furthermore, a genuinely friendly service provider may cross the line simply by behaving in an instinctive manner that is natural to most social interactions, (e.g., initiating a personal conversation with customers). Thus, while emotional regulation usually refers to the need by service providers to fake positive emotions and restrain themselves from displaying negative emotions or indifference, sometimes it might require faking formality and distance, while restraining the desire to engage in a friendlier or more flexible interaction with customers.

A major negative behavior of service providers – discrimination – reflects deep-rooted prejudices and stereotypes that are not exclusive to service and are displayed in many other social and work-related interactions. In service, as in other contexts, some of the manifestations of discrimination are likely to be unintentional and even unconscious. However, even relatively innocent behaviors contradict central themes of service, in addition to obvious violations of basic human rights. The notion of the customer as king is violated when some customers are perceived by service providers as inferior. Being different (e.g., ethnicity, gender, weight, sexual orientation, attire, etc.) may position the customer as having a low status in the eyes of the service provider. Consequently, the strict regulation of emotions and behavior which dictates most aspects of behavior towards customers, is overshadowed by negative behaviors. Although service providers are trained to control a large part of their behavior, their deepest beliefs and values are sometimes revealed in an uncontrolled manner. While some of these behaviors may seem minor, such as delayed service, the customers who are the target of the discrimination, and who are likely to experience it in other contexts as well, are probably especially sensitive to such discrimination.

Other negative behaviors, such as service sabotage, are deliberate and meant to cause harm to customers. However, unlike customers' negative behaviors towards service providers, which are almost always direct and explicit (e.g., verbal abuse), service providers show their hostility by acts that are sometimes quite unpleasant but are almost always concealed from customers. Since service providers are not in a position to express negative emotions in any direct way, they regulate the explicit expression of their emotions during the interpersonal interaction with customers, while freely acting upon their negative emotions behind the customers' backs.

Curiously, negative behaviors by service providers towards customers often are not acts of revenge caused by the way customers treat them, but are related to predispositions and attitudes towards the organization. The triangular relationship between service providers, customers and the organization is reflected in such behaviors with service providers 'paying back' the organization by harming its business and sabotaging the provision of service. Customers are innocent victims in these cases, in the same way that service providers may sometimes be victims of customer dissatisfaction with the organization.

Notes

1 Zabava Ford, W. S. (1998). *Communicating with Customers: Service Approaches, Ethics and Impact*. Cresskill, NJ: Hampton Press.
2 Suprenant, C. F. & Solomon, M. R. (1987). Predictability and personalization in the service encounter. *Journal of Marketing*, 2, 86–96.

3 Bettencourt, L. A. & Gwinner, K. (1996). Customization of the service experience: The role of the frontline employee. *International Journal of Service Industry Management*, 7, 3–20.

4 Mittal, B. & Lassar, W. M. (1996). The role of personalization in service encounters. *Journal of Retailing*, 72, 95–109.

5 Zabava Ford, W. S. (2001). Customer expectations for interactions with service providers: Relationship versus encounter orientation and personalized service communication. *Journal of Applied Communication Research*, 29, 1–29.

6 Adelman, M. B. & Ahuvia, A. C. (1995). Social support in the service sector: The antecedents, processes, and outcomes of social support in an introductory service. *Journal of Business Research*, 32, 273–282.

7 Barrera, M. & Balls, P. (1983). Assessing social support as a prevention resource: An illustrative study. *Prevention in Human Services*, 2, 59–74.

8 Kalyani, M. & Dube, L. (2004). Service provider responses to anxious and angry customers: Different challenges, different payoffs. *Journal of Retailing*, 80, 229–237.

9 Gwinner, K. P., Bitner, M. J., Brown, S. W. & Kumar, A. (2005). Service customization through employee adaptiveness. *Journal of Service Research*, 8, 131–148.

10 Hartline, M. D. & Ferrell, O. C. (1996). The management of customer-contact service employees: An empirical investigation. *Journal of Marketing*, 60, 52–70.

11 Solomon *et al.* (1985). Chapter 1 note 7.

12 Organ, D. W. (1988). Organizational citizenship behavior: The good soldier syndrome. *Issues in Organization and Management Series*. Lexington, MA, England: Lexington Books/D. C. Heath and Com.

13 Payne, S. C. & Webber, S. S. (2006). Effects of service provider attitudes and employment status on citizenship behaviors and customers' attitudes and loyalty behavior. *Journal of Applied Psychology*, 91, 365–378.

14 Bettencourt, L. A. & Brown, S. W. (2003). Role stressors and customer-oriented boundary-spanning behaviors in service organizations. *Academy of Marketing Science Journal*, 31, 394–408.

15 Bowen, Gilliland and Folger (1999). Chapter 3 note 40.

16 Yoon, M. H. & Suh, J. (2003). Organizational citizenship behaviors and service quality as external effectiveness of contact employees. *Journal of Business Research*, 56, 597–611.

17 Yen, H. R., Gwinner, K. P. & Su, W. (2004). The impact of customer participation and service expectation on Locus attributions following service failure. *International Journal of Service Industry Management*, 15, 7–26.

18 Kelley, S. W. & Hoffman, K. D. (1997). An investigation of positive affect, prosocial behaviors and service quality. *Journal of Retailing*, 73, 407–427.

19 George, J. (1991). State or trait: Effects of positive mood on prosocial behaviors at work. *Journal of Applied Psychology*, 76, 299–307.

20 Donavan, D. T., Brown, T. J. & Mowen, J. C. (2004). Internal benefits of service-worker customer orientation: Job satisfaction, commitment, and organizational citizenship behaviors. *Journal of Marketing*, 68, 128–146.

21 Bettencourt, L. A., Gwinner, K. P. & Meuter, M. L. (2001). A comparison of attitude, personality, and knowledge predictors of service-oriented organizational citizenship behaviors. *Journal of Applied Psychology*, 86, 29–41.

22 Gotlieb, J., Levy, M., Grewal, D. & Lindsey-Muillikan, J. (2004). Attitude toward the service firm. *Journal of Applied Social Psychology*, 34, 825–847.
23 Zabava Ford (1995). Chapter 2 note 53.
24 Mohr, L. A. & Bitner, M. J. (1995). The role of employee effort in satisfaction with service transactions. *Journal of Business Research*, 32, 239–252.
25 Goodwin, C. & Smith, K. L. (1990). Courtesy and friendliness: Conflicting goals for the service provider? *The Journal of Services Marketing*, 4, 5–20.
26 Dobni, D. Z., Wilf, R. & Brent, J. R. (1997). Enhancing service personnel effectiveness through the use of behavioral repertoires. *The Journal of Services Marketing*, 11, 427–445.
27 Rosenthal and Peccei (2006). Chapter 2 note 41.
28 King, E. B., Shapuiro, J. R., Hebl, M. R., Singletary, S. L. & Turner, S. (2006). The stigma of obesity in customer service: A mechanism for remediation and bottom-line consequences of interpersonal discrimination. *Journal of Applied Psychology*, 91, 579–593.
29 Griffin, K. H. & Hebl, M. R. (2002). The disclosure dilemma for gay men and lesbians: 'Coming out' at work. *Journal of Applied Psychology*, 87, 1191–1199.
30 Martin, C. L. & Adams, S. (1999). Behavioral biases in the service encounter: Empowerment by default? *Marketing Intelligence & Planning*, 17, 192–201.
31 Gutek, Cherry, Bhappu, Schneider and Woolf (2000). Introduction note 12.
32 Lee, J. (2000). The salience of race in everyday life black customers' shopping experiences in black and white neighborhoods. *Work and Occupations*, 27, 353–376.
33 Being followed created an especially uncomfortable environment for Afro-American customers, making them feel that service providers treat them like criminals when they shop.
34 This type of preferential treatment stems from assumptions often made by service providers that Afro-American customers in general cannot afford to purchase expensive items found in upscale stores.
35 Mallinson, C. & Brewster, Z. W. (2005). 'Blacks and bubbas': Stereotypes, ideology, and categorization processes in restaurant servers' discourse. *Discourse & Society*, 16, 787–807.
36 Landrine, H., Klonoff, E. A. & Alcaraz, R. (1997). Racial discrimination in minors' access to tobacco. *Journal of Black Psychology*, 23, 135–147.
37 Weitzer, R. (1997). Racial prejudice among Korean merchants in African American neighborhoods. *The Sociological Quarterly* 38, 587–606.
38 Stead, B. A. & Zinkhan, G. M. (1986). Service priority in department stores: The effects of customer gender and dress. *Sex-Roles*, 15, 601–611.
39 Zinkhan, G. M. & Stoiadin, L. F. (1984). Impact of sex role stereotypes on service priority in department stores. *Journal of Applied Psychology*, 69, 691–693.
40 Especially when justification for the display of prejudice ostensibly existed (e.g., an obese customer was eating fattening food, thereby justifying the notion that obesity is a function of lack of willpower).
41 Pauley, L. L. (1989). Customer weight as a variable in salespersons' response time. *Journal of Social Psychology*, 129, 713–714.
42 Hebl, M. R. & Xu, J. (2001). Weighing the care: Physicians' reactions to the size of a patient. *Journal of Applied Psychology*, 91, 579–593.

43   Walters, A. S. & Curran, M. C. (1996). 'Excuse me, sir? May I help you and your boyfriend?' Salespersons' differential treatment of homosexual and straight customers. In *Journal of Homosexuality*, 31, 135–152.
44   Krapfel, R. E. (1988). Customer complaint and salesperson response: The effect of the communication source. *Journal of Retailing*, 64, 181–198.
45   Schwepker, C. H. & Hartline, M. D. (2005). Managing the ethical climate of customer-contact service employees. *Journal of Service Research*, 7, 377–397.
46   Scott, E. D. (2003). Plane truth: A qualitative study of employee dishonesty in the airline industry. *Journal of Business Ethics*, 42, 321–337.
47   Harris, L. C. & Ogbonna, E. (2002). Exploring service sabotage: The antecedents, types and consequences of frontline, deviant, antiservice behaviors. *Journal of Service Research*, 4, 163–183.
48   Harris, L. C. & Ogbonna, E. (2006). Service sabotage: A study of antecedents and consequences. *Academy of Marketing Science Journal*, 34, 543–558.

6
Service Provider Attributes

Employees' personality traits have been found to affect a broad range of work-related behaviors, including task performance, counterproductive behavior, turnover, absenteeism, tardiness, organizational citizenship behaviors, success in groups, job satisfaction, safety and leadership effectiveness (see review in Mount *et al.*, 2005).[1] Manufacturing organizations often hire for skills only, yet service organizations need to hire for positive service-oriented attitudes and train for specific skills. Service characteristics like intangibility and customer contact require service employees to cope effectively with stress, be sensitive and cooperative. Thus, service organizations place more emphasis on personality, energy, and attitude than on education and experience in their recruitment and strategies.[2]

Research shows that certain personality attributes may be categorized as service-oriented or customer-oriented – representing combinations of traits that are by definition related to better service. Researchers have also examined the effect of more general personality characteristics – mainly traits included in the five factor model along with self-efficacy – on service performance, customer orientation and service orientation. Gender too has been explored, especially in the context of the status of women in the service workforce and discrimination issues.

Attributes related specifically to service

Service orientation and customer orientation are distinctly relevant to behavior in the service context. Service orientation is made up of attributes thought to affect interpersonal interactions and thus related to service providers' performance in the service encounter. Customer orientation, which may be considered a subgroup of service orientation, consists of service providers' attitudes toward customers. It is defined not as a personality trait but rather as an attribute lying somewhere between a trait and a behavior. In view of these distinctive aspects, the literature discusses the antecedents of customer orientation, which are largely related to personality or to the organizational environment, in addition to exploring its outcomes. Service orientation and customer orientation are considered vital in the selection of service providers since these predispositions enhance individual performance as well as play an important role in creating a service-oriented organizational climate.[3]

Service orientation

Service orientation combines three basic personality traits – adjustment, sociability and agreeableness – which are reflected in attitudes and behaviors that affect the quality of the service provider-customer interaction. More specifically, '...It is the disposition to be helpful, thoughtful, considerate, and cooperative...a syndrome containing elements of good adjustment, likeability, social skill, and willingness to follow rules' (Hogan, Hogan & Busch, 1984, pp. 167, 173).[4]

Service orientation is measured in a variety of ways, but several traits are common to most measures: friendliness, reliability, responsiveness and courteousness.[5] In addition to its obvious effect on behavior towards customers, service orientation also affects service providers' willingness to receive service training and accept the need for supervision, thereby improving their effectiveness.[5,6,7]

While many service organizations tend to rely on training programs to develop employees' service abilities, managers report that some employees seem to have much more, or less, of the intangible service orientation attribute than others.[3] Ultimately, the manifestation of service-orientation personality characteristics in service-oriented behaviors largely depends on the perceived service orientation of the organization.[8] Moreover, incongruence between an employee's service orientation and the perceived orientation established by the organization and carried out by management may lead to job dissatisfaction, frustration and low-quality service performance.[5]

Customer orientation

While service orientation consists of general interpersonal attributes, customer orientation is reflected in a predisposition to put the customer's needs first. The concept, first developed in the context of sales, was described as 'the degree to which salespeople practice the marketing concept by trying to help their customers make purchase decisions that will satisfy customer needs' (Saxe & Weitz, 1982, p. 344).[9,10]

More recently, it has been described as beliefs that puts the customer's interest first;[11] a predisposition to meet customer needs in an on-the-job context;[12,13] the service provider's behavior in person-to-person interactions;[14] and the extent to which the employee's behavior meets customer needs.[15]

As such, employees with a predisposition toward customer orientation may be more inclined to engage in adaptive customer-satisfying behaviors due to their propensity for being helpful and cooperative.[16] Notably, however, there is a distinction, and possible inconsistencies, between customer-oriented attitudes and customer-oriented behaviors. Service providers might display superficial customer-oriented behaviors without having a strong commitment to customer service. While most definitions refer to customer orientation in terms of behavior, a customer-oriented attitude is defined as the amount of a service provider's affect for or against customers. It refers to such issues as affinity to be in contact with the customers and an understanding of the importance of customer orientation for both the individual and the organization's performance. Customer-oriented attitudes are distinct from customer-oriented behaviors and were found to reflect different facets of the customer-orientation construct. Both customer-oriented attitudes and behaviors have an impact on customer satisfaction.[17]

Customer orientation is viewed as a multi-dimensional construct. It has been conceptualized as composed of the following dimensions, presented in Table 6.1.

Antecedents and outcomes of customer orientation

A major factor that has been found to affect customer orientation is the perceived culture of the organization.[18,19] A customer-oriented organizational culture focuses outside the organization to acquire a customer perspective; empowers employees to ensure a flexible service process required for meeting dynamic customer expectations; generates creative and relevant solutions to customer problems; encourages the service provider to be procreative in adjusting service to the precise needs of the customer; and displays a sincere respect for both service providers and customers. These organizational characteristics provide an environment which fosters service providers' customer orientation reflected in information sharing, discovering the customer's needs and adaptation. Moreover, supportive organizations are more apt to utilize relational activities by service providers in performance evaluation.[19,20]

Table 6.1 Dimensions of customer orientation

Needs[13]	*Pamper the customer*: Desire to make customers believe they are special and individually important to the service provider.	*Read the customer*: A desire to grasp on customers' verbal and nonverbal communication.	*Maintain personal relationship*: A desire to know or connect with the customer on a personal level.	*Deliver*: A desire to perform the service successfully.
Cognitions	*Motivation*: A positive valence of customer-oriented behavior and the consequences associated with such behavior on the part of the employee; the employee's self-perception of being able to behave in a customer-oriented way; and his/her expectations of reaching the desired outcome through engaging in such behavior.[15]	*Self-perceived decision-making authority*: The extent to which service employees feel authorized to decide on issues that concern customers' interests and needs.[14,15]	*A belief in one's ability to fulfill customers' wishes.*[12]	
Emotions	*Enjoyment*: Derived from interaction with and serving customers.[12]			
Skills[15]	*Technical skill*: Skills required in order to fulfill the customer's needs during the personal interaction.	*Social skills*: The service provider's ability to adopt the customer's perspective visually, cognitively and emotionally during interactions.		

Additional factors that were found to enhance the employee's customer orientation are perceptions of support from colleagues,[18] perceived organizational justice,[21] the supervisor's service-oriented attitudes,[22] organizational commitment and job satisfaction.[23,24,25,26] However, another view which is empirically supported holds that customer orientation is the cause rather than the outcome of such organizational factors as commitment and organizational citizenship behavior.[13]

Customer-oriented employees fit roles that involve customer-contact because they are predisposed to enjoy the work of serving customers. Consequently, customer-oriented employees in service jobs experience job satisfaction and demonstrate organizational commitment. Additionally, customer-oriented employees are motivated to help colleagues as a means of ultimately satisfying customers because they recognize that successful exchanges with customers depend on effective internal exchanges. As a result, higher levels of customer orientation lead to higher levels of internal prosocial behaviors. Customer orientation was found to have a strong influence on the attitudes and behaviors of employees who have high frequency of contact with customers because employees with high levels of customer orientation are especially satisfied in services settings that allow for a high degree of contact time with customers.[13]

Additionally, customer orientation is seen as significantly related to personalization.[27] Customer-oriented service providers tend to demonstrate 'option personalization',[28] by offering several options to each customer. Service providers may also demonstrate 'customized personalization' by attending to the unique needs of a customer and providing helpful advice toward meeting those needs. Service providers in sales positions who are adept at customer-oriented selling may actually show a greater concern for customers' goals and interests than their own.[29]

Customer orientation has also been found to have a positive effect on a range of outcomes such as service providers' ethical behavior, sales performance, customer's perceived service quality, and building buyer-seller relationships (see reviews by Donavan, Brown & Mowen, 2004[13]; and Stock & Hoyer, 2005).[17] This orientation has been found to be positively related both to self-rating of service performance and supervisor rating of service performance.[12]

Customer orientation and sales-orientation behavior

Customer-oriented behaviors among sales people, however, may sometimes conflict with sales-oriented behaviors, because the eagerness to make a sale may lead the service provider to ignore the customer's needs. Saxe and Weitz (1982)[9] in devising a measure for a salesperson's sales orientation based upon relative amounts of selling orientation versus customer orientation (SOCO), found that in contrast to customer orientation which emphasizes the customer's needs, a sales-oriented approach emphasizes making the sale and/or selling as much as possible to every customer, while addressing the customer's best interests becomes secondary. Customer orientation and selling orientation also differ in their focus on long-term versus short-term customer needs. Customers have needs both in the immediate and the long term, but short-term needs are more pressing and clearly articulated, whereas long-term needs tend to be latent. A customer-oriented salesperson aims to discover and satisfy these latent needs[9,30], while the objective of sales orientation is to satisfy immediate articulated customer preferences. The two orientations also differ with respect to means. While customer orientation places an emphasis on listening to customers and on dialogue, sales orientation encourages opportunistic means, if these are necessary to make the sale. Customer orientation was found to create greater long-term performance benefits for the salesperson as compared to sales-oriented selling (see Thakor & Joshi, 2005 for review).[30] Another comparison between sales orientation and customer orientation showed that customer orientation was positively related to performance, while selling orientation was not related to performance.[18] However, in a comparison between the effect of customer orientation and that of adaptive selling, which enables salespeople to tailor messages to individual customers' needs, adaptive selling had a stronger effect on performance.[31]

There is considerable variance in the extent to which customer orientation is applied by service providers in the sales context, despite its benefits. A key reason for salespeople's affinity for sales orientation and their unwillingness to adopt a customer orientation is that a customer orientation demands greater effort in terms of developing the customer relationship. The motivation to adapt a customer orientation was found to be affected by the extent to which salespeople experience their work as meaningful, identify with the values of their organization, and are satisfied with the pay they receive.[30]

General personality characteristics that relate to job performance

In addition to specific service-related traits, research explored the effect of general predispositions on service performance, as described below.

The five-factor model of personality

Personality refers to attributes that consistently distinguish people from one another in terms of their basic tendencies to think, feel and act in certain ways, and that are stable over time and across situations and settings.[1,32] The five-factor model of personality,[33] which is currently the major theoretical framework for exploring personality, consists of the following dimensions of personality characteristics:

(1) Conscientiousness: the tendency to be responsible, organized, orderly, achievement-striving, dutiful and efficient.
(2) Agreeableness: the tendency to be altruistic, cooperative and warm. Individuals high on this dimension are oriented toward serving and helping others.
(3) Extraversion: exhibiting attributes such as sensation-seeking, sociability, affiliation, gregariousness, dominance, boldness and assertiveness.
(4) Emotional stability: the tendency to be poised, self-reliant and stable. Emotional stability is often discussed in the context of neuroticism, referring to individuals low on emotional stability and involving characteristics such as insecurity, indecisiveness, and tenseness.
(5) Openness to experience: exhibiting attributes such as intellect, imagination and curiosity.

Two of these traits, conscientiousness and emotional stability, were found to predict overall job performance through motivational components. The other three traits, agreeableness, extraversion, and openness to experience, are valid predictors of performance for specific occupations or for certain criteria only. When the criterion relates to 'getting ahead', the best personality predictors were a facet of extraversion, emotional stability, and conscientiousness. By contrast, when the criteria relate to getting along with people, the best predictors are conscientiousness, agreeableness and emotional stability.[1,32,34] Conscientiousness, which facilitates performance in jobs involving interpersonal interaction, is at the core of service provision. Successful service providers are described as being accurate, dependable, responsive and prompt, a description highly similar to the description of conscientiousness. Conscientiousness was found to be positively related to service performance[34] as well as to the service provider's self-direction, which is reflected in the performance of desirable behaviors even in the absence of external control.[35]

Agreeableness is an important predictor in jobs that involve significant interpersonal interactions, especially when that interaction involves helping, cooperation and nurturing.[36,34] Highly agreeable people are more likely to be cooperative rather than competitive, thereby facilitating service performance. However, an excess of cooperation may be dysfunctional in cases when service providers and customers have different goals. An example of this is seen when a service provider's goal may be to provide quality service at a price that results in profit for the organization, while the customer's goal may be to receive that service for the lowest possible price.

Service providers high on emotional stability are likely to be more relaxed and tolerant of stress, which helps them build credibility and trust with customers. Both emotional stability and agreeableness were found to be positively related to service performance.[12,34]

Extroversion has been found to be positively related to service performance mainly when the interaction is focused on influencing others and gaining status and power. In such jobs, especially sales and management jobs, being sociable, assertive and energetic is likely to contribute to success on the job.[37]

Personality characteristics are relevant not only to performance but also to subjective person-job fit, which refers to individuals' perceptions regarding how well suited they are to a particular job. A study of personality-job fit in service roles[38] found that extraversion was related to a better person-job fit in jobs that are perceived to involve a great quality and quantity of interpersonal interaction. Service providers who are high on extraversion are people-oriented and out-going, and therefore, when a job is perceived as more people-oriented, more interactive, and involving more frequent and higher quality interpersonal interaction, people high on extraversion perceive themselves as better suited to the job. For individuals high on agreeableness, person-job fit is greater with respect to jobs perceived as providing more opportunities for interactions that involve helping or serving customers.

Arguably, however, basic personality traits may be too far removed from service behaviors to be able to predict employee performance accurately.[12,36] Customer orientation, by contrast, is seen as closer in the personality hierarchy to the specific behaviors needed to achieve high performance and therefore may enhance the prediction of specific behaviors and performance ratings. Furthermore, customer orientation is affected by the interaction of basic traits with the service role. Two components of the five-factor model – agreeableness and emotional stability – were found to be related to customer orientation.[12] Employees high in agreeableness may naturally feel an empathy with their customers and have a desire to help them solve their problems through the service they provide. Such employees may derive personal satisfaction from being able to help others satisfy their needs. Emotional stability ensures the emotional consistency that is related to the ability and motivation to serve customers well.[12] Similarly, service orientation was found to be related to agreeableness, emotional stability and conscientiousness. Employees with a high service orientation are friendly, stable and dependable.[5]

Self-efficacy as it related to the employee

Self-efficacy is considered to affect performance in many types of occupations, but has a specific relevance to the service role. Self-efficacy refers to an employee's belief in his/her ability to perform job-related tasks (Bandura, 1977).[39] As self-efficacy increases, employees exert more effort, become more persistent, and learn how to cope with task-related obstacles, thereby enhancing their ability to manage service encounters successfully.[40] A service employee's performance typically involves responding to customer needs, handling special requests and performing under adverse circumstances (e.g., service failure). Because of the added effort involved in self-efficacy, employees who measure high in this attribute perform better in these service activities, thereby raising customers' perceptions of service quality.[40,41] Qualitative studies[42,43] have demonstrated that customers are typically more satisfied with the service encounter when the employee displays the ability, willingness and competence to solve problems.

Gender

Increasingly service providers are asked to 'inhabit' their jobs and bring their own personality into the delivery of service. Consequently, personal characteristics such as age, gender, ethnicity and appearance become an integral part of the service that is provided. Demographics shape what is expected of an employee by management and customers, how the employee adapts to the job, and his/her attitudes toward various aspects of the job.[44] Since professional skills are not always sufficient in radiating authority and competence to customers, characteristics such as age, gender, education and ethnicity serve an external signaling function toward customers. The impact of these dimensions, however, can vary between contexts. In particular, during a one-time service interaction, where there is no expectation of future interaction, such aspects can be especially important.[45]

Of the demographic variables, the effect of gender has been discussed in the literature most frequently in the service context. Nearly all service jobs below the level of 'knowledge workers' and professionals (e.g., care assistants, cleaners, sales assistants), are jobs in which women predominate and which are associated with a range of poor conditions, such as low wages and limited career prospects. Significantly, along with secretarial and clerical occupations, service occupations are generally those with the highest levels of female density.[46]

A study of gender issues in call centers[47] found that this area of employment offers women little in the way of career prospects. In this sense, call centers share many similarities with older female-dominated workplaces and occupations such as typing pools in large organizations which similarly involve a single highly repetitive work activity, with promotion prospects restricted to a role as a senior typist or supervisor. Call center work seems to bear many of the hallmarks of these traditional female employment 'ghettos', defined as places occupied mainly by women and offering low-skilled, low-status, undemanding jobs.[47]

The predominance of women in service jobs is related to recruitment motivated partly by the search for relatively cheap labor, and for employees with customer-oriented norms, both having gendered elements. The employment of women is attractive to management since women continue to be significantly underpaid in relation to men. Furthermore, many women are willing to behave in ways that correspond with the customer-service norm.[46] Gender stereotypes about women's willingness to engage in so-called 'softer' behaviors reinforce gender division in service organizations.[48] The stereotyped image of female service providers has its basis in the stereotyped image of female qualities such as caring, being empathic, behaving altruistically and being able to make people feel good.[49,50] These characteristics are also considered important in service. Additionally, due to socialization, women are more likely than men to perform emotion work to please the customer and are therefore perceived as more fit to perform service roles, for women are willing to reinforce their inferior position in order to please customers.[45]

Male workers interviewed at McDonald's explained that women were better at making contacts with guests and that men were too 'explosive' to deal with difficult customers.[51] Assumptions about 'natural' gender skills were found to prevail in the airline industry as well, reflected in the belief that women are 'by nature better at anticipating the needs and (exceeding the) expectations of others' (Leidner, 1993, p. 71), resulting in gender-typed front-office jobs.[48,52] The study of call centers[53] found that women were considered to be suited to call center work because they are perceived as more capable of dealing with work monotony and a regimented work environment, and because 'feminine' social skills play a central role in call center work. Paradoxically, however, the routinized environment of call centers allows women to use their social skills only to a very limited extent. A study in restaurants[54] shows that restaurants hire and allocate workers in a way that makes gender distinctions, using stereotypes to rationalize these distinctions and to structure interactions along gender lines. Basically, restaurants define service work as women's work, legitimize a gendered servant image and structure the interactions of waitresses as if they were sexual objects. As in other service contexts, being a waitress is considered an extension of the women's role in the home and a manifestation of women's supposed feminine nature. Indeed, waitresses themselves define their jobs as caring for others as a mother cares for her family. They are also perceived as friendlier than waiters and are more likely to be the subject of sexual approaches. Additionally, male servers are sometimes able to avoid conflicts with customers because the waiter's service style and the stereotypical meaning of maleness dictate a more reserved interaction norm.

Differences also exist in the management of male and female service providers. Male service providers are often implicitly allowed to focus on quantitative aims only, while women are more often expected to focus on qualitative as well as quantitative aims.[45] The predominance of women in service jobs contributes to management undervaluing and giving insufficient recognition to the skills involved in service work.[46] Furthermore, when the service interaction goes wrong customers use gendered reprimands in venting their anger at the service provider in question.[45] Moreover, in service quality evaluations, male service providers tend to receive higher service quality ratings than female service providers.[55]

Gender has also been found to affect the relationship of role stress with job performance: female service providers' performance is affected more negatively by increased role conflict or role ambiguity. A related difference is that job satisfaction affects the intent to quit differently among female and male service providers: the inclination to quit is stronger for men than for women. This might be due at least partially to the limited opportunities for mobility that women experience.[56]

Conclusion

The ideal service provider is described as well adjusted, sociable, agreeable, helpful, considerate, cooperative, likeable, having social skills, willing to follow rules, tactful, perceptive about customers' needs, pleasant, friendly, reliable, responsive, courteous, polite, and putting the customer's needs first. In terms of the five-factor model of personality, most of these traits are related to agreeableness, and a few are related to conscientiousness (being reliable, following rules) and emotional stability (being well adjusted). Notably, these are reactive rather than proactive skills. They are social skills that reflect the expectation that service providers be able to 'read' the customer and the situation and respond accordingly, but not take initiative themselves. Moreover, many of these traits are considered to be feminine traits, and traits that contrast with such highly regarded characteristics as assertiveness, independence and leadership skills. Such prestigious traits may actually be perceived by management as an obstacle to the successful performance of the service role and consequently be discouraged among service providers.

The conceptualization of the combination of traits that make for a good service provider is naturally dictated by the criterion of good service performance. Since the ultimate criterion of service performance is customer satisfaction, many traits required for good service seem to be determined with the customers' viewpoint in mind. This affects the description of service providers' traits in several ways. First, the adjectives listed above are mainly reflected in visible interpersonal behavior, and many of them may result from compliance with organizational display rules rather than from innate personality predispositions. Coneivably, therefore, in order to be a good service provider an employee does not have to be genuinely friendly and considerate, but only be able to pretend to have such traits.[57] Additionally, describing traits from the customers' viewpoint results in an emphasis on only one characteristic of the service provider role – that of interaction with customers, while another distinct characteristic – being boundary spanners (e.g., able to handle ambiguity and cope with conflict and stress) is not reflected at all in the traits considered relevant to the role. The dominance of the interpersonal interaction aspect of the service role results in describing service providers' attributes almost exclusively in terms of interpersonal skills or demographic variables with strict relevance to interpersonal skills.

Notes

1 Mount, M. K., Barrick, M. R., Scullen, S. M. & Rounds, J. (2005). Higher-order dimensions of the big five personality traits and the big six vocational interest types. *Personnel Psychology*, 58, 447–478.
2 Bowen and Ford (2002). Introduction note 7.

3   O'Connor, S. J. & Shewchuk, R. M. (1995). Doing more with less, and doing it nicer: The role of service orientation in health care organization. *Academy of Management Journal Proceedings*, 120–124.
4   Hogan, J., Hogan, R. & Busch, C. M. (1984). How to measure service orientation. *Journal of Applied Psychology*, 69, 167–173.
5   Frei, R. L. & McDaniel, M. A. (1998). Validity of customer service measures in personnel selection: A review of criterion and construct evidence. *Human Performance*, 11, 1–27.
6   Cran, D. J. (1994). Towards validation of the service orientation construct. *The Service Industries Journal*, 14, 34–44.
7   Rosse, J., Miller, H. & Barnes, L. (1991). Hiring for personality and ability: The case of service orientation. *Journal of Business and Psychology*, 5, 431–445.
8   Service orientation has been described as a dimension of the organization's overall climate, reflected in organizational practices and procedures that promote service excellence (Lytle *et al.*, 1998; Schneider and Bowen, 1995).
9   Saxe, R. & Weitz, B. A. (1982). The SOCO scale: A measure of the customer orientation of salespeople. *Journal of Marketing Research*, 19, 343–351.
10 Since the measure developed by Saxe and Weitz – SOCO or selling orientation-customer orientation – was the basis of many subsequent studies, much research on customer orientation was done with sales people.
11 Hartline, M. D., Maxham, J. G. III & McKee, D. O. (2000). Corridors of influence in the dissemination of customer-oriented strategy to customer contact service employees. *Journal of Marketing*, 64, 35–50.
12 Brown, T. J., Mowen, J. C., Donavan, D. T. & Licata, J. W. (2002). The customer orientation of service workers: Personality trait effects on self and supervisor performance ratings. *Journal of Marketing Research*, 39, 110–119.
13 Donavan, Brown and Mowen (2004). Chapter 5 note 25.
14 Hennig-Thurau, T. & Thurau, C. (2003). Customer orientation of service employees – Toward a conceptual framework of a key relationship marketing construct. *Journal of Relationship Marketing*, 2, 1–32.
15 Hennig-Thurau, T. (2004). Customer orientation of service employees: Its impact on customer satisfaction, commitment, and retention. *International Journal of Service Industry Management*, 15, 460–478.
16 Gwinner, Bitner, Brown and Kumar (2005). Chapter 5 note 9.
17 Stock, R. M. & Hoyer, W. D. (2005). An attitude-behavior model of salespeople's customer orientation. *Academy of Marketing Science Journal*, 33, 536–552.
18 Boles, J. S., Babin, B. J., Brashear, T. G. & Brooks, C. (2001). An examination of the relationships between retail work environments, salesperson selling orientation-customer orientation and job performance. *Journal of Marketing Theory and Practice*, 9, 1–13.
19 Williams, M. R. & Attaway, J. S. (1996). Exploring salespersons' customer orientation as a mediator of organizational culture's influence on buyer-seller relationships. *The Journal of Personal Selling & Sales Management*, 16, 33–52.
20 See Chapter 7.
21 Bettencourt, Brown and MacKenzie (2005). Chapter 3 note 29.
22 Jones, E., Busch, P. & Dacin, P. (2003). Firm market orientation and salesperson customer orientation: Interpersonal and intrapersonal influences on

customer service and retention in business-to-business buyer-seller relationships. *Journal of Business Research*, 56, 323–340.

23 Bettencourt, L. A. & Brown, S. W. (2003). Role stressors and customer-oriented boundary-spanning behaviors in service organizations. *Academy of Marketing Science Journal*, 31, 394–408.

24 Hoffman, K. D. & Ingram, T. N. (1992). Service provider job satisfaction and customer-oriented performance. *The Journal of Services Marketing*, 6, 68–78.

25 Joshi, A. W. & Randall, S. (2001). The indirect effects of organizational controls on salesperson performance and customer orientation. *Journal of Business Research*, 54, 1–9.

26 O'Hara, B. S., Boles, J. S. & Johnston, M. W. (1991). The influence of personal variables on salesperson selling orientation. *The Journal of Personal Selling & Sales Management*, 11, 61–67.

27 See Chapter 5.

28 Suprenant and Solomon (1987). Chapter 2 note 2.

29 Zabava Ford (2001). Chapter 5 note 5.

30 Thakor, M. V. & Joshi, A. W. (2005). Motivating salesperson customer orientation: Insights from the job characteristics model. *Journal of Business Research*, 58, 584–592.

31 Franke, G. R. & Park, J. E. (2006). Salesperson adaptive selling behavior and customer orientation: a meta-analysis. *Journal of Marketing Research*, 43, 693–702.

32 Viswesvaran, C., Ones, D. S. & Schmidt, F. L. (2005). Is there a general factor in ratings of job performance? A meta-analytic framework for disentangling substantive and error influences. *Journal of Applied Psychology*, 90, 108–131.

33 McCrae, R. R. & Costa, P. T. (1987). Validation of the five-factor model of personality across instruments and observers. *Journal of Personality and Social Psychology*, 52, 81–90.

34 Mount, M. K., Barrick, M. R. & Stewart, G. L. (1998). Five-Factor Model of personality and performance in jobs involving interpersonal interactions. *Human Performance*, 11, 145–165.

35 Stewart, G. L., Carson, K. P. & Cardy, R. L. (1996). The joint effects of conscientiousness and self-leadership training on employee self-directed behavior in a service setting. *Personnel Psychology*, 49, 143–164.

36 Hurley, R. F. (1998). Customer service behavior in retail settings: A study of the effect of service provider personality. *Academy of Marketing Science Journal*, 26, 115–127.

37 Barrick, M. R., Mount, M. K. & Judge, T. A. (2001). Personality and performance at the beginning of the new millennium: What do we know and where do we go next? *International Journal of Selection and Assessment*, 9, 9–30.

38 Holcombe-Ehrhart, K. (2006). Job characteristic beliefs and personality as antecedents of subjective person-job fit. *Journal of Business and Psychology*, 21, 193–226.

39 Bandura, A. (1977). Self efficacy: Toward a unifying theory of behavior change. *Psychological Review*, 84, 191–215.

40 Chebat and Kollias (2000). Chapter 1 note 23.

41 Ahearne, M., Mathieu, J. & Rapp, A. (2005). To empower or not to empower your sales force? An empirical examination of influence of leadership empower-

ment behavior on customer satisfaction and performance. *Journal of Applied Psychology*, 90, 945–955.

42   Bitner, M. J. (1990). Evaluating service encounters: The effects of physical surroundings and employee responses. *Journal of Marketing*, 54, 69–82.

43   Bitner, M. J., Booms, B. H. & Tetreault, M. S. (1990). The service encounter: diagnosing favorable and unfavorable incidents. *Journal of Marketing*, 54, 71–84.

44   Macdonald and Sirianni (1996). Introduction note 8.

45   Forseth, U. (2005). Gender matters? Exploring how gender is negotiated in service encounters. *Gender, Work and Organization*, 12, 440–459.

46   Kerfoot, D. & Korczynski, M. (2005). Gender and service work: New directions for the study of front-line service work. *Gender, Work and Organization*, 12, 387–399.

47   Belt, V. (2002). A female ghetto? Women's careers in call centres. *Human Resource Management Journal*, 12, 51–66.

48   Bradley, H. (1989). *Men's Work, Women's Work*. Cambridge: Polity Press.

49   Bradley, H., Erickson, M., Stephenson, C. & Williams, S. (2000). *Myths at Work*. Cambridge: Polity Press.

50   Gustavsson, E. (2005). Virtual servants: Stereotyping female front-office employees on the internet. *Gender, Work and Organization*, 12, 400–419.

51   Leidner (1993). Chapter 2 note 6.

52   Taylor, S. & Tyler, M. (2000). Emotional labor and sexual difference in the airline industry. *Work, Employment and Society*, 14, 77–95.

53   Belt, V., Richardson, R. & Webster, J. (2002). Women, social skill and interactive service work in telephone call centres. *New Technology, Work, and Employment*, 17, 20–34.

54   Hall, E. J. (1992). Smiling, deferring, and flirting: Doing gender by giving 'good service'. *Journal of Work and Occupations*, 20, 452–471.

55   Snipes, R. L., Thomson, N. F. & Oswald, S. L. (2006). Gender bias in customer evaluations of service quality: an empirical investigation. *The Journal of Services Marketing*, 20, 274–284.

56   Babin, B. J. & Boles, J. S. (1998). Employee behavior in a service environment: A model and test of potential differences between men and women. *Journal of Marketing*, 62, 77–91.

57   See Chapter 1 on the acting element in service work.

7
Organizational Perspectives of the Service Role

Certain distinctive characteristics of service indicate that it must be managed differently from production.[1] First, given its intangibility, the service process is difficult to measure, control or standardize. This is largely because of the role that employee attitudes and emotions play in customer service behaviors and subsequent customer satisfaction.[2] Additionally, service providers are not only being managed but are engaged in management activities themselves *vis-à-vis* customers. Service providers often supervise the customer in terms of assessing the customers' ability to participate in the co-production of the service, motivating customers, training them and helping them evaluate the success of their co-production. Additionally, service providers must examine whether or not the service meets the customer's expectations, and take corrective action if it does not. Human resource management concerns, therefore, focus on interpersonal relationship skills rather than on standardization.[1]

While a significant segment of service positions require extensive training and education (e.g., medical, legal, technical support, teaching, etc.), the majority of customer contact jobs are at the traditional entry level, where task complexity is minimal (e.g., hospitality, basic financial services, customer service representatives, retail) but the importance of attitude is paramount. Employee attitudes and behavior are thus more critical to service than to manufacturing organizations. The unpredictable ranges of customer demands, and the intangibility of service output, make it difficult for management to determine the behaviors required of service providers in advance or to control their behavior in service encounters by means of formal training. Moreover, employees in service organizations are expected to be marketers as well. When interacting with customers, service providers represent the organization and are often required to explain the attributes of the service they are producing. In order to generate positive customer attitudes toward the organization and its products, service providers themselves must have positive attitudes. Service organizations therefore rely on norms and values rather than rigid rules to affect service providers' attitudes and guide their behavior. Service organizations are also faced with the need to manage distinctive sources of employee stress such as emotional labor and role conflict related to contradictory demands by the organization and the customers. In meeting this challenge, service organizations must rely on supportive managerial measures.[1]

While previous chapters referred mainly to the service provider-customer interface, this chapter focuses on the organizational sphere of the service role, describing the manager-employee interface and the employee-role interface.[3] The first part of the chapter describes different levels of service provider management, namely service leadership, and organizational procedures. The second part describes the service role, focusing on service performance and various role stressors.

Managing service providers

Leadership and organizational procedures relating to service providers consist of universal components (supportive management, fair evaluation processes) which have specific applications in the service context (backing up the employee *vis-à-vis* the customer, basing evaluation on controllable service behaviors) and of operations specifically relevant to service (manager behavior with customers, evaluation based on service quality).

Service leadership

A key element in satisfying customers is the effective management and leadership of service providers. Given that higher levels of customer-oriented behavior on the part of service providers should result in higher levels of satisfaction on the part of the customers, the primary function of those responsible for the service sector is maximizing employee service behaviors. However, managers in the service sector are faced with various challenges. On the one hand, a major factor that reinforces employee service behavior is positive interactions, or moments of truth, between managers and service employees.[2] On the other hand, these managers are often responsible for many subordinates while also facing increasing demands for customer satisfaction. With many employees to manage and increasing demands on performance, service sector managers may be limited in their ability to develop relationships with employees on a dyadic level.[4]

However, leadership in the service context is reflected not only in the manager's relationship with the service provider, but also in his/her relationship with customers as well as the ability to enhance the service provider-customer interaction. Research on the positive and negative dimensions of service leadership identifies several leadership dimensions that are specifically relevant to the service context. Dimensions 1–5 are discussed in Testa and Ehrhart (2005).[2]

(1) *Customer assistance.* In its most positive form, the supervisor assists a customer with a personal or non-service-related problem (e.g., a flat tire, a medical problem). On the other end of the spectrum, negative leadership is reflected in a failure by the supervisor to help a dissatisfied customer (e.g., ignoring a customer's complaint and/or making little effort to resolve the issue).

(2) *Customer complaint or request for resolution.* The supervisor attempts to satisfy a customer who has a service-related complaint or special request (e.g., explaining policy to customers, offering an apology, altering policy).

(3) *Service recovery effort.* The supervisor attempts to save a failed service experience and facilitate satisfaction through personal attention, comparable merchandise, or other forms of compensation.

(4) *Employee protection.* Positive leadership is demonstrated by supervisor attempts to protect the employee from a disgruntled customer (e.g., redirecting customer anger toward him/herself, defending the employee's rights, removing the hostile customer from the work environment). Negative leadership is reflected in reprimanding the employee in front of customer, namely the supervisor conveys negative feedback to the employee in front of customers and humiliates the employee.

(5) *Employee back-up.* In the positive context, the supervisor supports the employee's decision regarding a customer-related issue (e.g., by addressing a customer who may be upset at the employee's decision). Negative leadership is reflected in a supervisor's failure to support the employee's decision in a customer-related issue (e.g., reversing the employee's decision in the presence of the customer, embarrassing the employee).[2]

(6) *Managerial communication with and consideration of the employee.*[5] Service providers, as all employees, look to their manager for guidance in handling work-related tasks, including the amount and

types of role ambiguity experienced. Underlying all leadership efforts are the supervisor's communication practices – the patterns of communication-related behaviors used when interacting with his/her employees. Because ambiguity refers to a lack of information and communication, supervisor communication practices may offer a powerful means to address employee role ambiguity and job outcomes. Greater use of two-way communication by supervisors was found to reduce service provider ambiguity.[5] Both the relationship and the productivity of the manager and the employee were found to improve as a result of sharing the same idea of what needs to be done, as well as accurate and timely communication directed toward problem solving.[6,7]

Organizational procedures

A distinction may be made between two types of managers – 'service enthusiasts' and 'service bureaucrats'. Service enthusiasts are service managers who are oriented toward satisfying the organization's customers, adopting customer-oriented policies and procedures, and otherwise engaging in behaviors that show concern for customers. Service bureaucrats, by comparison, are interested in system maintenance, routine, and adherence to uniform operational guidelines and procedures. The most important difference between these two orientations is the emphasis placed by the service enthusiast on good interpersonal relationships at work, and a flexible application of rules. This orientation contrasts with the bureaucrat's avoidance of interpersonal issues and an emphasis on formalized rules, formalized procedures, and system maintenance. The literature describes several managerial procedures relating to the service enthusiast style, which can evoke employee behaviors and responses that are more conducive to the delivery of service quality.[8]

Employee evaluation

Many service organizations use quantifiable behavioral standards of service outcomes (e.g. sales, response time) to assess productivity. Significantly, service marketing literature posits service quality and productivity as two related but distinct aspects of service performance.[9] While service quality often concerns process-oriented, subjective measures based on customer ratings, service productivity is frequently assessed by objectively verifiable and quantifiable service outcomes, such as response time or percentage of technical problems solved in one call.[10]

Nevertheless, in the service context, a behavior-based evaluation – that is, evaluating employees on the basis of how they behave or act rather than on the basis of the measurable outcomes they achieve – is recommended. In a behavior-based system, service providers are evaluated and compensated on the basis of criteria such as effort, commitment, teamwork, customer orientation, friendliness, the ability to solve customer problems, and/or other behaviors directed toward improved service quality.[3] Behavior-based evaluation is particularly suited to service providers in that their performance in serving customers' needs is directly related to customer-oriented behaviors (e.g., courtesy, friendliness, problem solving) rather than to specific work-related outcomes (e.g., quota, sales volume). Moreover, behavior-based evaluation encourages employee performance that is consistent with customer expectations of quality service.[11] Additionally, linking evaluations to service-related behavioral criteria gives employees more control over the conditions that affect their performance evaluations. While outcomes such as sales and profit can be influenced by several factors, service providers are solely responsible for their behavioral responses. Thus, the use of behavior-based evaluation is likely to have a positive influence on the attitudes and behaviors of service providers, enhancing their satisfaction and sense of competence, while simultaneously reducing role stress.[3]

Management commitment to service quality

Management commitment to service quality involves a strong personal commitment to improving quality demonstrated by visible and active involvement in such improvement. A management that exhibits this commitment is more likely to take initiative in helping the organization and its employees deliver high-quality service. Examples of such initiative include creating more flexible service procedures, dedicating resources to the improvement of service, promoting a quality-oriented vision throughout the organization, and rewarding employees for their efforts and commitment to the service process.[3]

Work group socialization

The process by which an employee acquires the social knowledge and organizational skills necessary to assume an organizational role is a critical component in the dissemination of a customer-oriented approach to service providers. Service organizations employ socialization techniques to teach service providers the norms and behaviors that are consistent with a customer-oriented approach because socialization increases the likelihood that employees will adopt the attitudes and behaviors desired by the organization. Employees who work in a customer-orientation atmosphere are more likely to engage in and enforce the professional/ social controls that stem from the work group. Moreover, work group socialization is a highly influential determinant of shared values between employees and the organization. Shared values are highly important in service organizations, since service providers who share the customer-oriented values of the organization are more likely to engage in behaviors that are consistent with those values and with the organization's approach. When employees share the organization's customer-oriented values, the organization's customer-oriented strategy is more likely to be implemented effectively.[11]

The service climate

The concept of an organizational climate is based on the notion that employees integrate their perceptions of workplace events into perceptions of climates which capture important themes in the work environment.[12] Often, multiple climates exist simultaneously within a single organization, so that the concept of climate is best regarded as a specific construct that has a referent – a climate must be a climate for something. When excellent service is an important theme in an organization, the climate is a positive service climate. A service climate is defined as 'employees' perceptions of the practices, procedures and behaviors that get rewarded, supported and expected with regard to customer service and customer service quality' (Schneider, White & Paul, 1998, p. 151).[13] A high level of service climate implies that providing qualitative service is perceived by employees as an important organizational objective.[13] So long as employees perceive that they are rewarded for delivering quality service, or that customer service is important to management, their organization's service climate will be stronger. The concept of service climate has emerged as the 'missing link' between internal and external service performance parameters.[10]

Building a service climate

Notably, service climate is a broad concept that goes beyond service provider-customer interaction, implying a range of procedures designed to implement the organizational vision, with some procedures emphasizing basic organizational issues and others focusing more specifically on service policies and practices[13] (see Table 7.1). If an organization is to deliver service along dimensions that customers perceive as important, then its internal environment and subsystems must be coordinated and managed to facilitate the attainment of the desired level of service. More specifically, both managerial practices (e.g., goal setting, merchandise management) and human resource-related practices (e.g., selection, training, compensation) need to be developed and work together to create a cohesive service system and deliver this desired level of service.[14,15,16] The establishment of a service climate thus strongly depends on top management, which influences perceptions of the importance of the service climate throughout the organization. The importance of service to senior management directly influences the perceived importance of customer service at successive levels in the management hierarchy (e.g., store management, immediate management). Senior level managers play a primary role in establishing policies oriented toward customer service and thus influence employee perceptions of service climate.[14] The supervisor's service quality behaviors such as planning for service and rewarding good service behaviors impact the way employees behave toward customers. Service leadership was found to be related to service climate; service climate, to employee organizational citizenship behaviors; and organizational citizenship behaviors to customer satisfaction.[17]

The organization's climate or culture, therefore, must stress service quality throughout the entire organizational hierarchy, and not just for those employees in physical contact with customers. Since services are produced and consumed simultaneously, no quality control check after production is possible. Rather, the total workplace environment needs to emphasize service quality which involves not only a focus on customers but a focus on service quality-oriented human resource management throughout the organization.[18]

Creating a climate for service begins with identifying what the market expects and needs for service quality. This involves measuring customer expectations and satisfaction, sharing the data with affected employees, generating goals and plans to ensure improvement in service delivery, and developing and communicating a service strategy that defines excellent service and how it will be delivered.[19,16] Research shows that a service climate is reflected in organizational practices that are explicitly tied to service and soliciting and paying attention to customer opinions.[20,21,13] In turn, a service climate yields service-provider behaviors that result in positive customer evaluations of service quality.[13]

A service climate rests on a foundation of organizational support in the areas of resources, training, managerial practices, and the assistance required to perform effectively. For service excellence to be delivered to customers, service providers must receive the support of those who serve them. Two categories of fundamental organizational support issues have been identified: (1) The quality of the service received from other departments within the organization, and (2) general conditions that facilitate service, namely efforts to remove obstacles to work, supervisory behaviors such as giving feedback and sharing information and human resource policies.[13] When employees' work is facilitated by support measures such as adequate resources and supportive supervision, they can devote themselves to meeting the demands of customers. By contrast, having to struggle against organizational policies diminishes the ability of employees to satisfy customers and makes it unlikely that a service climate will emerge.[18] When employees perceive that the availability of organizational resources removes obstacles at work, they feel more engaged in work, which in turn is related to a better climate for service.[22] Additionally, research shows that when employees report that they work in a setting where their own service delivery efforts are supported by the service of others, and where they receive performance feedback from the customers they serve, customer perceptions of service quality is positive.[23,13] This finding indicates that the assistance of others is a key internal link in the chain of events between organizational functioning and customer perceptions of service quality.

Additionally, shared perceptions of support among team members were found to be conducive to the creation of a service climate, which is related to internal cooperation among team members, and ultimately to better customer assistance. The dynamic of supportive behavior in teams results in coherent collective perceptions. This is important in

Table 7.1 Organizational foundation of service climate

Organizational operation	Description
Service strategy	Defining service excellence and the ways to achieve it.
Customer focus	Measuring customer expectations and satisfaction.
Internal service	Support from other departments.
Service facilitation	Providing resources and removing obstacles.
Human resources management	Ensuring service excellence and employee well-being through selection, training and reward systems.

the context of service because service delivery is heterogeneous across employees, and the delivery of consistent service quality is a constant challenge. Furthermore, nonroutine services are relatively complex and require procedures and group-embedded expertise when addressing complex, unpredictable customer demands. A collective understanding of one another's roles, and shared beliefs about the capability to perform various roles, were found to be particularly important for service-climate perceptions.[23]

Maintaining a service climate requires focused human resources practices. A service climate depends on having well-trained, service-oriented people at all levels of the organization,[19] which implies that the organization must hire people who are able and willing to deliver excellent service, train them in every aspect of service delivery, and reward them for providing excellent service.[13,21,24] These human resource practices were found to be positively related to customer perceptions of service quality,[20] and a positive relationship between service provider satisfaction and customer satisfaction (for reviews, see, e.g., Anderson, 2005[4]; Rust, Stewart, Miller & Pielack, 2001[25]).

Yet another requirement for maintaining a service climate is the condition that the organization treats service providers as it would want them to treat customers.[16] Essentially, this means that service organizations need to create two parallel climates: a climate for service and a climate for employee well-being. The former requires practices that create an organizational setting in which customers feel their needs are being met; the latter focuses on meeting the needs of employees through supportive human resource practices. A climate that supports employee well-being serves as a foundation for a climate that supports service. Employees need to feel that their own needs have been met within the organization before they can become enthusiastic about meeting the needs of customers.[15,16,18,26] This notion is supported by findings that service provider satisfaction is often positively related to customer satisfaction and evaluation of service quality, as will be discussed in Chapter 8.

The effect of service climate on employees and on customers

Employee perceptions of the service climate have a positive effect on their work effort. When service providers perceive that the organization emphasizes customer service, they are likely to respond by investing more time and energy in their work.[27] Service climate variables for example, were found to be positively related to sales personnel service performance.[14,23]

Ultimately, the notion of service climate assumes a positive relationship between the climate of service within the organization and customer satisfaction.[10,20] Several organizational variables (e.g., managerial functions, enthusiastic service orientation, the degree to which attempts are made to retain customers, and employee perceptions of customer satisfaction) were found to be significantly related to customer satisfaction with overall service quality.[8] Additionally, human resource policies regarding supervision, status, career facilitation, socialization, and work facilitation were found to be related to customer ratings of overall service quality.[16] This relationship has been supported in studies in a variety of contexts, such as insurance companies, banks, hospitals and retail stores (see Anderson, 2005[4] for review). These studies all suggest that customer perceptions of the quality of service are correlated with the service climate in the organization.[4,10,28]

Customers experience the organizational service climate through their interactions with service providers, which reflects the internal functioning of an organization. A strong climate of excellent service manifests itself in employee behaviors (e.g., attentiveness to customers, favorable references to the organization and its services). In situations of frequent employee-customer contact, customers are exposed to these positive behaviors more often, which, in turn, affects customer satisfaction.[12,13,29]

In summary, the service climate may be viewed as mediating the relationship between managerial practices aimed at employees and at the service system, on the one hand, and customer perceptions, on the other.[13] Working in an organization that facilitates customer services enhances service performance, which in turn is associated with customer satisfaction and loyalty.[22]

The service role

Because the service role is performed at the organization's boundary, it consists of responsibilities relating to both the organization and the customers. Having to constantly interact with organizational demands on the one hand and customers' demands on the other, generates a variety of role stressors for service providers.

Dimensions of service performance

Service performance, similar to performance in other work roles, is evaluated by its contribution to organizational goals.[30] Three key dimensions of service provider behaviors have been found to contribute to the attainment of organizational goals as follows:

(1) Service providers play an important role in representing the organization to outsiders enhancing the organization's image and legitimacy through their advocacy of the organization, its products and its services.

(2) The service providers' boundary-spanning position provides many opportunities to share information internally about evolving customer needs and possible improvements in service delivery. This internal-influence function is often reflected in taking individual initiative by communicating suggestions for improving service delivery by the organization, colleagues, and self to the organization and to colleagues.

(3) Service provider behaviors such as courtesy, personal attentiveness, responsiveness, and keeping promises affect service quality perceptions and customer satisfaction. Service delivery behaviors are likely to be visible and are the most role-prescribed behaviors, reflected in frequent reference to them in job descriptions, training materials and performance evaluation forms.[31,32]

Another perspective[33] views the service role as consisting of employee in-role performance and customer-directed extra-role performance. In-role performance reflects formally required behaviors that serve the goals of the organization, reflected in the employee's knowledge (of the company, competitor products, and customers), accurate management (of records, time, and expenses) and the quantity of work achieved. Customer-directed extra-role performance is the degree to which the service employee 'goes the extra mile' in serving customers during the employee-customer interface.

A major aspect of performance is effort, viewed as how hard one tries to achieve the desired performance level, or the amount of energy spent on an act per unit of time. Increased effort on the part of the service provider yields higher quality as perceived by the customer.[34] Customer satisfaction was found to increase with perceived employee effort during the service encounter, regardless of the outcome. Whether customers were happy or not with the outcome of service encounters, they tended to be more satisfied with the experience when they perceived higher effort on the part of the service employee.[35]

Notably, the interactive nature of the service provider-customer encounter implies that the display of some behaviors by the contact employee is more dependent on the customer than others because of their more reciprocal nature. Certain behaviors are produced and performed by the contact employee alone, and are termed employee-specific (e.g., competence, authenticity). Other behaviors are interaction-induced, as they are more reactive and reciprocal in nature and are co-produced with the customer (e.g., mutual understanding, extra attention, meeting minimum standards).[36]

Role stressors

Role stress is an issue that is particularly problematic among boundary-spanning employees[37,38,39] and has a major impact on their performance. This section elaborates on two types of role stressors – role conflict, and role ambiguity – which have been discussed most often in regard to service providers (see Figure 7.1).

Role conflict

Role conflict in the work context is the incompatibility between one or more roles within an employee's role set, such that fulfilling one role makes fulfilling the others more difficult.[39] This conflict may occur when employees are constrained from taking the actions they feel are most productive; when they are expected to meet increasing role demands without a proportionate increase in resources; or when the course of action suggested by one party is inconsistent with the demands of another.[9,37]

The more the role partners with whom an employee interacts differ, the greater the likelihood that the actor will be faced with competing expectations, and the greater the likelihood that role conflict will arise. This is particularly relevant to customer work, as service providers act as intermediaries, attending to the needs of individuals on both sides of a transaction, and their role set therefore includes different role partners. Furthermore, service providers are not only agents of the organization but of the customer as well. The customer, therefore, represents an additional set of interests and demands to which the service provider must respond. The service role places employees in the unique position of answering to two bosses: the organization, which represents legitimate authority, and the customer, with whom service providers often identify psychologically.

The needs of organizations and customers may often represent contradictions (e.g., the organization wants a brief interaction between the customer and the service provider, whereas the customer wants enough interaction time to express his/her needs and views). In many cases, a demand by the customer will be met by resistance on the part of the organization (i.e., when it is considered an inappropriate diversion of the organization's resources), and as an agent of the organization, the service provider may be required to turn down the customer's request. In doing so, the employee fails to meet the needs of the customer, and if success is defined in terms of meeting both the organization's and the customer's expectations, then the employee also fails to successfully enact the role as mediator in the customer-organization exchange.

Since service providers experience greater role conflict due to having a broader and more diverse role set than non-customer employees, often being confronted with competing demands from the organization and the customers, they are at a high risk of becoming frustrated and confused in their search for the best ways to fulfill their multiple roles.[37,40,41] Role conflict was found to emerge when there is a discrepancy between what service providers think customers expect of them and what they report management rewards them for doing.[42]

Variations of role conflict that service providers might experience are:

Person-role conflict.   This is reflected in conflicts between what service providers are asked to do by the organization and their own personalities, attitudes or values. Such a conflict generates a discrepancy between role requirements and the self-image or self-esteem of the service provider. Person-role conflict for example, may arise when service providers are required to change some aspect of their appearance or wear a particular type of clothing to conform to the job requirement.[43]

Quality-quantity conflict.   Another conflict service providers frequently experience is the quality-quantity trade-off, which is reflected in the requirement to provide high quality service and at the same time serve as many customers as possible. The trade-offs between quality and quantity, and between maximum effectiveness and efficiency, place real-time demands and pressures on service providers.[43]

Inter-client conflict.   Service providers experience inter-client conflicts which result from incompatible needs, expectations and requirements from two or more customers. Such conflict occurs when the service provider attempts to satisfy one customer's needs by customizing the service, and may cause dissatisfaction in other customers who do not receive a similar service. Additionally, different customers may prefer different modes of service delivery, such as varying degrees of familiarity.[43]

Role ambiguity

Role ambiguity occurs when salient information is lacking regarding (1) the scope and limits of the employee's responsibilities, (2) the expectations associated with the role and the methods and behaviors for fulfilling job responsibilities, (3) what role expectations are most important, and (4) the standards by which performance is appraised.[44,45] Role ambiguity is reflected in employees' uncertainty about appropriate actions in commonly occurring job situations.[37]

Ambiguity is inherent in boundary-spanning roles because providing clear guidelines for all possible situations is difficult in such complex environments.[38] In addition to sources of ambiguity experienced by the general employee population, service providers face several specific types of ambiguity relating to modes of interpersonal interaction (i.e., how to interact with various customers), handling objections (i.e., how to deal with customers' complaints), and forms of presentation (i.e., the product benefits that should be presented to the customer).[46,47]

The ambiguity experienced by service providers stems from both internal and external sources. Internal ambiguity is reflected in the lack of sufficient information concerning role definitions, expectations, responsibilities, tasks, required behaviors and ethical issues in dealing with organizational personnel (e.g., supervisor, colleagues). In contrast, external role ambiguity refers to service provider ambiguity concerning role definitions, expectations, responsibilities, tasks, required behaviors and ethical issues in dealing with customers.[46,47]

Viewed another way, ambiguity is attributed to input and output uncertainty. Input uncertainty is reflected in the lack of sufficient information about the processing of customer input.[48] Since service providers have limited control over many of the issues with which they must deal, as they originate from customer demand, the input to their role, both in terms of content and volume, remains uncertain. By way of example, predicting how many service requests will be made within a particular time frame is difficult. Additionally, the desired outcome of a service transaction is not always made clear. Service providers, therefore, are confronted with output uncertainty, or incomplete information regarding performance criteria. This incompatibility between multiple performance criteria is a result of the conflicting demands by the organization, co-workers and customers.

Stress in call centers

The distinctive characteristics of work in call centers have been found to generate high levels of stress among employees. Call centers are designed

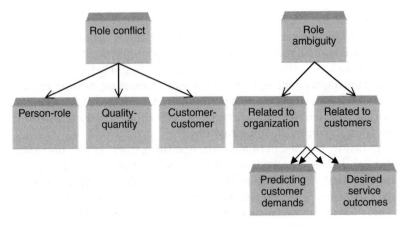

Figure 7.1   Role stressors in service

to help organizations achieve economies of scale in service delivery and sales/marketing efforts. The size of their staff may range from five to several hundred workers who conduct customer transactions by telephone, initiated either by the customer or the employee.[49] Many call centers adopt a mass service model which aims at high market volume and low added value with the primary goal of cost minimization. Consequently, service jobs are characterized by routine, low complexity and low control.[50,51] Employees are often required to follow a scripted dialogue when interacting with customers and are provided with explicit operational guidelines in the form of 'talk time' (i.e., the phrase used in call centers referring to targeted average call length) and customer interaction scripts. Scripts may specify phrases to be used at different points in the conversation (e.g., 'Thank you for calling Company A. How may I help you?') as well as display rules (e.g., customers should be addressed in a friendly tone).[49]

Service providers in call centers were found to experience higher levels of emotional exhaustion than service providers in other roles (e.g., social and welfare workers, mental health workers, medical residents, or law enforcement officers).[38,52,53] Following is a description of distinctive characteristics of call centers which contribute to employee stress beyond the stress experienced by other service providers.

Frequency and variety of interactions

Employees who have the most frequent and intense interpersonal contact experience the highest level of emotional exhaustion (Maslach & Jackson

1981).[54] The focus on limited talk time and customer interaction scripts, which reflects the performance criteria common to call centers, is a major source of stress for employees. Call center employees are expected to handle a specified number of calls daily along with a target for average call length. The percentage of customers who hang up before being answered (call abandonment rate) is often a major criterion of managerial performance. Accordingly, the speed and volume of calls comprise an important criterion of employee performance.[38]

Call center demands on employees for constant and varied interpersonal interactions with customers make this job emotionally demanding. Workers in call centers must continually engage in differing types of calls, interacting with customers who may be, in turn, polite, angry, friendly, upset, frustrated or chatty.[49,55] The pressure to handle calls quickly while simultaneously following scripts and conveying the appropriate emotion to create a positive customer experience leads to stress.[49,56,57]

Role ambiguity and role conflict

While call center employee performance is evaluated by volume of calls, employees are also required to deliver quality service by showing care and concern for the customer.[38] Therefore, the quality-productivity trade-off[43] is especially acute in call centers. Employees receive contradictory messages about the importance of quality service to customers: despite the rhetoric of service quality, management appears to place a greater emphasis on the quantity of calls, often at the expense of the service rendered to the customer.[57] This double message reduces role clarity and results in stress. Since employees operate with dual and often conflicting objectives – the need to be cost efficient and the goal to be customer oriented – they often fail to serve customers to their satisfaction, as they are preoccupied with the cost control and efficiency targets (e.g., attending to a larger number of calls with quick response time and short waiting time).

Moreover, call centers reduce the call abandonment rate by attempting to resolve customer problems on the first call. This requires service providers to immediately address customer concerns to their satisfaction. Customers may call with a wide range of problems or requests, many of which are complicated or unexpected. Being able to resolve these customer problems on the first call without abandonment or transferring requires a high level of spontaneity and role clarity on the part of service providers.[52] Furthermore, managers may encourage call center employees to resolve customer complaints but at the same time uphold a policy of performance evaluation based on criteria such as number of calls taken or made. Such evaluation measurements may be contradictory to the desired behavior of solving complex and time-consuming customer complaints or problems on the first call.[58]

Call centers also frequently implement high-commitment management by means of a combination of incompatible control strategies. Service providers are encouraged to adhere to scripts as closely as possible while at the same time adapting to customer requirements and, in addition, 'getting to know' their customers better. Such a combination of tight management controls and customer relationship expectations leads to employees experiencing tension and dealing with contradictions when carrying out their jobs.[52]

Routine work and lack of control

Job simplification by division of labor is inevitably accompanied by low task variety (repetition of the same task over extended periods), low task complexity (little necessity for own decisions), and consequential low utilization of qualifications (knowledge, skills and abilities). Most jobs in call centers are characterized by relatively short-cycle routine interactions with customers, generally controlled by automatic call distribution systems and supported by networked information technologies which allow little control of when and with whom to speak. Service providers must repeat the same activities continuously, with scarcely an opportunity to make use of their skills. Work complexity is often systematically restricted due to the help of standardized computer programs, with the more complicated inquiries diverted to specialists.[53,59] This lack of variety of work tasks was found to affect the level of experienced emotional exhaustion,[56,57] satisfaction and affective commitment.[59]

Many service providers have a low level of job control not only over work pace (i.e., time point, succession and duration of actions), but also with regard to planning and organizing their work[59] (see Deery, Iverson & Walsh, 2002[57] for review). Lack of control also results from the requirement to manage a tightly scripted dialogue with customers and conform to highly detailed instructions. The close monitoring of words and manners and the limited variation that employees are allowed in service interactions implies that call center employees have a low level of control over their self-presentation to customers. Scripts inhibit service provider autonomy and the ability to provide customized service and can restrict the employees' latitude to personalize the organization's display rules.[53,57] Employees who experience greater dialogue scripting and more intensive performance monitoring show higher levels of strain[51] (see discussion of performance monitoring below).

Performance monitoring

Performance monitoring involves the observation, examination and recording of employee work behaviors and usually involves feedback processes. Traditional forms of monitoring, such as direct observation, listening to calls, work sampling and self-report, tend to be episodic and to collect both qualitative and quantitative data. By contrast, electronic performance monitoring involves the automatic and remote collection of quantitative data and permits the continuous monitoring of performance.[60] Nevertheless, since computer technology can be used to monitor the speed of work, regulate the level of downtime, and assess the quality of the interaction between the service provider and the customer, it is viewed as a particularly invasive form of workplace control.[57] Empirical studies have provided strong evidence linking electronic performance monitoring with increased stress. Monitored employees have complained about increases in workload and loss of control over their job performance. Along with the increase in the demand for productivity and the decline in decision latitude, electronic performance monitoring transforms ordinary jobs into high-stress positions.[56,61]

The effect of role stressors

Continuous coping with role stressors has a negative effect on service providers in terms of performance, organizational attitudes and well-being. Although these stressors cannot be totally eliminated, organizational practices can buffer their effect to a certain extent.

Performance

The effect of role stressors on performance is complex. Role stressors are viewed as major contributors to employee inability to deliver good service and, indirectly, to customers' negative perceptions of service quality.[37,40,44] Role ambiguity, a major stressor, negatively affects performance because of its negative relationship to employee self-efficacy, job satisfaction,[3] knowledge of the most effective role behaviors[9,44] and effort.[37] Furthermore, research has shown that service providers may 'disengage' from performing customer-directed extra-role performance because job stress drains emotional and cognitive resources such as patience and empathy, which are integral in prompting persuasive performance in the employee-customer interface,[33] although some studies indicate weak or no relationships between role stressors and performance,[46] or curvilinear and interactional influences.[45] Job stress was found to have a more pronounced effect on employee in-role performance than on customer-directed extra-role,[31,33] although one study showed it to have a negative effect on service quality but not on productivity.[9] Furthermore, the direction of the relationship (negative/positive) between role conflict and performance is unclear. While some employees may respond to role stressors negatively by showing reduced customer-oriented behaviors, others may respond positively with citizenship-type behaviors designed to alter the situation within the organization.[31,37] Additionally, role stress was found to affect job performance differently among men than among women: female service providers' performance was affected more negatively by increased role conflict or role ambiguity.[62]

Notably, the relationship between role ambiguity and job outcomes may vary by the type of ambiguity facing the service provider. Ambiguity concerning one's role with colleagues for example, may have little impact on performance but may impact job satisfaction. In contrast, ambiguity concerning customer expectations and demands are likely to be more deleterious to job performance. Furthermore, ambiguity related to organizational personnel was found to be related to job tension and turnover intentions, while both internal and external (customer-related) ambiguity was related to performance, job satisfaction and commitment.[46]

Burnout

Burnout consists of emotional exhaustion, reduced personal accomplishment and depersonalization.[54] Emotional exhaustion, which reflects a sense of energy depletion due to excessive psychological demands, primarily occurs in people-oriented occupations in which job tasks involve charged interpersonal interactions. Reduced personal accomplishment is reflected in declining feelings of achievement in work while depersonalization is reflected in the tendency to treat human beings as things; Burnout arises from the cumulative impact of role stressors, namely role conflict, role ambiguity and work overload. Role conflict may generate a sense of failure due to the employee's inability to satisfy incongruent expectations and may lead to high levels of distress, frustration and anxiety, and consequently to burnout. Role ambiguity contributes to burnout in that the performance of roles without clear goals requires excessive levels of energy and mental resources. Work overload involves demands that exceed the ability and resources of the service provider, and thereby also leads to emotional drain and burnout. Burnout, in turn, was found to mediate the relationship of role stressors with psychological and behavioral outcomes.[38]

Job satisfaction

High levels of the role ambiguity stressor lead to reduced job satisfaction because uncertainty about the expectations and demands in the work environment impedes rewards and leads to low self-confidence and morale.[3,31,37,42,44,46,48] Similarly, high incompatibility between various job performance criteria (e.g., quantity/quality) leads to decreased job satisfaction.[3]

Turnover

Role conflict and role ambiguity have an indirect effect on employee turnover through their negative effects on job satisfaction, organizational commitment and burnout – that is, role stress leads to psychological withdrawal in the form of reduced job satisfaction, organizational commitment and increased burnout, which in turn lead to behavioral withdrawal from the organization, namely turnover. Additionally, role ambiguity leads to turnover because concerns about how to proceed with critical tasks lead to frustration, which enhances turnover intentions.[31,38,42,44]

Reducing the negative effect of role stressors

Several managerial practices were found to reduce the negative effect of role stressors, as follows:

(1) Job autonomy and empowerment may be beneficial when workers are faced with conflicting expectations that are not easily prioritized, since autonomy and empowerment enable employees to renegotiate their roles in a manner that reduces role conflict.[3,41,42,44,48]

(2) At the same time, clear rules and regulations regarding work procedures and performance criteria may help define employee role expectations and reduce ambiguity.[48] Such organizational control identifies the behaviors that the service provider should adopt for attaining organizational goals as well as the rewards for goal attainment. Organizational control thereby increases the service providers' performance motivation. Role ambiguity is thus viewed as mediating the effects of organizational controls on outcomes: by reducing role ambiguity, organizational controls affect service providers' outcomes in a positive fashion.[63]

(3) Supervisor consideration, consisting of concern, trust, friendliness and helpfulness, is also viewed as reducing perceived role ambiguity. Since consideration is generally shown by supervisors after the

employee performs well, it clarifies and reinforces what is expected by rewarding employees for desired behaviors.[44]

(4) Role ambiguity may be prevented as a result of a high level of team commitment to service quality, reflected in such steps as service improvement initiatives, promoting service quality standards, and exhibiting extra-role behaviors aimed at customer satisfaction. Employee commitment to service quality defines performance and hence potentially reduces uncertainty. An active involvement with service quality may lead to the clear knowledge and understanding of what high-quality customer service performance entails and how it can best be provided.[48,64]

Conclusion

As with other organizational roles, the ultimate purpose of the management of service providers is to produce optimal performance. However, a major managerial dilemma underlies the definition of criteria for good service performance – the conflict between quantity (serving as many customers as possible) and quality (providing each customer with optimal service). This quantity-quality dilemma may be viewed as an intra-organizational representation of the conflict inherent in the broader organization-customer relationship, namely that while the customer wants to receive high quality service regardless of what is required of the organization to provide it, the organization's interest is to economize its resources. Although the proportional weight assigned to each goal depends largely on type of service offered (e.g., fast food restaurants emphasize quantity, while hairdressers emphasize quality), this dilemma is likely to exist to some degree in all customer service organizations.

Managerial preferences regarding the quantity-quality dilemma are reflected in the allocation of resources, in human resource practices, and in verbal messages to employees, all of which signify the organization's priorities to employees. Managerial decisions about the amount of time that should be allocated to each customer, or how comprehensive the training of service providers regarding customer needs should be, affect the organization's financial gains in both the short and the long terms and therefore indicate basic managerial preferences regarding quantity versus quality. Management may send double messages to employees which lead to role ambiguity, by repeating slogans regarding the importance of quality service (which might actually be designed to affect customers' perceptions more than employees' behavior) but at the same time rewarding employees according to number of served customers.

The notion of service climate represents a comprehensive management model that ultimately transcends this managerial dilemma. A fundamental element that underlies service climate is that climate signifies to the service providers that the organization is literally willing to pay a price in order to satisfy customers. This willingness is reflected in the allocation of resources for service and the willingness to cut back on profits if necessary (e.g., preferring quality over quantity, compensating customers). In this way the organization not only conveys a highly convincing message regarding the organizational vision, but also provides a model for service providers. Their acceptance of hardships in their interactions with both the organization and the customers, and their willingness to solve dilemmas of immediate self-interest versus customer interests in favor of the customer, are likely to be enhanced by the realization that the organization also puts customer interests first.

Another common managerial dilemma in service organizations is the issue of control versus flexibility or empowerment. The need for control arises because many service providers are non-professional, unskilled employees who spend most of their work hours with people outside the organization. Yet, because they work with people, the service providers' job is inevitably characterized by uncertainty and unpredictability, which cannot be solved by control but rather by relying on the service providers and empowering them. Yet, the case of call centers seems to suggest that while empowerment is discussed in the literature as a desirable approach to service management, in practice it is applied only when there is no way to exert a high level of control. The tight control and surveillance applied in call centers, for example, demonstrates that when extreme control is an option, it is preferred to empowerment.

These two dilemmas, and the fact that management tends to prefer mechanical solutions, are likely to contribute to the stress experienced by service providers. The inevitable stressful aspects of the service job might be compensated by a sense of employee self-fulfillment in the ability to help people solve their problems and to generate satisfaction. However, this positive aspect of the job is consistently suppressed when customers must be processed quickly and control is so high at all levels that interpersonal skills are hardly demonstrated. Thus, the unique characteristics of the service role are discussed in the literature most often in the context of stress, while the positive aspects of this work are less pronounced.

Notes

1 Bowen and Ford (2002). Introduction note 7.
2 Testa, M. R. & Ehrhart, M. G. (2005). Service leader interaction behaviors: Comparing employee and manager perspectives. *Group & Organization Management*, 30, 456–486.
3 Hartline and Ferrell (1996). Chapter 5 note 10.
4 Anderson, J. R. (2005). Managing employees in the service sector: A literature review and conceptual development. *Journal of Business and Psychology*, 20, 501–523.
5 Johlke, M. C. & Duhan, D. F. (2001). Supervisor communication practices and boundary spanner role ambiguity. *Journal of Managerial Issues*, 13, 87–101.
6 Gittell, J. H. (2000). Paradox of coordination and control. *California Management Review*, 42, 101–117.
7 Gittell, J. H. (2001). Supervisory span, relational coordination, and flight departure performance: A reassessment of postbureaucracy theory. *Organization Science*, 12, 468–483.
8 Schneider, B. (1980). The service organization: Climate is crucial. *Organizational Dynamics*, 9, 52–65.
9 Singh, J. (2000). Performance productivity and quality of frontline employees in service organizations. *Journal of Marketing*, 64, 15–34.
10 de Jong, A., de Ruyter, K. & Lemmink, J. (2005). Service climate in self-managing teams: Mapping the linkage of team member perceptions and service performance outcomes in a business-to-business setting. *The Journal of Management Studies*, 42, 1593–1620.
11 Hartline, Maxham, and McKee (2000). Chapter 6 note 11.
12 Dietz, J., Pugh, S. D. & Wiley, J. W. (2004). Service climate effects on customer attitudes: An examination of boundary conditions. *Academy of Management Journal*, 47, 81–92.
13 Schneider, White and Paul (1998). Chapter 4 note 4.
14 Borucki, C. C. & Burke, M. J. (1999). An examination of service-related antecedents to retail store performance. *Journal of Organizational Behavior*, 20, 943–962.
15 Sergeant, A. & Frenkel, S. (2000). When do customer contact employees satisfy customers? *Journal of Service Research*, 3, 18–34.
16 Schneider, B. & Bowen, D. E. (1985). Employee and customer perceptions of service in banks: Replication and extension. *Journal of Applied Psychology*, 70, 423–433.
17 Schneider, B., Erhart, M. G., Mayer, D. M., Saltz, J. L. & Niles-Jolly, K. (2005). Understanding organization-customer links in service settings. *Academy of Management Journal*, 48, 1017–1032.
18 Schneider and Bowen (1993). Chapter 3 note 41.
19 Zemke, R. & Albrecht, K. (1985). Service management: A new game plan for the post-industrial era. *Training*, 22, 54–60.
20 Johnson, W. (1996). Linking employee perceptions of service climate to customer satisfaction. *Personnel Psychology*, 49, 831–851.
21 Schneider, B., Wheeler, J. K. & Cox, J. F. (1992). A passion for service: Using content analysis to explicate service climate themes. *Journal of Applied Psychology*, 77, 705–716.

22 Salanova, M., Agut, S. & Peiro, J. M. (2005). Linking organizational resources and work engagement to employee performance and customer loyalty: The mediation of service climate. *Journal of Applied Psychology*, 90, 1217–1227.

23 de Jong, A., de Ruyter, K. & Lemmink, J. (2004). Antecedents and consequences of the service climate in boundary-spanning self-managing service teams. *Journal of Marketing*, 68, 18–35.

24 Schneider and Bowen (1995). Introduction note 5.

25 Rust, R. T., Stewart, G. L., Miller, H. & Pielack, D. (2001). The satisfaction and retention of frontline employees: A customer satisfaction measurement approach. *International Journal of Service Industry Management*, 7, 62–80.

26 Burke, M. J., Borucki, C. C. & Hurley, A. E. (1992). Reconceptualizing psychological climate in a retail service. *Journal of Applied Psychology*, 77, 717–729.

27 Yoon, M. H., Beatty, S. E. & Suh, J. (2001). The effect of work climate on critical employee and customer outcomes: An employee-level analysis. *International Journal of Service Industry Management*, 12, 500–521.

28 Organizational practices most highly related to customer satisfaction are seeking and sharing information about customers' needs and expectations, training in delivering quality service, and rewarding and recognizing excellent service (Johnson, 1996).

29 The relationship between climate and customer satisfaction appears to be reciprocal: service climate predicts customer satisfaction, which in turn predicts service climate (Dietz, Pugh & Wiley, 2004; Schneider, White & Paul, 1998).

30 Churchill, G. A., Ford, N. M. & Walker, O. C. (1990). Organizational climate and job satisfaction in the salesforce. *Journal of Marketing Research*, 13, 323–332.

31 Bettencourt and Brown (2003). Chapter 5 note 19.

32 Bettencourt, Brown and MacKenzie (2005). Chapter 3 note 29.

33 Netemeyer, R. G., Maxham, J. G. III & Pullig, C. (2005). Conflicts in the work-family interface: Links to job stress, customer service employee performance, and customer purchase intent. *Journal of Marketing*, 69, 130–143.

34 Testa, M. R. (2001). Organizational commitment, job satisfaction, and effort in the service environment. *The Journal of Psychology*, 135, 226–236.

35 Mohr and Bitner (1995). Chapter 5 note 14.

36 van Dolen, W., de Ruyter, K. & Lemmink, J. (2004). An empirical assessment of the influence of customer emotions and contact employee performance on encounter and relationship satisfaction. *Journal of Business Research*, 57, 437–444.

37 Babin, J. S. & Boles, B. J. (1996). On the front lines: Stress, conflict, and the customer service provider. *Journal of Business Research*, 37, 41–50.

38 Singh, J., Goolsby, J. R. & Rhoads, G. K. (1994). Behavioral and psychological consequences of boundary spanning burnout for customer service representatives. *Journal of Marketing Research*, 31, 558–569.

39 Weatherly and Tansik (1993). Introduction note 17.

40 Chebat and Kollias (2000). Chapter 1 note 23.

41 Troyer, L., Mueller, C. W. & Osinsky, P. I. (2000). Who's the boss?: A role-theoretic analysis of customer work. *Work and Occupations*, 27, 406–429.

42 Chung, B. G. & Schneider, B. (2002). Serving multiple masters: Role conflict experienced by service employees. *Journal of Services Marketing*, 16, 70–85.

43   Zeithaml and Bitner (1996). Introduction note 2.
44   Singh, J. (1993). Boundary role ambiguity: Facts, determinants, and impacts. *Journal of Marketing*, 57, 11–31.
45   Singh, J. (1998). Striking a balance in boundary-spanning positions: An investigation of some unconventional influences of role stressors and job characteristics on job outcomes of salespeople. *Journal of Marketing*, 62, 69–86.
46   Rhoads, G. K., Singh, J. & Goodell, P. W. (1994). The multiple dimensions of role ambiguity and their impact upon psychological and behavioral outcomes of industrial salespeople. *The Journal of Personal Selling & Sales Management*, 14, 1–23.
47   Singh, J. & Rhoads, G. K. (1991). Boundary role ambiguity in marketing-oriented positions: A multidimensional, multifaceted operationalization. *Journal of Marketing Research*, 28, 328–338.
48   de Jong, A., de Ruyter, K., Streukens, S. & Ouwersloot, H. (2001). Perceived uncertainty in self-managed service teams: An empirical assessment. *International Journal of Service Industry Management*, 12, 158–183.
49   Witt, L. A., Andrews, M. C. & Carlson, D. S. (2004). When conscientiousness isn't enough: Emotional exhaustion and performance among call center customer service representatives. *Journal of Management*, 30, 149–160.
50   Holman, D. J. (2003). Call centres. In D. J. Holman, T. D. Wall, C. W. Clegg, P. Sparrow & A. Howard (eds), *The New Workplace: A Guide to the Human Impact of Modern Working Practices*. Chichester, UK: Wiley.
51   Sprigg, C. A. & Jackson, P. R. (2006). Call centers as lean service environments: Job-related strain and the mediating role of work design. *Journal of Occupational Health Psychology*, 11, 197–212.
52   Avinandan, M. & Neeru, M. (2006). Does role clarity explain employee-perceived service quality?; A study of antecedents and consequences in call centres. *International Journal of Service Industry Management*, 17, 444–473.
53   Zapf, D., Isic, A., Bechtoldt, M. & Blau, P. (2003). What is typical for call centre jobs? Job characteristics, and service interactions in different call centers. *European Journal of Work and Organizational Psychology*, 12, 311–340.
54   Maslach, C. & Jackson, S. E. (1981). The measurement of experienced burnout. *Journal of Occupational Behavior*, 2, 99–113.
55   Wilk and Moynihan (2005). Chapter 1 note 35.
56   Bakker, A. B., Demerouti, E. & Schaufeli, W. B. (2003). Dual processes at work in a call centre: An application of the job demands-resources model. *European Journal of Work and Organizational Psychology*, 12, 393–417.
57   Deery, Iverson and Walsh (2002). Chapter 4 note 47.
58   Tuten, T. L. & Neidermeyer, P. E. (2004). Performance, satisfaction and turnover in call centers: The effects of stress and optimism. *Journal of Business Research*, 57, 26–34.
59   Grebner, S., Semmer, N. K., Lo Faso, L., Gut, S., Kalin, W. & Elfering, A. (2003). Working conditions, well-being, and job-related attitudes among call centre agents. *European Journal of Work and Organizational Psychology*, 12, 341–365.
60   Holman, D. J., Chissick, C. & Totterdell, P. (2002). The effects of performance monitoring on emotional labor and well-being in call centers. *Motivation and Emotion*, 26, 57–81.

61 Aiello, J. R. & Kolb, K. J. (1995). Electronic performance monitoring and social context: Impact on productivity and stress. *Journal of Applied Psychology*, 80, 339–353.
62 Babin and Boles (1998). Chapter 6 note 56.
63 Joshi and Randall (2001). Chapter 6 note 25.
64 Peccei and Rosenthal (2001). Chapter 2 note 6.

8
Service Relationships: The Impact of Service Providers on Customers

Customer satisfaction and evaluation of service quality have a strong positive effect on customer loyalty intentions as well as on their willingness to speak highly of the organization to others. This in turn influences the organization's ability to retain current customers and attract new ones,[1,2,3] thereby increasing overall profitability.[4] Customer outcomes are thus good measure of the viability and success of an organization.[5]

Satisfaction and service-quality evaluations are affected by two major factors: the service outcome (what the customer receives during the exchange), and the process of service delivery (the manner in which the outcome is transferred to the customer).[6,7,8] The process of service delivery consists of the service provider's core tasks and socio-emotional behaviors. Core tasks include product knowledge, fulfilling customer service needs, and helping customers achieve their goals. The socio-emotional aspect of service comprises those employee behaviors that foster interpersonal relationships and satisfy customers' emotional needs (e.g., being friendly, enthusiastic and attentive, and showing empathy for the customer). Customer perceptions of all aspects of the employee's performance are important drivers of customer satisfaction.[9,10] The customer may stay with a certain service provider not necessarily because of superiority of performance but more because of a sense of commitment and friendship toward a service provider.[11,12]

The quality of service provider-customer relations is given special attention in all service organizations because of their intangible nature and the extent to which the customer is involved in the production process.[6,13,14] Studies of various types of service interactions found that customers reacted positively to such positive service provider behaviors as adaptability, prosocial behavior,[9,15,16] listening to the customer,[17] concern, civility, congeniality, caring, courtesy, friendliness, personal-ization,[18] customer orientation (see review in Hennig-Thurau, 2004),[12] exerting effort,[9] thoroughness, knowledgeableness, preparedness,[19] friendliness and empathy.[8,20]

Beyond these specific behaviors, most of which were presented in previous chapters, close personal relationships with service providers have a distinctly positive effect on customers which transcend rational calculations of desirability. In forming such close relationships, service providers are able to utilize their interpersonal skills intuitively and provide customers with a truly personal and meaningful service exper-ience. The present discussion examines behaviors and processes that are relevant primarily to evolving long-term relationships between customers and service providers, followed by a review of the effects of the service provider's emotional state on customer emotions and satisfaction.

Service relationships

The term service relationships usually describes repeated contact by the customer with the same service provider (Gutek, 1995)[21] (see Table 8.1). In a service relationship, a customer identifies a particular person as his/her service provider, contacting this particular service provider when in need of service and expecting to return to the same service provider if in need of service again. Customers often refer to these providers as their own (e.g., 'my doctor', 'my travel agent').[22]

Service relationships tend to evolve and change over time, with the parties developing greater trust and interdependence as the relation-ship progresses. Aspects of the development of the relationship include: (1) cumulative satisfactory encounters and the expectation of future encounters; (2) active participation of both parties in the service process based on mutual disclosure and trust; (3) the creation of a dual bond between the parties – personal and economic; and (4) psycholo-gical loyalty to the relationship.[6] Customers may be segmented based on their desire for a functional relationship, a social relationship, or a combination of the two, although sometimes relationships tend to move from functional to social, and from superficial to meaningful.[23]

Service relationships bear a surface resemblance to social ties of friendship.[24] A service relationship with a physician, insurance agent or teacher constitutes a continuing pattern of interaction, with a history and a future. Over time, the customer and service provider develop a history of shared interaction upon which they can draw whenever they interact in the service context. This history of interaction allows customers to feel comfortable with their service providers and guides them regarding what to expect. Service relationships can satisfy both the customer's instrumental as well as expressive needs, namely the service interaction itself can be satisfying, and may also develop into friendship with the service provider becoming a part of the customer's social support system. In the service relationship the service provider is expected to be actively involved and share feelings with customers, while the customer believes that the service provider is interested in him/her as an individual because the service encounter transcends commercial transaction parameters. Extended service relationships, moreover, provide more time for the service provider and the customer to display emotions and self-revelation, the key to feelings of intimacy.[25]

Significantly, in service relationships the customer and provider can typically accommodate each other's interests and needs. There is no requirement to treat all customers the same way: especially good customers can be given special treatment. Thus, customers in service relationships can receive customized service and can complain directly to the service provider if they are dissatisfied with the service.[21,22] Additionally, greater contact between service provider and customer results in heightened customer awareness of the service provider's capabilities. The customer's more accurate service expectations leads to a closer alignment between expectations and performance, thus resulting in higher levels of customer satisfaction.[26] Furthermore, customers in service relationships often believe that 'their own' service provider has greater expertise than other service providers. Customers in service relationships for instance, may believe their hairstylists know their hair best and can cut or treat it better than other hairstylists, or customers believe that their car mechanics are especially well qualified and will do a thorough job in taking care of their car relative to other mechanics. In short, customers perceive them as having expertise in their domain.[22]

When the customer expects to interact with the same service provider again in the future (and vice versa), the two become interdependent and both benefit from cooperation (e.g., the service provider gives good service and the customer responds appropriately by paying on time).[6,23,24] The longer a relationship lasts, the more likely it is to continue, as over time social and economic adjustments are made so that sustained dyads achieve a high degree of fit. In addition, time, emotional energy, personal sacrifice and other indirect investments are made which raise the price of ending the relationship.[27] Furthermore, long-term relationships have the potential to create more satisfying experiences for customers than single service encounters because the service provider is motivated to provide good service and to meet the customer's specific needs in order to retain him/her.[6,23,24]

Notably, service relationships may have some disadvantages. In such relationships, the knowledge that a service provider and customer gain about the other is specific to the particular dyad and not transferable to other customers or service providers. Thus, customers may remain in service relationships that are not satisfactory because of high switching costs and the uncertainty of acquiring a better service provider. Furthermore, in the beginning the relationship might be inefficient and frustrating because it takes time and effort to establish a good service relationship. Additionally, the customer is limited to seeing the service provider when he/she is available, and may sometimes be forced to wait for quite awhile.[24]

Yet, such relationships are generally advantageous for customers[28] because, in addition to the core service, customers in long-term relationships with service providers experience several types of relational benefits: (1) benefits related to a sense of comfort or feelings of security, reduced anxiety, trust in the service provider and knowing what to expect in the service encounter; (2) social benefits which include understanding, familiarity, and the development of friendship; and (3) benefits that are reflected in special treatment which may include discounts or price breaks, time savings, preferential treatment, special added services, or consideration and recognition of customers' needs.[11]

The beneficial effect of service relationships is significantly reflected in customer reactions: customers who have a service relationship with a provider were found to be more satisfied and reported higher levels of trust and a willingness to refer their service provider to others as compared to customers who did not have a long-lasting service relationship with a particular provider.[22,24]

Personal connections and friendships

If a broad definition of relationships as any interaction between people over an extended period of time is accepted, many interactions between customers and service providers could be considered 'relationships.' However, not all interactions constitute relationships. Rather, in the same sense that a relationship between friends involves some deeper meaning beyond frequency of interaction, the notion of an employee-customer relationship goes beyond repeated encounters.[29,30]

Table 8.1   Customers' experiences in service relationships

Identifying a particular person as his/her service provider

Expecting to return to the same service provider in the future

Experiencing psychological loyalty

Feeling trust

Feeling comfortable

Believing the service provider is interested in him/her as an individual

Participating actively in the service process

Displaying emotions

Engaging in self-revelation

Being aware of the service provider's capabilities

Believing the service provider's expertise

Being dependent on the service provider

In the course of the service process, all employees and customers become mutually involved to some degree as they exchange information regarding the provision of the service as well as other issues not directly related to service delivery. However, mutual interest on a more personal level is likely to build stronger bonds between customers and service providers, and may result in the development of personal connections and friendships. A personal connection in a service relationship, which represents a strong affiliation between the customer and the service provider, may facilitate the development of relationships because it can contribute to the parties' sense of self-image. Thus, to the extent that a personal connection with a service provider positively contributes to a customer's sense of identity, it enhances the consumer's relationship satisfaction and increases his/her desire to maintain the relationship.[31]

Closeness is likely to occur not only as a result of repeated encounters but also in the case of a single extended, affectively charged and intimate service encounter. In a study on a river rafting excursion[32] performance was found to be related to managing emotionally charged situations and providing service encounter benefits; displaying authentic understanding (i.e., the service provider and customer show self-revelation, expend emotional energy and connect as individuals rather than simply performing their respective roles); and providing extras that transcend the standard transactional exchange, including benefits neither expected not purchased.[32]

Generally, two types of service interactions have high affective content which evokes closeness between the parties in the service encounter, motivating self-revelation and enhancing intimacy: (1) A situation in which the customer is primarily interested in the functional benefits of the service encounters, but emotional content is also an important component of the interaction and affects customer satisfaction (e.g., services in which risks are associated with credibility and trust, such as financial advice); (2) A situation in which the customer is primarily interested in the affective benefits offered by the service (e.g., psychotherapy).[25]

Personal connections and friendships are associated with customer satisfaction, loyalty, positive word of mouth,[26,31,33,34,35] perception of service quality and willingness to overlook service failures in close relationships.[34,36]

The factors discussed below were found to affect the development of a personal connection within the service interaction.

Trust

The notion of trust as a critical success factor in service relationships was introduced by Parasuraman *et al.* (1985),[8] who emphasized that customers should be able to trust their service providers and feel safe in their dealings with them. Trust in the service provider is reflected in the customer's confidence in the service provider's reliability, integrity, confidentiality, honesty, credibility, benevolence and high ethical standards.[30,37,38]

The need for trust arises in any situation characterized by a high degree of risk, uncertainty and/or a lack of knowledge or information on the part of the parties in the interaction. The inherent intangibility of service means that customers are often faced with uncertainty as to what to expect of the service until they have used it, and hence initially perceive it as risky. Uncertainty implies a potential for service failure and negative outcomes. Thus, customers have an inherent need to trust their service provider to deliver the desired service outcome. From the customers' perspective, relationship quality is achieved through the service provider's ability to reduce perceived uncertainty.[20,37,38,39]

Trust is a multidimensional construct with cognitive, emotional and behavioral dimensions. The cognitive dimension is the customer's conscious decision to trust based on belief in the service provider's qualities stemming from accumulative knowledge.[38] This means that the customer is able to rely on the service provider's integrity and has confidence in the service provider's future performance because the level of past performance has been consistently satisfactory.[27,38] Emotional trust refers to the confidence the customer places in a service provider on the basis of feelings generated by the level of care and concern the service provider demonstrates, and the belief that the service provider's actions are beneficially motivated. This dimension is characterized by feelings of security and perceived strength of the relationship and is more confined to personal experiences with the service provider than cognitive trust. Behavioral trust refers to actions that flow from a state of cognitive and affective trust (e.g., disclosing personal information to the service provider).[38]

Trust is primarily cognitive in the first stages of a service relationship because emotional bonds are yet to be established. However, as the encounter progresses, both customer and service provider become actively involved in sharing their feelings and reacting to each other's emotional behavior. Thus, affective trust is more likely to develop in a relationship involving frequent and extended interactions with the same service provider.[38,39] Cognitive trust, too, may develop with repeated encounters. At the beginning of the relationships the level of trust between customer and service provider is minimal because of lack of opportunity to look at each other's qualifications. As the relationship develops and exchanges take place, both customer and service provider have the opportunity to compare the exchange to the promises made by the respective parties. Trust is established when perceived performance matches promised performance. Therefore, trust increases with repeated encounters as a customer comes to rely on the predictability and consistency of a service provider's actions.[27]

Additionally, trust develops as the customer acquires information about the service provider which concerns both 'offer-related' (competence, customization, reliability, promptness) and 'person-related' (similarity, empathy, politeness) characteristics of the service provider.[37,40] Among these characteristics, expertise is considered central to the development of trust. A customer's perception of a service provider's expertise reflects the identification of relevant competencies associated with the service exchange, namely a service provider's level of skill, knowledge and experience concerning the focal service. A service provider's perceived level of expertise enhances his/her credibility and trustworthiness.[38,39] Customer evaluations of a service provider's competence tend to be higher for extended personal encounters (e.g., hairstylists) than for brief, non-personal encounters due to the higher levels of mutual understanding, extra attention and service provider authenticity perceived by the customer in extended, physically close personal encounters.[27] Customer trust is also affected by service provider interpersonal characteristics – empathy (the degree to which the service provider possesses a warm and caring attitude) and politeness (the degree to which the service provider is perceived as being considerate, tactful, and courteous). Similarity, namely the degree to which a customer perceives himself/herself to have shared attributes with the service provider, was also found to contribute to trust.[37]

These characteristics are particularly important determinants of trust for customers with little experience and in the first stages of the service relationship due to a lack of knowledge of what to expect of the service, how to evaluate it and how to judge the quality of the exchange. As knowledge is gained over the course of the relationship, the initial uncertainty associated with a particular service provider may recede and customers will no longer rely on inferences about service quality from the personal qualities of the service provider. In other words, as knowledge is gained over time, the 'person-related' characteristics (similarity, politeness and an empathetic attitude) become less important as 'surrogate cues' on which to base trust evaluations.[37]

Trust was found to affect customer loyalty[23,27,37,38] and customer propensity to engage in positive word of mouth communication behaviors.[30]

Rapport

Rapport in the service context is described as the customer's perception of having an enjoyable interaction with a service provider, characterized by a personal connection and a feeling of care, friendliness and liking. Rapport can be seen as one of the interpersonal interaction elements related to the provision of service, which also include eye contact, language and nonverbal gestures. Because rapport is a relationship-based construct, it is likely to have a greater influence on the evaluation of the interpersonal customer-employee interaction than on the evaluation of the service outcome. In actuality, the evaluation of enjoyable interactions may be quite distinct from the evaluation of the service outcome, especially when the technical aspect and the interaction aspect of the service are entirely distinct (e.g., hairstyling). In these situations, it is possible for a customer to have an enjoyable interaction but rate the service outcome as unsatisfactory, and vice versa.[31]

Psychological closeness and involvement

Service encounters can be conceptualized and managed as planned social interactions that have the objective of achieving a temporary sense of closeness between customers and service providers, referred to as rites of integration.[41] Such rites help establish the appropriate level of psychological involvement, namely the degree of psychological closeness with the service provider experienced by the customer during the service encounter. Psychological involvement can range from a low level (customer experiencing the service provider as polite but essentially indifferent toward him/her as a person), to medium level (customer experiencing the service provider as empathetic), to high level (customer experiencing the service provider as concerned, caring and sympathetic). The experience of a high level of psychological involvement is associated with a customer's belief that the service provider is interested in him/her as a person. Such encounters resemble a meeting between friends in which service providers are expected to be actively involved and to share their feelings. In contrast, low psychological involvement encounters reflect clear boundaries for the participants, with the service provider expected to be pleasant but not necessarily friendly.

The degree of psychological closeness is determined by such factors as language, gestures, physical setting, and the displayed emotions of the service provider. Low involvement is characterized by task-related comments, little eye contact or facial expression and blocked visibility of the service provider from the customer. Service providers in a low involvement situation are placid and generally display a pleasant approach toward the customer. Medium involvement is characterized by a pleasant quality of the conversation (e.g., small talk), eye contact, pleasant facial expressions (e.g., smiling) and expressions of personal caring, empathy and enthusiasm. High involvement is characterized by an intimate conversational quality (conversation that is directly relevant to the customer), sustained eye contact, varied facial expressions, expressions of compassion, and high levels of empathy and trust.[41] Since the level of closeness or intimacy in the relationship is affected by the quality and quantity of the parties' self-disclosure, a relationship exists between self-disclosure and the parties' view of the relationship as friendship.[35]

Communality

Interpersonal relationships may be conceptualized in terms of motives, and may be described as either exchange or communal relationships.[42]

Some service transactions, such as with a dry cleaner or an automated car wash, come close to being purely economic exchanges. At the opposite pole are communal relationships which are characterized by an awareness of the other's needs and incorporate a degree of intimacy, such as teacher-student relationships.[29] Communally motivated service interactions were found to have a positive impact on positive word of mouth.[30]

Notably, the association between service role requirements and reciprocity norms is not always clear, because the service provider's role might not define the nature of this relationship sufficiently. A bartender for example, can be a source of help and advice, or simply a person who serves drinks. A tip can be similarly ambiguous, rewarding the bartender for either serving drinks or for friendly listening. However, evidence of service communality can be found in the degree to which service providers and consumers conduct conversations on topics that are not linked to service delivery, and offer and receive self-disclosure and assistance beyond what is required for service delivery.[29]

Caring and social regard

Caring behavior in a service exchange is reflected in three groups of giving behaviors: obligatory behaviors – normative in nature and thus expected; instrumental behaviors – caring behaviors exhibited solely to induce a customer to purchase more; hedonic behaviors – motivated by the desire to make others feel good.[43] The degree to which caring shown by the service provider leads to customer trust is likely to be based on the motivation ascribed to the employee for the caring behaviors. Thus, caring behaviors that are ascribed to hedonistic motivations are likely to result in the formation of greater levels of trust.[30] Furthermore, evidence shows that customers respond negatively to friendship behaviors they view as opportunistic. Once a relationship has been established, however, attributions of opportunistic motives will be less likely since relationships tend to be guided by norms of trust rather than opportunism.[29] Caring develops over time as the service provider-customer relationship becomes closer. As the relationship evolves, service providers show they care by remembering details about their customers and their lives. Yet, even in the early stages of the relationship, such minor gestures as remembering the customer's name and sending thank-you messages may show that the service provider thinks the customer is important.[6,23]

Additionally, social regard, defined as genuine respect, deference, and interest shown to the customer by the service provider, so that the customer feels valued or important in the social interaction, was found to play a central role in determining customer satisfaction and loyalty. Furthermore, social regard was shown to have a greater effect on customer satisfaction than value for money.[14]

Familiarity

A personal connection between a customer and a service provider, and consequently the customer's sense of being cared for, depend on the service provider having some knowledge of the customer. Such knowledge is developed mainly through repeated encounters, during which service providers gain familiarity with a customer and his/her specific service needs either from explicit verbal information provided by the customer or by observing the customer's behavior during the encounters. Thus, familiarity is determined by the frequency and depth of the interaction. Interactions on a weekly basis (e.g., with a waitress at the customer's favorite restaurant) will enhance the amount of personal knowledge gained about the individual to a greater degree than interactions that occur every three months (e.g., with a technician at a car service center). A sense of familiarity is reflected in the customer's perception that the service provider has personal recognition of him/her and knows specific details about his/her service needs.[30,44]

Personal loyalty to the service provider

The object of customer loyalty in a service context may be either the service organization or a particular service provider, or both. Customer loyalty to the organization is defined as service loyalty, while customer loyalty to a service provider is defined as personal loyalty.[34] Regardless of its object, customer loyalty is a two-dimensional construct consisting of attitudes and behaviors. The attitudinal dimension of service loyalty refers to the customer's attitude towards the organization relative to other organizations offering the same service, and the behavioral dimension refers to the proportion of the customer's patronage of the organization relative to total service category purchases over a defined period of time. Similarly, the attitudinal dimension of personal loyalty to a service provider is reflected in the customer's attitude towards a service provider relative to other service providers he/she is aware of in the field, and the behavioral dimension is reflected in the customer's level of using the provider's services over a defined period of time.[45]

Customer relationships with service providers are influential in the development of customer loyalty to the service organization[6,23] (see review in Bove & Johnson, 2006).[45] Customers who are committed to an employee in an affective way will typically want to sustain the interpersonal relationship, which can be attained by maintaining the relationship with the service organization. Additionally, when the customer evaluates the service provider in the service relationship to be superior to others, greater commitment results from a perceived lack of alternatives.[45,46,47]

However, personal loyalty to a service provider might also have disadvantages for the organization. Personal loyalty is likely to develop when the customer perceives the service provider as unique compared to other service providers in the same field. This implies that the customer's attitude towards a service provider is positive relative to other service providers in the same organization, and that the customer's level of using this employee's services is very high, if not exclusive.[34] Such a high level of personal loyalty might limit the operational flexibility of the service organization, as customers may choose to wait, or even forgo the service until 'their' service provider is available. Additionally, the customer's loyalty to the organization is subject to the service provider continuing to serve the customer (see review in Bove & Johnson, 2001, 2006).[34,45] Thus, although close relationships between service providers and customers are generally encouraged by organizations, the development of strong relationships between customers and one particular service employee is not. The fear is that strong relationships will lead to customer loyalty to the service provider rather than to the organization. In fact, customer loyalty to a single service provider is often actively discouraged by organizations by a variety of methods such as not allowing the service employee to serve a customer for longer than a specific period; job rotation; the use of teams; ensuring that the customer has multiple contacts with the organization; and organizing informal events that expose customers to employees beyond those with whom they normally interact.[34,45]

The effect of service provider satisfaction and positive emotions

Service providers' satisfaction

Because service providers and customers work together, observe each other and interact, the employee experience at the workplace is transmitted to customers. Research has shown that service provider appraisals of climates of well-being and service are positively related to intentions to provide quality service to customers, which are in turn positively related to customer service behavior.[48,49,50,51] Service organizations in which employees have positive perceptions of human resources practices are those in which employees can devote their energies and resources to serving customers. Put another way, when employees perceive their organization as facilitating performance, providing positive supervision and enhancing career opportunities, they are free to perform the organization's main work of serving customers.[52] Additionally, happy and satisfied service providers who have positive appraisals of their work environment tend to radiate these emotions to customers and to engage in prosocial and helping behavior, leading to high levels of customer satisfaction and loyalty.[51,53] Thus, how service providers experience their work environment is reflected in customer perceptions of service quality.[3,54] A relationship has also been found between employee and customer perceptions of service climate as well as service quality.[55]

The relationship between service provider attitudes and customer attitudes reflects the broader reciprocal influence that develops in the service relationship. Long-term personal relationships with customers are the foundation for a reinforcing cycle of positive interactions between employees and customers. Customers who receive better service express fewer complaints and thus create fewer problems for employees. Employees in turn react more favorably to encounters with customers. These reactions result in better service which in turn leads to higher customer satisfaction.[56] Notably, while this reciprocal effect may be more pronounced in long-term relationships, it may also be reflected in one-time service encounters, as both customer and service provider are inevitably influenced by the characteristics, behavior or perception of the other.[10]

Displayed positive emotions

While satisfied service providers may display authentic positive emotions, organizational display rules require service providers to display positive emotions even if their internal emotional state is negative.[57] Although the type of affect displayed by a service provider varies, depending on the job, most commonly a pleasant type of emotion is called for, reflected in behaviors such as smiling, greeting, thanking, and making eye contact.[58] Such positive emotional displays were found to result in customer satisfaction, positive mood, purchasing behavior, willingness to return to the organization, and willingness to recommend the service to others.[59,60,61]

However, the positive effect of an emotional display occurs only to the extent that the display is perceived as authentic. In actuality, the authenticity of the service provider's emotional display (e.g., smiling) affects the customer's emotional state more than the frequency of the display.[62] Since the authenticity of service provider emotions depends on the customer's perception that the emotions are spontaneous responses to environment, activities and social interaction, the service provider may attempt to hide underlying commercial intentions from the customer.[25] Ultimately, behaviors that come across as authentically positive demonstrate high motivation by going beyond role requirements, thus enhancing the evaluation of overall performance.[63]

Several reasons have been suggested for the positive effect of employees' displayed positive emotions on customers. First, the effect may be attributed to emotional contagion, namely an individual's tendency to imitate the attitude and style of another person and, consequently, to converge emotionally.[64] In the context of service interactions, emotional contagion creates a ripple effect of emotions from service provider to customer.[59,61,63,65,66] Service providers who smile at customers may have the ability to change the customers' affective state and thus influence their perceptions and evaluations of the service encounter.[59,62] Additionally, the positive influence exerted by employees who display positive emotions may relate to customer expectations regarding service quality. The evaluation of service quality involves a comparison of customer expectations with customer perceptions of actual service performance. Conceivably, the positive emotions displayed by service providers meet or exceed customer expectations of appropriate treatment, thereby leading to high service quality evaluations. Lastly, emotions might affect customer behavior due to reciprocity norms. When service providers display positive emotions to customers, a type of debt is created which customers can repay by an accommodating behavior. Customers may for instance, feel guilty leaving a store without buying anything if employees have displayed positive emotions to them so they make a purchase.[58] Figure 8.1 summarizes the effects of service provider experiences in the workplace on customers.

Conclusion

The service encounter often proceeds according to defined rules regarding the purpose, content and duration of the interaction as well as the parties' role in it. However, when a personal connection is formed

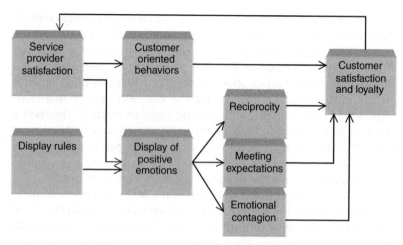

Figure 8.1 The effect of service provider satisfaction and positive emotions on customers

between a service provider and a customer, the rigid boundaries between service relations and other types of social connections are blurred and changes may occur in the purpose, content and duration of the encounter as well as in the parties' roles. The service provider-customer relationship becomes more complex and less predictable in that it is no longer determined by defined rules.

Certain key aspects in the service provider-customer relationship are likely to develop distinctive characteristics when the parties form personal connections and friendships. First, similar to long-term friendships in which the parties gradually allow themselves to display their less representative aspects, the acting component of service provision may be reduced in time as self-disclosure develops. The service provider becomes an identifiable individual for the customer and is perceived as separate from his/her work role and from the organization. While a certain amount of emotional display would still be required, even in a close service relationship (e.g., the service provider is still not allowed to show anger), the expression of emotions that service providers do not usually display, such as sadness, or fear, may become legitimate as a result of the intimacy and trust that have developed. Once the service provider is 'allowed' by the customer to have an identity, he/she might actually be expected to display genuine emotions, inasmuch as self-disclosure is an important part of close relationships. Thus, in close relationships authenticity might be appreciated not only with regard to pleasant emotions but with regard to a full range of displayed emotions.

The power relationship between the parties is also likely to change. While normally the service provider has little power *vis-à-vis* the customer, largely due to the fact that he/she can be easily substituted by another service provider, a personal connection is unique to the customer, difficult to replace, and therefore empowering the service provider. Additionally, the high level of trust that characterizes close relationships imbues the service provider with more influence on the customer (e.g., a medical recommendation, suggesting a new hairstyle). Customer loyalty also grants the service provider more power *vis-à-vis* the organization by increasing his/her value for the organization. This probably means higher levels of skill and higher pay for the service providers relative to skill and pay for providers delivering service in encounters.

With the formation of close relationships, the exchange between the service provider and the customer becomes multidimensional and more equitable. Once the service provider has an identity, he/she is perceived not only in the role of the giver but as someone who is entitled to receive various tangibles (e.g., gifts) and intangibles (e.g., listening, emotional support, consideration) from the customer. Thus, in close relationships the behavior of the service provider and the customer toward each other is likely to be both more authentic and more considerate.

Conceivably, both the customer and the service provider benefit from a close relationship which satisfies the basic human need for relatedness and gives them an advantage over other customers and service providers. Yet, the parties also pay a certain price for a sustained personal connection. The customer might be expected to relinquish the convenient position of 'being always right', show more tolerance for service failures on the part of the employee, restrict his/her complaining behavior and remain with the service provider even if the service is not very good. The service provider, for his/her part, is likely to be expected to invest more time, pay more attention, exert more emotional energy and provide various extra benefits in a relationship characterized by a personal connection. As in other forms of friendship, each party has to trust that the other is aware of his/her interests and will not take advantage of the friendship.

From the organization's perspective, long-term relationships, friendships and personal connections between service providers and customers present a dilemma. On the one hand, service organizations often strive to provide the customer with 'something extra' that will tie him/her to the organization. Additionally, organizations promote the notion of personalized service, an awareness that this is often the optimal form of service for the customer. A close relationship with a service provider might be considered a significant extra which guarantees a sense of personal service. In fact, the ability to form personal connections with customers might be the service provider's strongest asset because once such relationships are formed, they are so powerful that they may transcend gain-loss calculations in affecting customer loyalty. On the other hand, however, when customer and service provider become close, the organization is removed from the usual triadic relationship in the service context. Consequently, the organizational and social rules that usually dictate the service interaction become less relevant and organizational control is loosened. Service providers, for example, might express emotions that do not accord with organizational display rules, spend too much time with one customer, provide him/her with extras, or take his/her side in the event of an organization-customer conflict. Eventually, and worst of all, if the service provider should leave the organization, so might the customer.

Notes

1   Zemke, R. & Albrecht, K. (1985). See Chapter 7 note 19.
2   Bitner, M. J. (1990). Chapter 6 note 42.
3   Schneider and Bowen (1985). Chapter 2 note 17.
4   Reichheld, F. F. & Sasser, W. E. (1990). Zero defections: Quality comes to services. *Harvard Business Review*, 68, 105–111.
5   Anderson (2005). Chapter 7 note 4.
6   Czepiel, J. A. (1990). Service encounters and service relationships: Implications for research. *Journal of Business Research*, 20, 13–21.
7   Gronroos (1990). Introduction note 3.
8   Parasuraman, A., Zeithaml, V. A. & Berry, L. L. (1985). A conceptual model of service quality and its implications for future research. *Journal of Marketing*, 49, 41–50.
9   Mohr and Bitner (1995). Chapter 5 note 14.
10 van Dolen, W., Lemmink, J., de Ruyter, K. & de Jong. A., (2002). Customer-sales employee encounters: A dyadic perspective. *Journal of Retailing*, 78, 265–279.
11 Gwinner, K. P., Gremler, D. D. & Bitner, M. J. (1998). Relational benefits in services industries: The customer's perspective. *Academy of Marketing Science Journal*, 26, 101–114.
12 Hennig-Thurau (2004). Chapter 6 note 15.
13 Bitner, Booms and Tetrault (1990). Chapter 6 note 43.
14 Butcher, K. Sparks, B. & O'Callaghan, F. (2003). Beyond core service. *Psychology & Marketing*, 20, 187–208.

15 Chebat and Kollias (2000). Chapter 1 note 23.
16 George, J. M. & Bettenhausen, K. (1990). Understanding prosocial behavior, sales performance, and turnover: A group-level analysis in a service context. *Journal of Applied Psychology*, 75, 698–709.
17 Ramsey, R. P. & Ravipreet, S. S. (1997). Listening to your customers: The impact of perceived salesperson listening behavior on relationship outcomes. *Academy of Marketing Science Journal*, 25, 127–128.
18 Frazer-Winsted, K. (2000). Service behaviors that lead to satisfied customers. *European Journal of Marketing*, 34, 399–417.
19 Froehle, C. M. (2006). Service personnel, technology, and their interaction in influencing customer satisfaction. *Decision Sciences*, 37, 5–38.
20 Crosby, L. A., Evans, K. R. & Cowles, D. (1990). Relationship quality in services selling: An interpersonal influence perspective. *Journal of Marketing*, 54, 68–81.
21 Gutek, B. (1995). Introduction note 10.
22 Gutek, Cherry, Bhappu, Schneider and Woolf (2000). Introduction note 12.
23 Beatty, S. E., Mayer, M., Coleman, J. E., Reynolds, K. E. & Lee, J. (1996). Customer-sales associate retail relationships. *Journal of Retailing*, 72, 223–245.
24 Gutek, Bhappu, Liao-Troth & Cherry (1999). Introduction note 11.
25 Price, L. L., Arnould, E. J. & Tierney, P. (1994). Going to extremes: Managing service encounters and assessing provider performance. *Journal of Marketing*, 59, 83–97.
26 Ennew, C. T. & Binks, M. R. (1999). Impact of participative service relationships on quality, satisfaction and retention: An exploratory study. *Journal of Business Research*, 46, 121–132.
27 Bove, L. L. & Johnson, L. W. (2000). A customer-service worker relationship model. *International Journal of Service Industry Management*, 11, 491–511.
28 Notably, single encounters also have advantages, because encounters are often easy, quick, inexpensive, and readily available at the customer's convenience (Gutek, Bhappu, Liao-Troth & Cherry, 1999).
29 Goodwin, C., Grove, S. J. & Fisk, R. P. (1996). 'Collaring the Cheshire cat': Studying customers' services experience through metaphor. *The Service Industries Journal*, 16, 421–442.
30 Gremler, D. D., Gwinner, K. P. & Brown, S. W. (2001). Generating positive word-of-mouth communication through customer-employee relationships. *International Journal of Service Industry Management*, 12, 44–59.
31 Gremler, D. D. & Gwinner, K. P. (2000). Customer-employee rapport in service relationships. *Journal of Service Research*, 3, 82–104.
32 Arnould, E. J. & Price, L. L. (1993). River magic: Extraordinary experience and the extended service encounter. *Journal of Consumer Research*, 20, 24–25.
33 Barnes, J. G. (1997). Closeness, strength, and satisfaction: Examining the nature of relationships between providers of financial services and their retail customers. *Psychology & Marketing*, 14, 765–790.
34 Bove, L. L. & Johnson, L. W. (2001). Customer relationships with service personnel: Do we measure closeness, quality or strength? *Journal of Business Research*, 54, 189–197.
35 Price, L. L. & Arnould, E. J. (1999). Commercial friendships: Service provider–client relationships in context. *Journal of Marketing*, 63, 38–56.

36   Goodwin, C. & Gremler, D. D. (1996). Friendship over the counter: How social aspects of service encounters influence consumer service loyalty. In T. A. Swartz, D. E. Bowen & S. W. Brown (eds), *Advances in Services Marketing and Management*, Vol. 5 (pp. 247–282). Greenwich, CT: JAI.

37   Coulter, K. S. & Coulter, R. A. (2002). Determinants of trust in a service provider: The moderating role of length of relationship. *The Journal of Services Marketing*, 16, 35–50.

38   Johnson, D. & Grayson, K. (2005). Cognitive and affective trust in service relationships. *Journal of Business Research*, 58, 500–507.

39   Swan, J. E., Bowers, M. R. & Richardson, L. D. (1998). Customer trust in the salesperson: An integrative review and meta-analysis of the empirical literature. *Journal of Business Research*, 44, 93–107.

40   Coulter, K. S. & Coulter, R. A. (2003). The effects of industry knowledge on the development of trust in service relationships. *International Journal of Research in Marketing*, 20, 31–43.

41   Siehl, C., Bowen, D. E. & Pearson, C. M. (1992). Service encounters as rites of integration: An information processing model. *Organization Science*, 3, 537–555.

42   Clark, M. S., Powell, M. C. & Mills, J. (1979). Keeping track of needs in communal and exchange relationships. *Journal of Personality and Social Psychology*, 51, 333–338.

43   Miller, L. C. and Berg, J. H. (1984). Selectivity and urgency in interpersonal exchange, in V. Derlega (ed.), *Communication, Intimacy, and Close Relationships*. Orlando FL: Academic Press.

44   Familiarity can be regarded as a necessary but not sufficient condition for the development of a personal connection with a service provider (Gremler, Gwinner & Brown, 2001).

45   Bove, L. L. & Johnson, L. W. (2006). Customer loyalty to one service worker: Should it be discouraged? *International Journal of Research in Marketing*, 23, 79–91.

46   Bitner, Booms and Mohr (1994). Chapter 1 note 22.

47   Hansen, Sandvik and Selnes (2003). Chapter 3 note 25.

48   Hartline and Ferrell (1996). Chapter 5 note 10.

49   Hoffman and Ingram (1992). Chapter 6 note 24.

50   Jones, Busch and Dacin (2003). Chapter 6 note 22.

51   Schmidt, M. J. & Allscheid, S. P. (1995). Employee attitudes and customer satisfaction: Making a theoretical and empirical connection. *Personnel Psychology*, 48, 521–537.

52   Schneider and Bowen (1985). Chapter 2 note 17.

53   Payne and Webber (2006). Chapter 5 note 18.

54   Schneider and Bowen (1993). Chapter 3 note 41.

55   Schneider, B., Parkington, J. J. & Buxton, V. M. (1980). Employee and customer perceptions of service in banks. *Administrative Science Quarterly*, 25, 252–267.

56   Rust, Stewart, Miller and Pielack (2001). Chapter 7 note 25.

57   See Chapter 1.

58   Tsai, W. C. (2001). Determinants and consequences of employee displayed positive emotions. *Journal of Management*, 27, 497–512.

59   Pugh (2001). Chapter 1 note 54.

60 Rafaeli and Sutton (1987). Chapter 1 note 32.
61 Tsai, W. C. & Huang, Y. M. (2002). Mechanisms linking employee affective delivery and customer behavioral intentions. *Journal of Applied Psychology*, 87, 1001–1008.
62 Hennig-Thurau, T., Groth, M., Paul, M. & Gremler, D. D. (2006). Are all smiles created equal? How emotional contagion and emotional labor affect service relationships. *Journal of Marketing*, 70, 58–73.
63 Grandey, A. A., Fisk, G. M., Mattila, A. S., Jansen, K. J. & Sideman, L. A. (2005). Is 'service with a smile' enough? Authenticity of positive displays during service encounters. *Organizational Behavior and Human Decision Processes*, 96, 38–55.
64 Hatfield, E., Cacioppo, J. T. & Rapson, R. L. (1994). *Studies in Emotion and Social Interaction*. New York, NY: Cambridge University Press.
65 Barger, P. B. & Grandey, A. A. (2006). Service with a smile and encounter satisfaction: Emotional contagion and appraisal mechanisms. *Academy of Management Journal*, 49, 1229–1238.
66 Verbeke, W. (1997). Individual differences in emotional contagion of salespersons: Its effect on performance and burnout. *Psychology & Marketing*, 14, 617–636.

9
Conclusion: Managerial Implications and Future Research Directions

Managerial implications

Managerial implications in the service provider context center on such human resource procedures as selection, training and rewards which are designed to enhance both service providers' performance and their well-being. Many managerial practices are based on the recognition of the stress involved in the service role as well as the demands generated by the service providers' sometimes complex relationship with the customers and the organization. The implications discussed in this chapter are based on the results of studies reviewed in previous chapters and thus refer specifically to aspects of human resource procedures that are relevant to the service role rather than to more general implications. Still, the specific practices adopted by each organization must be tailored to its characteristics, goals and environment.[1]

Selection and placement

A well thought out policy should be adopted regarding the challenge of recruiting and hiring suitable service personnel to ensure high quality service. Service providers need to have two complementary attributes: service competencies and service inclination. Service competencies are skills and knowledge required to do the job. Service inclination is the interest in doing service-related work.[2] Beyond these general qualities recommended for employees in service roles, organizations should consider the candidate's ability and willingness to satisfy the needs of the customers in the particular service organization.[3]

Considering traits and attitudes relating to service performance

The main attributes that predict service performance are related to service orientation – namely adjustment, sociability, along with general traits of conscientiousness, agreeableness, emotional stability and self-efficacy.[4] Additionally, organizational attempts to foster customer orientation at the level of individual employees must focus not only on customer-oriented behaviors but must also be aware of underlying attitudes. Because changing attitudes is more difficult than influencing behaviors, organizations should concentrate on customer-oriented attitudes when hiring new employees and seek candidates with positive attitudes or candidates who are neutral in this regard but would be responsive to training.[5,6]

Besides enhancing service performance, appropriate selection can contribute to the prevention of some of the problems that are distinct to the service role, namely emotional dissonance, service sabotage and discrimination as discussed in Chapter 5 and below.

Matching employee characteristics with organizational display rules

In addition to organizational attempts to select employees who fit the organization in general terms (e.g., values, competitiveness, sociability), service organizations should attempt to select employees whose expressive style matches the organization's display norms. Thus, the organization will not have to force employees to comply with display norms that violate strongly felt emotions. In all likelihood, employees who have a tendency to think positively will be better suited for work roles that require the expression of positive emotion (e.g., salespeople, flight attendants). By contrast, employees who have a tendency to project negative emotions may be better suited for work roles that require the expression of negative emotion (e.g., bill collectors).[7]

A particular personality variable that may predict the stability of expressive behavior is affectivity, namely a general tendency to react to people and events in an emotionally consistent way (e.g., to be happy or sad). Notably, organizations that articulate their emotional labor requirements explicitly during the selection process can help candidates decide beforehand whether their expressive behavior matches the organization's display rules.[7]

Detecting the potential for service sabotage and discrimination

Because service sabotage is related to personality characteristics (e.g., risk taking, need for social approval), the relevant traits should be considered during the hiring process, especially for employees to fill positions in which service sabotage is more likely.[8] Moreover, the selection process should be able to detect applicants with prejudicial attitudes toward others or who are otherwise intolerant of people different from them. Measures of adaptive behavior or behavioral flexibility may be used to identify prospective service providers who can maintain self-control during service encounters and avoid negative reactions to undesirable customer behaviors.[9]

Placing employees according to their customer orientation level

Obviously, customer-oriented employees will experience the greatest level of satisfaction and commitment when placed in high customer-contact positions. When they are placed in low-contact positions, the internal drive to satisfy customer needs has much less effect on their job satisfaction and commitment to the organization. Similarly, employees who have a low degree of customer orientation will experience less satisfaction and commitment in a high customer-contact position than in a low-contact position. Thus, managers who fail to adequately consider their employees' degree of customer orientation may miss an important non-salary-based driver of satisfaction and commitment. The organization of job tasks ought to allow highly customer-oriented employees to spend the maximum amount of time possible in contact with customers, while non-customer-contact tasks should be shifted to other employees in the organization if possible. Furthermore, although it might seem natural to move the better-performing service providers into supervisory positions, the shift from a high-contact line position to a position with less direct customer interaction may be counterproductive both for the organization and for the employee. If such a move is unavoidable, the employee's job satisfaction, previously derived from customer contact, may have to be provided in other channels.[5]

Training

To provide quality service, employees require ongoing training in the necessary technical skills and the acquisition of knowledge (e.g., accounting systems), along with interactive skills (e.g., listening).[2] While each organization must develop training for its unique competencies in particular jobs, several general competencies are relevant for all service providers, namely in ensuring customer security, ethical behavior and treating customers fairly.[3] Additionally, because many service jobs are repetitive and routine, service providers should be periodically trained to accept and perform new and more complex service roles with the potential to enhance job satisfaction and provide them with a broader range of skills and responses to service encounters. From a managerial perspective, the key issue is to identify and measure the impact of these graduated roles on employee satisfaction and ultimately on the consumer experience.[10] Notably, training programs do more than provide the necessary skills to do the job: the very existence of training programs sends a message to employees about how much the organization values service quality.[11,3]

Conducting 'acting workshops'

While the need to pretend within the service interaction is sometimes seen as a negative aspect of the job, it may provide opportunities for variety and interest. Training can provide employees with the opportunity to experiment with different roles defined in the organizational service script. Using improvisation techniques, they can extend their individual role repertoire as well as develop scenarios for difficult or unexpected situations. The interpretative process (exploring and experimenting with the service script) can sensitize service providers to customer needs. As a result of working through the various roles and observing their impact, employees will develop a sense of ownership in the experiences that the organization is trying to create for the customers. Such training may be based on a critical incident approach which elicits service situations described in the employees' own words.[12]

Teaching adaptive behaviors

Training programs designed for increasing adaptive behaviors should emphasize the two mutually compatible routes to customization, available for service providers: interpersonal customization (i.e., adapting the service process to the customer's preferences) and service-offering customization (i.e., adapting the service outcome to the customer's preferences). Moreover, such training should focus on teaching methods that increase the employees' customer knowledge: which customer traits to observe, how to recognize these traits, and which interpersonal behavioral strategies and service-offering combinations would be most appropriate for specific customer categories.[11]

Enhancing personalization among professional service providers

Customers expect professional service providers (e.g., physicians, lawyers) to spend sufficient time listening to them, advising them of their options, sharing technical information in simple terms, giving encouragement and support, and engaging in additional communication behaviors that reflect service tailored to the customer. Professional service providers thus benefit from supplementary programs that foster personalized service communication by enhancing advanced communication skills such as interactive involvement, information sharing, and social support.[13]

Eliminating employee discrimination and customer misbehaviors

Because service behaviors are sometimes determined by employee reactions to such customer characteristics as age, gender and race, the effectiveness of traditional training programs designed to teach service providers how to behave in the presence of customers may be doomed to failure if the training does not adequately overcome the prejudicial attitudes and stereotypical beliefs that often underlie discriminatory service behaviors. Furthermore, informal training approaches may actually perpetuate service biases by institutionalizing the spread of discriminatory practices from more experienced to less experienced employees. Thus, formal training may be necessary to make employees aware of and confront their prejudicial attitudes. Continuous programs in diversity and empathy training are obvious examples. Additionally, interpersonal skills training programs can sensitize service providers to the undesirable aspects of their responses to customers. Heightened self-awareness of behavioral biases is a key step toward self-control of these tendencies. The goal of such training is be to equip service providers with a broader range of appropriate behavioral responses.[9]

Side by side with raising service providers' awareness of unethical behaviors toward customers, customers too can be educated to behave ethically toward service providers. Customer education can be attained by the use of promotional messages to persuade consumers to unlearn patterns of misconduct and to strengthen moral constraints which inhibit misbehavior (for example, by portraying consumer misbehaviors as unacceptable and describing the consequences of these misbehaviors for service providers).[14]

Encouraging training by colleagues

Employees consider peer-based learning to be their most important source of education for service work. Experienced employees can teach newcomers various methods of providing good service and coping with hardships. Such employees have the advantages of a wide personal knowledge of the 'tricks of the trade' and the ability to provide a personal model of successful performance.[15]

Evaluation and feedback

The implications of research about service provider evaluation and feedback mainly concern process considerations, namely the type of criteria that should be used to evaluate the performance of service providers. Content considerations (what type of behavior to evaluate) are described below, under rewards and penalties, which are closely tied to the evaluation process.

Using behavior based criteria

Because employees can control their own behaviors more easily than they can control work-related outcomes, a behavior-based evaluation gives employees more control over their performance, which in turn reduces role conflict and ambiguity.[16] In the evaluation of service providers' performance, therefore, managers should focus on behavioral criteria rather than on the outcomes they achieve.[17]

Balancing customer- and organization-based parameters

A trade-off should be made in performance evaluation between customer-based performance parameters (e.g., customer satisfaction) and organization-based parameters (e.g., productivity). Too much emphasis on customer satisfaction, or the maximization of customer relationships, might result in sub-goal optimization, where employee productivity does not increase or is even reduced. Too much emphasis on productivity, however, might lead to low-quality service, which will ultimately result in negative customer-related outcomes. An appropriate balance in relation to customer and productivity issues may be achieved by adopting a dual-goal approach, setting explicit productivity-oriented as well as customer-oriented targets.[18]

Using customer data

Fair performance evaluation processes consist of accuracy in information gathering, feedback and explanation of results; consistent application of standards; and a clear understanding of the evaluation criteria by employees being evaluated. Incorporating customer satisfaction data into evaluations of service providers, therefore, must be done with the employees' perceptions in mind. The evaluation system should emphasize (a) gathering valid and reliable information from customers, (b) conveying those elements of customer satisfaction that can be controlled by the employees, (c) conveying information that is easily understandable by the employees, (d) providing regular and timely feedback to employees, and (e) offering guidance to employees on how to improve.[19]

Of the various types of feedback provided by customers, complaints constitute the most sensitive issue, with the potential to significantly improve service quality but also to be rejected by service providers in an attempt to defend their self-image. Complaints, therefore, should not be communicated to employees directly, under the mistaken assumption that the employees will respond by immediately improving their performance. Managers should consider how to project customer complaints so that a positive reaction is fostered among employees. One possibility is by combining complaints feedback with problem-solving workshops. Another is to present complaints alongside customer compliments, thereby enabling employees to interpret the complaints in the context of a more positive picture of customer feedback. Because individuals are likely to respond in different ways to performance feedback, and especially to negative feedback, managers should consider the personality and coping strategies of the individual service employee when communicating this information.[20]

Evaluating discriminatory behaviors

Discriminatory tendencies can be subtle and difficult to reveal. Because supervisors cannot be physically present to monitor discriminatory behaviors at all times, management must find alternative methods to monitor and measure service encounters systematically. Particular attention should be paid to customer characteristics that may prompt unjustified discriminatory practices. Classifiable variables for example, such as gender, age and race/ethnicity can be included on customer feedback devices (e.g., periodic service quality surveys or customer comment cards). This information can be supplemented with feedback from mystery shoppers embodying diverse customer characteristics.[9]

Rewards and penalties

In many organizations, service providers are the lowest on the corporate ladder, working for a minimum wage and not well rewarded for their efforts.[2] Although extrinsic rewards are not the only means of employee retention, lack of appropriate reward is a major cause of employee turnover. In service organizations, turnover has a cyclical effect whereby customer retention and employee retention sustain one another, with high employee turnover resulting in low productivity, poor service, angry customers, and even more discontented workers, thereby perpetuating high turnover.[21] The cost of attractive rewards, therefore, is often more than offset by the financial benefits of retaining existing employees over the costs of winning new ones.[15]

In addition to affecting employee retention, rewards can be used to channel employees' behavior toward achieving desirable organizational goals and preventing undesirable behaviors, as described below.

Rewarding based on organizational goals

Service organizations tend to link rewards to goals that are quantifiable rather than to service quality. Often, therefore, the organization's reward system is not set up to reward service excellence, and in fact may value productivity, quantity, sales or some other dimension that can potentially work against good service. Consequently, intrinsically motivated employees may become discouraged and leave or stop providing high levels of service if their efforts are not rewarded.[2]

Service providers must be rewarded in a way that sends a clear message that providing quality service holds the key to rewards.[3] Additionally, the reward system must be linked to the organization's vision and outcomes. If customer retention is viewed as important, service behaviors that enhance retention need to be recognized and rewarded. In organizations where customer satisfaction in each service encounter is a goal, this should be the criterion by which employee performance is judged. Linking rewards to goals sometimes means shifting from a total emphasis on productivity data to other means of assessment (e. g., team analyses of complaint data). Organizations can use a variety of rewards (e.g., higher pay, peer awards, team celebrations) in developing new systems to measure customer focus and customer satisfaction.[3,2]

Linking type of reward to behavior

The specific type of reward used by the organization should be determined by the type of behavior management wishes to encourage. The most effective dimensions of workplace fairness in rewarding pro-social behaviors involve defined rules for pay and promotion and their implementation by customer service managers.[19] By contrast, adaptive behavior is often reinforced by intrinsic rather than extrinsic rewards. Such behavior may be encouraged by emphasizing to employees how desirable behaviors can lead to opportunities for creativity, personal growth, and working in a stimulating environment.[11]

Penalizing unethical behaviors

An organization's ethical climate is primarily a function of the internalization of ethical rules along with penalties for ethical violations.

The understanding that the organization will punish employees for ethical lapses can produce an environment where ethical values are fostered, supported and shared among employees. Thus, managers should be ready to penalize employees for unethical behaviors that violate customer trust and undermine the organizational customer orientation.[22]

Empowerment, flexibility and control

Rigid rules and procedures generally stand in contrast to the adoption of a customer-oriented strategy in a customer-oriented service organization, in that service providers must be able to adapt and respond quickly to customer needs. For this to occur, the organization must foster an environment in which employees feel they are not constantly watched. Yet, the implementation of empowering and flexible practices needs to be guided by a contingency approach. Although empowerment and flexibility are generally considered to be positive managerial practices, research suggests that the amount of empowerment granted to service providers, as well as the flexibility of organizational rules, must be carefully thought out.[23,24]

Balancing empowerment and flexibility with rules

A high level of empowerment is recommended mainly when the business strategy is personalized, the tie to the customer is long term, the technology is complex, and employees have high growth needs and strong interpersonal skills.[25] A major consideration in determining when consistent application of formal, standardized rules and procedures is more desirable than flexibility is the degree of complexity and change in the internal and external organizational environments. In low-complexity and stable environments (e.g., fast food restaurants), strict procedure-driven employee behavior is the key to delivering what customers want. In such businesses, employees who are free to exercise personal discretion in service encounters can actually be disruptive, or at the least can slow down the operation.

As the environment becomes more complex and more unpredictable (e.g., health care, education), empowerment and flexibility will be more appropriate.[26,1] Yet, increasing autonomy in a high role-ambiguity environment requires care, as additional autonomy has the potential to overstimulate service providers exposed to high role stress.[27] Management should therefore become familiar with the customer-contact stress elements experienced by the service and clarify the degree to which employees can bend rules in performing their job duties. Rather than creating a single type of control environment, service management might consider a blend in which employees are motivated by certain outcomes but are also given clear guidance regarding how much deviation from accepted procedures will be tolerated and/or rewarded.[28] In such a blended environment management can help employees perceive that they have control over their behavior even if major structural or policy changes are not possible. By way of example, managers might avoid overt attempts to control employees' emotional displays by overly specific display expectations and rigid rules about necessary behaviors.[29]

When appropriate, empowerment can enrich the service role and help service providers cope with the stressful aspects of their job by allowing more flexibility and greater latitude in employee decision making, problem solving and the display of emotions.[7] Such empowerment allows employees to feel responsible for their job and view it as meaningful.[25] Additionally, helping service providers feel that they have control in their jobs may aid in decreasing the stress of abusive customers. For example, employees may be allowed to take a break after dealing with an unpleasant customer, or tell customers when they have crossed the line.[30] At the same time, strict rules should guide management in preventing customer aggression. Management needs to supervise the service encounter and develop adequate guidelines for coping with all forms of dysfunctional customer behaviors encountered by service providers on a daily basis.[31]

Using control to eliminate employee sabotage and discriminatory behaviors

In the case of undesirable employee behaviors, organizational control rather than empowerment and flexibility is called for. Employee sabotage, for example, may be reduced by using direct control through surveillance as well as more subtle control exerted by means of organizational culture. The use of direct control mechanisms (e.g., overt surveillance techniques) can control employee behavior, while the use of cultural control efforts might affectively change the employees' mind-set and thus curb the actions of service personnel when direct controls are ineffective.[8] Additionally, without managerial control, some service providers may let stereotypical beliefs and prejudicial attitudes affect their behavior, and consequently respond to customers' characteristics inappropriately. Management must therefore set clear and strict rules to guide service providers' behavior in this area.[9]

Organizational communication

Service providers' willingness and ability to improve service aspects depends largely on effective information exchanges with upper management and other work units. Therefore, attention must be given to providing a communication infrastructure that is conducive to the seamless sharing of information, using mediated (e.g. e-mail and intranet) as well as face-to-face communication opportunities.[18]

Encouraging communication from service providers

Uniquely, communication with customers in service organizations constitutes an added channel of organizational communication. The service providers' boundary role means that not only do they communicate with two distinctly separate parties – the organization and the customers – but they can serve an intermediary role in communication between the organization and the customers. Service providers know the customers better than anyone else in the organization and have a unique perspective of both the organization and the customers. Furthermore, the advantage of customer information provided by service providers rather than the customers themselves is that such information is unaffected by customer self-interest. Nevertheless, many organizations rely mainly on direct communication with customers, requesting information from them about themselves and about the service providers, rather than questioning service providers about customers. Thus, the management of service providers as boundary spanners seems to emphasize only one direction – that of representing the organization *vis-à-vis* the customers. Service providers are selected, trained and supported primarily in this aspect of their role. The opposite direction – that of representing the customers *vis-à-vis* the organization – is often neglected by management.

Yet, customer knowledge acquired by service providers may be used to improve service in two important ways: (a) This knowledge can be useful to service providers themselves in facilitating their interactions with customers, as employees often modify their behavior from moment to moment on the basis of feedback they receive while serving customers; and (b) It can be used by the organization in making strategic decisions, especially decisions regarding service development and service modifications. Open communication between service providers and managers is thus important in achieving service quality.[32,33,34] Furthermore, a management that demonstrates faith in employee reports about organizational functioning sends a strong message of its intent to function in partnership with its employees.[35]

Communicating organizational themes to service providers

For employees to remain motivated and committed to the organization, they need to share an understating of the organization's vision. Employees who deliver service day in and day out need to know how their work fits into the broader organizational picture and its goals. Additionally, organizational norms of high service quality enhance employee involvement with the organization's working procedures. The organizational vision, therefore, should be communicated to employees frequently by all management levels[2,18]. Similarly, efforts to eliminate discriminatory service biases should be sufficiently widespread to identify and address stereotypical beliefs that may affect the organizational culture and possibly even established practices and policies. Toward this end, management should produce communication that challenges unwarranted corporate beliefs.[9] Table 9.1 summarizes managerial implications in the context of the service provider themes presented in the previous chapters.

Future research directions

The research on service providers is extensive. Yet, while some issues have been explored in some detail (e.g., service providers' burnout, emotional labor, customer orientation), other areas call for further study, as discussed below.

Differentiation between service providers

Further research is needed to establish the similarities and differences between professional and nonprofessional service providers. While most research has addressed nonprofessional employees, some observers have found that professional service providers (e.g. physicians, nurses, teachers) have similar experiences in certain areas (e.g., a sense of inequity in the relationship with customers). One obvious direction would be to examine which facets of the role of nonprofessional service providers can be generalized to professionals, and how they apply to that group (e.g., what are the organizational display rules for high-status professional service providers). A related aspect for exploration is whether/which professionals view the role of providing service as central to their professional identity, and how this self-concept affects their interaction with customers. Would physicians, lawyers or architects be less likely to view the role of service provision as central in their professional identity, as the professional content of their job might overshadow the service part? Would financial

Table 9.1 Managerial implications of service provider variables

Service provider themes	Managerial implications					
	Selection	Training	Evaluation and feedback	Rewards and penalties	Empowerment and control	Communication
Dissembling and pretending	Match of employee characteristics and display rules	Acting workshops			Allowing autonomy in displayed emotions	
Influence					Empowerment to generate a sense of influence	
Social exchange				Providing fair rewards		
Customer misbehavior		Public education			Empowerment to cope with customer aggression	
Service providers' adaptiveness and personalization		Interpersonal and service-offer customization; personalized communication				
Service providers' misbehavior	Considering potential for misbehavior	Diversity and empathy; self-awareness	Measuring discriminatory behaviors	Punishing unethical behaviors	Control to eliminate sabotage and discrimination	

Table 9.1 Managerial implications of service provider variables – *continued*

Service provider themes	Managerial implications				
	Selection	Training	Evaluation and feedback	Rewards and penalties	Empowerment and control	Communication
Service providers' attributes	Conscientiousness, agreeableness, emotional stability, self-efficacy, adjustment, sociability; customer oriented attitudes					
Organizational perspectives			Behavior based criteria; balancing customer and organization-based parameters	Linking rewards to organizational goals	Empowerment to enrich the service role and reduce stress	Communicating service-related messages; encouraging communication from service providers
Impact on customers			Communicating customer feedback fairly and sensitively			

consultants or psychologists, by comparison, be more likely to high-light service provision?

While the professional/nonprofessional differentiation is a major one in service, other categorizations are of interest as well, for example:

1. Service providers who are organizational employees vs. self-employed. The presence/absence of the organization as a third party is likely to affect the functioning of service providers and their inter-action with customers.
2. Service providers who have authority over their audience (teachers, police officers, prison wardens) are unique because their 'customers' are not 'always right'. Such service providers often have more power in the service interaction than do their customers, which might generate a distinctive relationship between the service provider and customers as well as with the organization.
3. Service providers who develop close emotional contact with cus-tomers (psychiatrists, psychologists, social workers) or physical contact with customers (physicians, nurses, physiotherapists, hair-dressers) constitute a group of employees that does not comply with the usual interpersonal norms of emotional/physical proximity (e.g., no touching between strangers, gradual and reciprocal emotional disclosure only). Studying the mechanisms that allow for the disre-gard of such norms can be an illuminating research area.

Differentiation between customers' needs and expectations

Customers are often differentiated according to preferences for services, but not in terms of their interpersonal needs and expectations in the service context. Research shows that service providers react differently to customers based on their characteristics, but extant studies focus mostly on discrimination rather than on constructive behaviors. The effect of customer characteristics (e.g., age, gender, education) on the desired service interaction in terms of such factors as closeness, amount and form of required information, wish for familiarity, or need for control merits further exploration.

Customers' attitudes and behaviors

Both positive and negative behaviors of service providers towards cus-tomers, as well as the effect of such behaviors on customers, have been studied extensively. However, research about customer behavior towards service providers has focused mainly on aggressive behaviors. Conceivably, in their daily interaction with service providers, customers exhibit a range of interpersonal behaviors that affect the service provider as well as the interaction itself. While customers are often viewed as subjected to depersonalization by service providers, it is equally likely that customers themselves demonstrate depersonalization, especially towards nonprofessional service providers and in one-time service encounters. Customers may fail to see the person, perceiving the service provider as a faceless entity whom they might notice only in the case of exceptionally good service or, alternatively, a service failure. From the service providers' perspective, being the constant target of such impersonal behavior is likely to affect his/her well-being and sense of self-worth.

Service provider and customer dyads

The service provider-customer dyad in long-term service relationships is a neglected research area that could provide valuable information regarding mutual emotions, perceptions, attributions, and behavioral reciprocity. Such dyads reflect the dynamic nature of service and provide a fuller picture of interpersonal processes than studying interaction from one party's perspective only.

The organization – service provider – customer dynamic

In a similar vein, dynamic three-way interrelationships in the service context merit further study in terms of the mediating role of service and the variables related to the three participants in the service interaction. Specifically, collecting data about service leadership in this context would be a useful contribution. Supervisors of service providers face the challenge of managing their subordinates' behavior while often not being on the scene in real time. Research on leadership style and the leader-employee relationship, along with service provider attitudes/behavior and customer reactions, is needed.

Group dynamics and teamwork

The provision of service is a lonely task in the sense that the service provider faces the customer by him/herself. However, when not engaged in interaction with customers, service providers interact with their colleagues both socially and for purposes of providing service (e.g., the exchange of work-related information). While social support provided by colleagues and by group cohesion is always important, it may be especially vital in light of the lonely nature of the service role. Additionally, effective teamwork, which occurs mostly behind the scenes, affects the performance of each service provider. The group

202 *The Service Providers*

thus constitutes yet another partner in the service context, influencing service providers' attitudes and behavior both towards customers and the organization.

Positive aspects of the service role

Current research shows that the service role is laden with stressful characteristics. Further research is needed regarding work aspects that may buffer the effect of such stress and how to maximize these aspects. Positive aspects such as enjoyable interactions with customers, the satisfaction derived from being able to help others, and the interest provided by interpersonal interactions, could be explored with the aims of enhancing. Additionally, various positive personality attributes may be found to help service providers cope with the stress involved in their job, namely resilience, hopefulness and optimism.

Notes

1 Schneider and Bowen (1993). Chapter 3 note 41.
2 Zeithaml and Bitner (1996). Introduction note 2.
3 Schneider and Bowen (1995). Introduction note 5.
4 See Chapter 6.
5 Donavan, Brown, and Mowen (2004). Chapter 5 note 25.
6 Stock and Hoyer (2005). Chapter 6 note 17.
7 Morris and Feldman (1997). Chapter 1 note 49.
8 Harris and Ogbonna (2006). Chapter 5 note 48.
9 Martin and Adams (1999). Chapter 5 note 30.
10 Baron, Harris and Harris (2001). Chapter 1 note 16.
11 Gwinner, Bitner, Brown and Kumar (2005). Chapter 5 note 9.
12 Harris, R., Harris, K. & Baron, S. (2003). Service experiences: Dramatic script development with employees. *International Journal of Service Industry Management,* 14, 184–199.
13 Bettencourt, Brown and MacKenzie (2005). Chapter 3 note 29.
14 Fullerton and Punj (2004). Chapter 4 note 26.
15 Redman, T. & Mathews, B. P. (1998). Service quality and human resource management: A review and research agenda. *Personnel Review,* 27, 57–77.
16 See Chapter 7.
17 Chebat and Kollias (2000). Chapter 1 note 23.
18 de Jong, de Ruyter & Lemmink (2005). Chapter 7 note 10.
19 Bettencourt and Brown (1997). Chapter 3 note 45.
20 Bell and Luddington (2006). Chapter 4 note 6.
21 Schlesinger, L. A. & Heskett, J. L. (1991). Breaking the cycle of failure in service. *Sloan Management Review,* 32, 17–28.
22 Schwepker and Hartline (2005). Chapter 5 note 45.
23 Chebat, J. C., Babin, B. & Kollias, P. (2002). What makes contact employees perform? Reactions to employees perceptions of managerial practices. *The International Journal of Bank Marketing,* 325–332.

24 Hartline, Maxham and McKee (2000). Chapter 6 note 11.
25 Bowen and Lawler (1992). Chapter 2 note 10.
26 Bowen, Gilliland and Folger (1999). Chapter 3 note 40.
27 Singh (1998). Chapter 6 note 45.
28 Babin and Boles (1998). Chapter 6 note 56.
29 Grandey, Fisk and Steiner (2005). Chapter 1 note 63.
30 Grandey, Dickter and Sin (2004). Chapter 4 note 31.
31 Harris and Reynolds (2003). Chapter 4 note 35.
32 Bitner, Booms and Mohr (1994). Chapter 1 note 22.
33 Bowen, D. E. & Schneider, B. (1988). Services marketing and management: Implications for organizational behavior. *Research in Organizational Behavior*, 10, 43–80.
34 Schneider and Bowen (1985). Chapter 2 note 17.
35 Schneider, White and Paul (1998). Chapter 4 note 4.

Appendix: Bibliographic List of Electronically Available Questionnaires

Questionnaires administered to service providers

Emotional labor

Brotheridge, C. M. & Lee, R. T. (2003). Development and validation of the emotional labour scale. *Journal of Occupational and Organizational Psychology*, 76, 365–379.

http://goliath.ecnext.com/coms2/summary_0199-3388443_ITM

Diefendorff, J. M., Croyle, M. H. & Gosserand, R. H. (2005). The dimensionality and antecedents of emotional labor strategies. *Journal of Vocational Behavior*, 66, 339–357.

http://www.sciencedirect.com/science?_ob=ArticleURL&_udi=B6WMN-4CB017M-2&_user=10&_coverDate=04%2F30%2F2005&_rdoc=1&_fmt=&_orig=search&_sort=d&view=c&_acct=C000050221&_version=1&_urlVersion=0&_userid=10&md5=a0c3c6ffe9c14da526959de6a8b41858

Grandey, A. A., Dickter, D. N. & Sin, H. P. (2004). The customer is not always right: Customer aggression and emotion regulation of service employees. *Journal of Organizational Behavior*, 25, 397–418.

http://www.personal.psu.edu/aag6/JOB252.pdf

Social exchange

Equity

van Dierendonck, D., Schaufeli, W. B. & Buunk, B. P. (1998). The evaluation of an individual burnout intervention program: The role of inequity and social support. *Journal of Applied Psychology*, 83, 392–407.

Lack of reciprocity

Bakker, A. B., Schaufeli, W. B., Sixma, H. J., Bosveld, W. & van Dierendonck, D. (2000). Patient demands, lack of reciprocity, and burnout: A five-year longitudinal study among general practitioners. *Journal of Organizational Behavior*, 21, 425–441.

http://www.google.co.il/search?hl=iw&q=Patient+demands%2C+lack+of+reciprocity%2C+and+burnout%3A+A+five-year+longitudinal+study+among+general+practioners.&btnG=%D7%97%D7%99%D7%A4%D7%95%D7%A9+%D7%91-Google&meta=

Customer behavior

Customer related social stressors

Dormann, C. & Zapf, D. (2004). Customer-related social stressors and burnout. *Journal of Occupational Health Psychology*, 9, 61–82.

http://direct.bl.uk/bld/PlaceOrder.do?UIN=143648616&ETOC=RN&from=search engine

Customer aggression

Shields, G. & Kiser, J. (2003). Violence and aggression directed toward human service workers: An exploratory study. *Families in Society*, 84, 13–21.

Service provider behavior

Adaptive behavior

Gwinner, K. P., Bitner, M. J., Brown, S. W. & Kumar, A. (2005). Service customization through employee adaptiveness. *Journal of Service Research*, 8, 131–248.
http://jsr.sagepub.com/cgi/reprint/8/2/131
Hartline, M. D. & Ferrell, O. C. (1996). The management of customer-contact service employees: An empirical investigation. *Journal of Marketing*, 60, 52–70.
http://links.jstor.org/sici?sici=0022-2429(199610)60%3A4%3C52% 3ATMOCSE%3E2.0.CO%3B2-1

Adaptive selling

Gwinner, K. P., Bitner, M. J., Brown, S. W. & Kumar, A. (2005). Service customization through employee adaptiveness. *Journal of Service Research*, 8, 131–248.
http://jsr.sagepub.com/cgi/reprint/8/2/131
Spiro, R. L. & Weitz, B. A. (1990). Adaptive selling: Conceptualization, measurement and nomological validity. *Journal of Marketing Research*, 27, 61–69.
http://www.cba.ufl.edu/mkt/crer/docs/papers/Spiro1990.pdf

Ethical behavior

Schwepker, C. H. & Hartline, M. D. (2005). Managing the ethical climate of customer-contact service employees. *Journal of Service Research*, 7, 377–397.
http://jsr.sagepub.com/cgi/reprint/7/4/377

Service sabotage

Harris, L. C. & Ogbonna, E. (2006). Service sabotage: A study of antecedents and consequences. *Academy of Marketing Science Journal*, 34, 543–558.
http://intl-jam.sagepub.com/cgi/reprint/34/4/543.pdf

Service provider attributes

Customer orientation

Brown, T. J., Mowen, J. C., Donavan, D. T. & Licata, J. W. (2002). The customer orientation of service workers: Personality trait effects on self and supervisor performance ratings. *Journal of Marketing Research*, 39, 110–119.
http://www.atypon-link.com/AMA/doi/abs/10.1509/jmkr.39.1.110.18928
Saura, I. G., Berenguer, G., Taulet, C. A. & Velázquez, B. M. (2005). Relationships among customer orientation, service orientation and job satisfaction in financial services. *International Journal of Service Industry Management*, 16, 497–125.
http://www.ingentaconnect.com/content/mcb/085/2005/00000016/ 00000005/art00005?crawler=true

Saxe, R. & Weitz, B. A. (1982). The SOCO scale: A measure of the customer orientation of salespeople. *Journal of Marketing Research*, 19, 343–351. http://www.msi.org/publications/publication.cfm?pub=143

Stock, R. M. & Hoyer, W. D. (2005). An attitude-behavior model of salespeople's customer orientation. *Academy of Marketing Science Journal*, 33, 536–552. http://jam.sagepub.com/cgi/reprint/33/4/536

Service orientation

Saura, Berenguer, Taulet & Velázquez (2005) – see customer orientation.

Organizational perspectives of the service role

Service climate

Andrews, T. L. & Rogelberg, S. G. (2001). A new look at service climate: Its relationship with owner service values in small businesses. *Journal of Business and Psychology*, 16, 119–131. http://www.springerlink.com/content/ h288j004755136t0/

de Jong, A., de Ruyter, K. & Lemmink, J. (2004). Antecedents and consequences of the service climate in boundary-spanning self-managing service teams. *Journal of Marketing*, 68, 18–35. http://www.atypon-link.com/AMA/doi/abs/ 10.1509/jmkg.68.2.18.27790

Dietz, J., Pugh, S. D. & Wiley, J. W. (2004). Service climate effects on customer attitudes: An examination of boundary conditions. *Academy of Management Journal*, 47, 81–92. http://www.ivey.uwo.ca/faculty/Dietz_AMJ-2.pdf

Hartline & Ferrell (1996) – see adaptive behavior.

Role modeling and leadership style

Peccei, R. & Rosenthal, P. (2001). Delivering customer-oriented behaviour through empowerment: An empirical test of HRM assumptions. *The Journal of Management Studies*, 38, 831–857. http://www.ingentaconnect.com/content/bpl/joms/2001/00000038/00000006/ art00004

Saura, Berenguer, Taulet & Velázquez (2005) – see customer orientation.

Schneider, B., White, S. S. & Paul, M. C. (1998). Linking service climate and customer perception of service quality: Test of a causal model. *Journal of Applied Psychology*, 83, 150–163. http://cat.inist.fr/?aModele=afficheN&cpsidt= 2244264

Social support

de Jong, de Ruyter & Lemmink (2004) – see service climate.

Service performance

Customer oriented boundary spanning behaviors

Bettencourt, L. A., Brown, S. W. & MacKenzie, S. B. (2005). Customer-oriented boundary-spanning behaviors: Test of a social exchange model of antecedents. *Journal of Retailing*, 81, 141–157. http://www.sciencedirect.com/science?_ob= MImg &_imagekey=B6W5D-4G1WYG915&_cdi=6568&_user=10&_orig=search &_cover Date=12%2F31%2F2005&_sk=999189997&view=c&wchp=dGLzVzz-zSkWW&md5=de5cdf57fbb18c6ceb772c3263147ce0&ie=/sdarticle.pdf

Social competence and task competence
van Dolen, W., Lemmink, J., de Ruyter, K. & de Jong, A. (2002). Customer sales employee encounters: A dyadic perspective. *Journal of Retailing*, 78, 265–279. http://www.ingentaconnect.com/content/els/00224359/2002/00000078/0000 0004/art00067

Service oriented organizational citizenship behaviors
Bettencourt, L., Gwinner, K. P. & Meuter, M. L. (2001). A comparison of attitude, personality, and knowledge predictors of service-oriented organizational citizenship behaviors. *Journal of Applied Psychology*, 86, 29–41.
http://www.ncbi.nlm.nih.gov/sites/entrez?cmd=Retrieve&db=PubMed&list_uids =11302230&dopt=Abstract

Self-report job performance
Babin, B. J. & Boles, J. S. (1996). The effects of perceived co-worker involvement and supervisor support on service provider role stress, performance and job satisfaction. *Journal of Retailing*, 72, 57–76.
http://www.ingentaconnect.com/content/els/00224359/1996/00000072/000000 01/art90005
Singh, J., Verbeke, W. & Rhoads, G. K. (1996). Do organizational practices matter in role stress processes? A study of direct and moderating effects for marketing-oriented boundary spanners. *Journal of Marketing*, 60, 69–86.

Performance evaluation
Netemeyer, R. G., Maxham, J. G. III & Pullig, C. (2005). Conflicts in the work-family interface: Links to job stress, customer service employee performance, and customer purchase intent. *Journal of Marketing*, 69, 130–143.
Hartline & Ferrell (1996) – see adaptive behavior.

Role conflict and role ambiguity

Hartline & Ferrell (1996) – see adaptive behavior.
Schwepker & Hartline (2005) – see ethical behavior.

Relationship quality

Rapport

Harris & Ogbonna (2006) – see service sabotage.

Questionnaires administered to customers

Service provider behavior

Organizational citizenship behavior

Payne, S. & Webber, S. S. (2006). Effects of service provider attitudes and employment status on citizenship behaviors and customers' attitudes and loyalty behavior. *Journal of Applied Psychology*, 91, 365–378.
http://www.ncbi.nlm.nih.gov/sites/entrez?db=pubmed&list_uids=16551189 &cmd=Retrieve&indexed=google

Bettencourt, L., Gwinner, K. P. & Meuter, M. L. (2001). A comparison of attitude, personality, and knowledge predictors of service-oriented organizational citizenship behaviors. *Journal of Applied Psychology*, 86, 29–41.
http://www.ncbi.nlm.nih.gov/sites/entrez?cmd=Retrieve&db=PubMed&list_uids=11302230&dopt=Abstract

Service provider attributes

Customer orientation

Hennig-Thurau, T. (2004). Customer orientation of service employees: Its impact on customer satisfaction, commitment, and retention. *International Journal of Service Industry Management*, 15, 460–478.

Michaels, R. E. & Day, R. L. (1985). Measuring customer orientation of salespeople: A replication with industrial buyers. *Journal of Marketing Research*, 22, 443–446.
http://links.jstor.org/sici?sici=0022-2437(198511)22%3A4%3C443%3AMCOOSA%3E2.0.CO%3B2-U

Stock & Hoyer (2005) – see customer orientation/service providers.

Service orientation

Bell, S. J. & Luddington, J. A. (2006). Coping with customer complaints. *Journal of Service Research*, 8, 221–233. http://jsr.sagepub.com/cgi/reprint/8/3/221

Saura, Berenguer, Taulet & Moliner (2005) – see customer orientation/service providers.

Schwepker, C. H. & Hartline, M. D. (2005). Managing the ethical climate of customer-contact service employees. *Journal of Service Research*, 7, 377–397. http://jsr.sagepub.com/cgi/reprint/7/4/377

Organizational perspectives of the service role

Service climate

Dietz, Pugh & Wiley (2004) – see service climate administered to service providers.

Service provider performance

Brady, M. K., Cronin, J. J. & Brand, R. R. (2002). Performance-only measurement of service quality: A replication and extension. *Journal of Business Research*, 55, 17–31.
http://www.sciencedirect.com/science/article/B6V7S-44GR1XW-2/2/03234e56389c1fca0d32b75f4317d405

Dietz, Pugh & Wiley 2004 – see service climate administered to service providers.

de Jong, de Ruyter & Lemmink (2004) – see service climate/service providers.

Parasuraman, A., Zeithaml, V. A. & Berry, L. L. (1988). Servqual: A multiple-item scale for measuring consumer perceptions of service quality. *Journal of Retailing*, 64, 12–40. http://soma.byu.edu/somad/?q=node/66

van Dolen, W., Lemmink, J., de Ruyter, K. & de Jong, A. (2002). Customer-sales employee encounters: A dyadic perspective. *Journal of Retailing,* 78, 265–279. http://goliath.ecnext.com/coms2/summary_0198-115124_ITM

Relationship quality

Roberts, K., Varki, S. & Brodie, R. (2003). Measuring the quality of relationships in consumer services: An empirical study. *European Journal of Marketing,* 37, 169–196.
http://www.emeraldinsight.com/Insight/viewContentItem.do?contentType= Article&hdAction=lnkhtml&contentId=853840

Mittal, B. & Lassar, W. M. (1996). The role of personalization in service encounters. *Journal of Retailing,* 72, 95–109.
http://www.ingentaconnect.com/content/els/00224359/1996/00000072/000000 01/art90007

Crosby, L. A., Evans, K. R. & Cowles, D. (1990). Relationship quality in services selling: An interpersonal influence perspective. *Journal of Marketing,* 54, 68–81. http://links.jstor.org/sici?sici=0022-2429(199007)54%3A3%3C68% 3ARQISSA%3E2.0.CO%3B2-K

Trust

Coulter, K. S. & Coulter, R. A. (2002). Determinants of trust in a service provider: The moderating role of length of relationship. *The Journal of Services Marketing,* 16, 35–50.
http://www.emeraldinsight.com/Insight/viewContentItem.do?contentType= Article&hdAction=lnkhtml&contentId=855927

Johnson, D. & Grayson, K. (2005). Cognitive and affective trust in service relationships. *Journal of Business Research,* 58, 500–507.
http://www.sciencedirect.com/science?_ob=ArticleURL&_udi=B6V7S-49H15B11 &_user=10&_coverDate=04%2F30%2F2005&_rdoc=1&_fmt=&_orig=search &_sort=d&view=c&_acct=C000050221&_version=1&_urlVersion=0&_userid= 10&md5=78a6776bcda3f208c854863525f443e1

van Dolen, W., de Ruyter, K. & Lemmink, J. (2004). An empirical assessment of the influence of customer emotions and contact employee performance on encounter and relationship satisfaction. *Journal of Business Research,* 57, 437–444.
http://www.sciencedirect.com/science/article/B6V7S-459J9SB-1/2/93 cde297d6cde98dc9d682d410d98e80

Rapport

Gremler, D. D. & Gwinner, K. P. (2000). Customer-employee rapport in service relationships. *Journal of Service Research,* 3, 82–104.
http://www.gremler.net/personal/research/2000_Rapport_JSR.pdf

Social regard

Butcher, K., Sparks, B. & O'Callaghan, F. (2003). Beyond core service. *Psychology and Marketing,* 20, 187–208.
http://www3.interscience.wiley.com/cgi-bin/abstract/104519590/ ABSTRACT? CRETRY=1&SRETRY=0

Listening behavior

Ramsey, R. P. & Sohi, R. S. (1997). Listening to your customers: The impact of perceived salesperson listening behavior on relationship outcomes. *Academy of Marketing Science Journal*, 25, 127–137.

Personal loyalty to service provider

Bove, L. L. & Johnson, L. W. (2006). Customer loyalty to one service worker: Should it be discouraged? *International Journal of Research in Marketing*, 23, 79–91.
http://www.sciencedirect.com/science?_ob=ArticleURL&_udi=B6V8R-4JCSJVH-2&_user=10&_coverDate=03%2F31%2F2006&_rdoc=1&_fmt=&_orig=search&_sort=d&view=c&_acct=C000050221&_version=1&_urlVersion=0&_userid=10&md5=2ccc6ef7e87f2bf30fc492d5de559250

References

Abraham, R. (1998). Emotional dissonance in organizations: Antecedents, consequences, and moderators. *Genetic, Social, and General Psychology Monographs*, 124, 229–246.

Adams, J. S. (1965). Inequity in social exchange. In L. Berkowitz (ed.), *Advances in Experimental Social Psychology*, Vol. 2 (pp. 267–299).

Adelman, M. B. & Ahuvia, A. C. (1995). Social support in the service sector: The antecedents, processes, and outcomes of social support in an introductory service. *Journal of Business Research*, 32, 273–282.

Ahearne, M., Mathieu, J. & Rapp, A. (2005). To empower or not to empower your sales force? An empirical examination of influence of leadership empowerment behavior on customer satisfaction and performance. *Journal of Applied Psychology*, 90, 945–955.

Aiello, J. R. & Kolb, K. J. (1995). Electronic performance monitoring and social context: Impact on productivity and stress. *Journal of Applied Psychology*, 80, 339–353.

Anderson, J. R. (2005). Managing employees in the service sector: A literature review and conceptual development. *Journal of Business and Psychology*, 20, 501–523.

Andrews, T. L. & Rogelberg, S. G. (2001). A new look at service climate: Its relationship with owner service values in small businesses. *Journal of Business and Psychology*, 16, 119–131.

Arnould, E. J. & Price, L. L. (1993). River magic: Extraordinary experience and the extended service encounter. *Journal of Consumer Research*, 20, 24–25.

Aron, D. (2001). Consumer grudgeholding: Toward a conceptual model and research agenda. *Journal of Consumer Satisfaction, Dissatisfaction and Complaining Behavior*, 14, 108–119.

Ashforth, B. E. & Humphrey, R. H. (1993). Emotional labor in service roles: The influence of identity. *The Academy of Management Review*, 18, 88–115.

Avinandan, M. & Neeru, M. (2006). Does role clarity explain employee-perceived service quality? A study of antecedents and consequences in call centres. *International Journal of Service Industry Management*, 17, 444–473.

Babin, B. J. & Boles, J. S. (1996). On the front lines: Stress, conflict, and the customer service provider. *Journal of Business Research*, 37, 41–50.

Babin, B. J. & Boles, J. S. (1998). Employee behavior in a service environment: A model and test of potential differences between men and women. *Journal of Marketing*, 62, 77–91.

Bain, P. & Taylor, P. (2004). Call centers and human resource management: A cross-national perspective. *Employee Relations*, 26, 569–571.

Bakker, A. B., Demerouti, E. & Schaufeli, W. B. (2003). Dual processes at work in a call centre: An application of the job demands-resources model. *European Journal of Work and Organizational Psychology*, 12, 393–417.

Bakker, A. B., Schaufeli, W. B., Sixma, H. J., Bosveld, W. & van Dierendonck, D. (2000). Patient demands, lack of reciprocity, and burnout: A five-year longitudinal study among general practitioners. *Journal of Organizational Behavior*, 21, 425–441.

Bandura, A. (1977). Self efficacy: Toward a unifying theory of behavior change. *Psychological Review*, 84, 191–215.

Barbee, C. & Bott, V. (1991). Customer treatment as a mirror of employee treatment. *S.A.M. Advanced Management Journal*, 56, 27–32.

Barger, P. B. & Grandey, A. A. (2006). Service with a smile and encounter satisfaction: Emotional contagion and appraisal mechanisms. *Academy of Management Journal*, 49, 1229–1238.

Barling, J., Rogers, K. A. & Kelloway, E. K. (1995). Some effects of teenagers' part-time employment: The quantity and quality of work make the difference. *Journal of Organizational Behavior*, 16, 143–154.

Barnes, J. G. (1997). Closeness, strength, and satisfaction: Examining the nature of relationships between providers of financial services and their retail customers. *Psychology & Marketing*, 14, 765–790.

Baron, S., Harris, K. & Harris, R. (2001). Retail theater: The 'intended effect' of the performance. *Journal of Service Research*, 4, 102–117.

Barrera, M. & Balls, P. (1983). Assessing social support as a prevention resource: An illustrative study. *Prevention in Human Services*, 2, 59–74.

Barrick, M. R., Mount, M. K. & Judge, T. A. (2001). Personality and performance at the beginning of the new millennium: What do we know and where do we go next? *International Journal of Selection and Assessment*, 9, 9–30.

Bateson, J. E. G. (1985). Perceived control and the service encounter. In A. Czepiel, M. R. Solomon & C. F. Suprenant (eds), *The Service Encounter: Managing Employee/Customer Interaction in Service Business* (pp. 67–82). Massachusetts: Lexington Books.

Bateson, J. E. G. (2000). Perceived control and the service experience. In T. A. Swartz & D. Iacobucci (eds), *Handbook of Service Marketing and Management* (pp. 127–145). Thousand Oaks: Sage.

Bateson, J. E. G. & Hui, M. (1992). The ecological validity of photographic slides and videotapes in simulating the service setting. *Journal of Consumer Research*, 19, 271–282.

Bateson, P. & Martin, P. (2000). Why all work and no play can be bad for business: Organisations with problems should look to where people have stopped having fun, advise Patric Bateson and Paul Martin. *Financial Times*, 8 April, 9.

Beatty, S. E., Mayer, M., Coleman, J. E., Reynolds, K. E. & Lee, J. (1996). Customer-sales associate retail relationships. *Journal of Retailing*, 72, 223–245.

Bell, C. & Zemke, R. (1988). Do service procedures tie employees' hands? *Personnel Journal*, 67, 76–83.

Bell, S. J. & Luddington, J. A. (2006). Coping with customer complaints. *Journal of Service Research*, 8, 221–233.

Bell, S. J. & Menguc, B. (2002). The employee-organization relationship, organizational citizenship behaviors, and superior service quality. *Journal of Retailing*, 78, 131–146.

Bell, S. J., Menguc, B. & Stefani, S. L. (2004). When customers disappoint: A model of relational internal marketing and customer complaints. *Academy of Marketing Science Journal*, 32, 112–126.

Belt, V. (2002). A female ghetto? Women's careers in call centres. *Human Resource Management Journal*, 12, 51–66.

Belt, V., Richardson, R. & Webster, J. (2002). Women, social skill and interactive service work in telephone call centres. *New Technology, Work, and Employment*, 17, 20–34.

Bennet, R. (1997). Anger, catharsis, and purchasing behavior following aggressive customer complaints. *Journal of Consumer Marketing*, 14, 156–172.

Ben-Zur, H. & Yagil, D. (2005). The relationship between empowerment, aggressive behaviours of customers, coping, and burnout. *European Journal of Work and Organizational Psychology*, 14, 81–99.

Berry, L. L. (1980). Services marketing is different. *Business*, 30, 24–33.

Berry, L. L. (1995). Relationship marketing of services – Growing interest, emerging perspectives. *Academy of Marketing Science Journal*, 23, 236–245.

Bettencourt, L. A. & Brown, S. W. (1997). Contact employees: Relationships among workplace fairness, job satisfaction and prosocial service behaviors. *Journal of Retailing*, 73, 39–61.

Bettencourt, L. A. & Brown. S. W. (2003). Role stressors and customer-oriented boundary-spanning behaviors in service organizations. *Academy of Marketing Science Journal*, 31, 394–408.

Bettencourt, L. A., Brown, S. W. & MacKenzie, S. B. (2005). Customer-oriented boundary-spanning behaviors: Test of a social exchange model of antecedents. *Journal of Retailing*, 81, 141–157.

Bettencourt, L. A. & Gwinner, K. (1996). Customization of the service experience: The role of the frontline employee. *International Journal of Service Industry Management*, 7, 3–20.

Bettencourt, L. A., Gwinner, K. P. & Meuter, M. L. (2001). A comparison of attitude, personality, and knowledge predictors of service-oriented organizational citizenship behaviors. *Journal of Applied Psychology*, 86, 29–41.

Bies, R. J. & Moag, J. S. (1986). Interactional justice: Communication criteria of fairness. In R. J. Lewecki, B. H. Sheppard & M. H. Blazerman (eds), *Research in Negotiation in Organizations*, Vol. 1, 43–55. Greenwich, CT: JAI Press.

Bishop, V., Korczynski, M. & Cohen, L. (2005). The invisibility of violence: Constructing violence out of the job centre workplace in the UK. *Work, Employment & Society*, 19, 583–602.

Bitner, M. J. (1990). Evaluating service encounters: The effects of physical surroundings and employee responses. *Journal of Marketing*, 54, 69–82.

Bitner, M. J. (1992). Servicescapes: The impact of physical surroundings on customers and employees. *Journal of Marketing*, 56, 57–71.

Bitner, M. J., Booms, B. H. & Mohr, L. A. (1994). Critical service encounters: The employee's viewpoint. *Journal of Marketing*, 58, 95–106.

Bitner, M. J., Booms, B. H. & Tetreault, M. S. (1990). The service encounter: Diagnosing favorable and unfavorable incidents. *Journal of Marketing*, 54, 71–84.

Blau, P. M. (1964). *Exchange and Power in Social Life*. New York: Wiley.

Boles, J. S., Babin, B. J., Brashear, T. G. & Brooks, C. (2001). An examination of the relationships between retail work environments, salesperson selling orientation-customer orientation and job performance. *Journal of Marketing Theory and Practice*, 9, 1–13.

Bolton, S. C. & Houlihan, M. (2005). The (mis)representation of customer service. *Work, Employment & Society*, 19, 685–703.

Borucki, C. C. & Burke, M. J. (1999). An examination of service-related antecedents to retail store performance. *Journal of Organizational Behavior*, 20, 943–962.

Bove, L. L. & Johnson, L. W. (2000). A customer-service worker relationship model. *International Journal of Service Industry Management*, 11, 491–511.

Bove, L. L. & Johnson, L. W. (2001). Customer relationships with service personnel: Do we measure closeness, quality or strength? *Journal of Business Research*, 54, 189–197.

Bove, L. L. & Johnson, L. W. (2006). Customer loyalty to one service worker: Should it be discouraged? *International Journal of Research in Marketing*, 23, 79–91.

Bowen, J. & Ford, R. C. (2002). Managing service organizations: Does having a 'thing' make a difference? *Journal of Management*, 28, 447–469.

Bowen, D. E., Gilliland, S. W. & Folger, R. (1999). HRM and service fairness: How being fair with employees spills over to customers. *Organizational Dynamics*, 27, 7–23.

Bowen, D. E. & Lawler, E. E. (1992). The empowerment of service workers: What, why, how, and when. *Human Resource Management and Industrial Relations*, 33, 31–39.

Bowen, D. E. & Lawler, E. E. (1995). Empowering service employees. *Sloan Management Review*, 36, 73–84.

Bowen, D. E. & Schneider, B. (1988). Services marketing and management: Implications for organizational behavior. *Research in Organizational Behavior*, 10, 43–80.

Boyd, C. (2002). Customer violence and employee health and safety. *Work, Employment & Society*, 16, 151–169.

Bradley, H. (1989). *Men's Work, Women's Work*. Cambridge: Polity Press.

Bradley, H., Erickson, M., Stephenson, C. & Williams, S. (2000). *Myths at Work*. Cambridge: Polity Press.

Brady, M. K., Cronin, J. J. & Brand, R. R. (2002). Performance-only measurement of service quality: A replication and extension. *Journal of Business Research*, 55, 17–31.

Broderick, A. J. (1998). Role theory, role management, and service performance. *Journal of Services Marketing*, 12, 348–361.

Brotheridge, C. M. & Grandey, A. A. (2002). Emotional labor and burnout: Comparing two perspectives of 'people work'. *Journal of Vocational Behavior*, 60, 17–39.

Brotheridge, C. M. & Lee, R. T. (1988). On the dimensionality of emotional labour: Development and validation of the emotional labour scale. *Paper presented at the First Conference on Emotions in Organizational Life*, San Diego.

Brotheridge, C. M. & Lee, R. T. (2003). Development and validation of the emotional labour scale. *Journal of Occupational and Organizational Psychology*, 76, 365–379.

Brown, T. J., Mowen, J. C., Donavan, D. T. & Licata, J. W. (2002). The customer orientation of service workers: Personality trait effects on self-and supervisor performance ratings. *Journal of Marketing Research*, 39, 110–119.

Burke, M. J., Borucki, C. C. & Hurley, A. E. (1992). Reconceptualizing psychological climate in a retail service. *Journal of Applied Psychology*, 77, 717–729.

Butcher, K., Sparks, B. & O'Callaghan, F. (2003). Beyond core service. *Psychology & Marketing*, 20, 187–208.

Buunk, B. P. & Schaufeli, W. B. (1993). Professional burnout: A perspective from social comparison theory. In W. B. Schaufeli, C. Maslach & T. Marck (eds), *Professional Burnout: Recent Developments in Theory and Research* (pp. 53–69). New York: Taylor & Francis.

Chebat, J. C., Babin, B. & Kollias, P. (2002). What makes contact employees perform? Reactions to employees perceptions of managerial practices. *The International Journal of Bank Marketing*, 20, 325–332.

Chebat, J. C. & Kollias, P. (2000). The impact of empowerment on customer contact employees' role in service organizations. *Journal of Service Research*, 3, 66–81.

Chung, B. G. & Schneider, B. (2002). Serving multiple masters: Role conflict experienced by service employees. *Journal of Services Marketing*, 16, 70–85.

Churchill, G. A., Ford, N. M. & Walker, O. C. (1990). Organizational climate and job satisfaction in the salesforce. *Journal of Marketing Research*, 13, 323–332.

Clark, M. S., Powell, M. C. & Mills, J. (1979). Keeping track of needs in communal and exchange relationships. *Journal of Personality and Social Psychology*, 51, 333–338.

Clark, R. E. & LaBeff, E. E. (1982). Death telling: Managing the delivery of bad news. *Journal of Health and Sociological Behavior*, 23, 366–380.

Clark, T. & Salaman, G. (1998). Creating the 'right' impression: Towards a dramaturgy of management consultancy. *Services Industries Journal*, 18, 18–38.

Colquitt, J. A. (2001). On the dimensionality of organizational justice: A construct validation of a measure. *Journal of Applied Psychology*, 86, 386–400.

Conger, J. A. & Rabindra, N. (1988). The empowerment process: Integrating theory and practice. *The Academy of Management Review*, 13, 471–482.

Côté, S. (2005). A social interaction model of the effects of emotion regulation on work strain. *The Academy of Management Review*, 30, 509–530.

Coulter, K. S. & Coulter, R. A. (2002). Determinants of trust in a service provider: The moderating role of length of relationship. *The Journal of Services Marketing*, 16, 35–50.

Coulter, K. S. & Coulter, R. A. (2003). The effects of industry knowledge on the development of trust in service relationships. *International Journal of Research in Marketing*, 20, 31–43.

Coulter, R. A. & Ligas, M. (2000). The long good-bye: The dissolution of customer-service provider relationships. *Psychology & Marketing*, 17, 669–695.

Coulter, R. & Ligas, M. (2004). A typology of customer-service provider relationships: The role of relational factors in classifying customers. *Journal of Services Marketing*, 18, 482–493.

Cran, D. J. (1994). Towards validation of the service orientation construct. *The Service Industries Journal*, 14, 34–44.

Cropanzano, R. & Ambrose, M. L. (2001). Procedural and distributive justice are more similar than you think: A monistic perspective and a research agenda. In J. Greenberg & R. Cropanzano (eds), *Advances in Organization Justice* (pp. 119–151). Stanford, CA: Stanford University Press.

Crosby, L. A., Evans, K. R. & Cowles, D. (1990). Relationship quality in services selling: An interpersonal influence perspective. *Journal of Marketing*, 54, 68–81.

Curson, D. L. & Enz, C. A. (1999). Predicting psychological empowerment among service workers: The effect of support-based relationships. *Human Relations*, 52, 205–224.

Czepiel, J. A. (1990). Service encounters and service relationships: Implications for research. *Journal of Business Research*, 20, 13–21.

Czepiel, J. A., Solomon, M. R. & Surprenant, C. F. (1985). *The Service Encounter: Managing Employee/Customer Interaction in Service Business*. Massachusetts: Lexington Books.

de Jong, A., de Ruyter, K. & Lemmink, J. (2004). Antecedents and consequences of the service climate in boundary-spanning self-managing service teams. *Journal of Marketing*, 68, 18–35.

de Jong, A., de Ruyter, K. & Lemmink, J. (2005). Service climate in self-managing teams: Mapping the linkage of team member perceptions and service performance outcomes in a business-to-business setting. *The Journal of Management Studies*, 42, 1593–1620.

de Jong, A., de Ruyter, K., Streukens, S. & Ouwersloot, H. (2001). Perceived uncertainty in self-managed service teams: An empirical assessment. *International Journal of Service Industry Management*, 12, 158–183.

Deery, S., Iverson, R. & Walsh, J. (2002). Work relationships in telephone call centers: Understanding emotional exhaustion and employee withdrawal. *Journal of Management Studies*, 39, 471–496.

Deighton, J. (1992). The consumption of performance. *Journal of Consumer Research*, 19, 362–371.

Diefendorff, J. M. & Gosserand, R. H. (2003). Understanding the emotional labor process: A control theory perspective. *Journal of Organizational Behavior*, 24, 945–959.

Diefendorff J. M., Croyle, M. H. & Gosserand, R. H. (2005). The dimensionality and antecedents of emotional labor strategies. *Journal of Vocational Behavior*, 66, 339–357.

Dietz, J., Pugh, S. D. & Wiley, J. W. (2004). Service climate effects on customer attitudes: An examination of boundary conditions. *Academy of Management Journal*, 47, 81–92.

Dobni, D. Z., Wilf, R. & Brent, J. R. (1997). Enhancing service personnel effectiveness through the use of behavioral repertoires. *The Journal of Services Marketing*, 11, 427–445.

Donavan, D. T., Brown, T. J. & Mowen, J. C. (2004). Internal benefits of service-worker customer orientation: Job satisfaction, commitment, and organizational citizenship behaviors. *Journal of Marketing*, 68, 128–146.

Dormann, C. & Kaiser, D. (2002). Job conditions and customer satisfaction. *European Journal of Work and Organizational Psychology*, 11, 257–283.

Dormann, C. & Zapf, D. (2004). Customer-related social stressors and burnout. *Journal of Occupational Health Psychology*, 9, 61–82.

Emerson, R. M. (1962). Power-dependence relations. *American Sociological Review*, 27, 31–41.

Ennew, C. T. & Binks, M. R. (1999). Impact of participative service relationships on quality, satisfaction and retention: An exploratory study. *Journal of Business Research*, 46, 121–132.

Erickson, R. J. & Wharton, A. S. (1997). Inauthenticity and depression: Assessing the consequences of interactive service work. *Work and Occupations*, 24, 188–213.

Fine, L. M., Shepherd, C. D. & Josephs, S. L. (1994). Sexual harassment in the sales force: The customer is NOT always right. *The Journal of Personal Selling & Sales Management*, 14, 15–30.

Finlay, W. & Coverdill, J. E. (2000). Risk, opportunism, and structural holes: How headhunters manage clients and earn fees. *Work and Occupations*, 27, 377–407.

Folger, R. & Cropanzano, R. (1998). *Organizational Justice and Human Resource Management. Foundations for Organizational Science*. Thousand Oaks, CA: Sage Publications, Inc.

Forseth, U. (2005). Gender matters? Exploring how gender is negotiated in service encounters. *Gender, Work and Organization*, 12, 440–459.

Franke, G. R. & Park, J. E. (2006). Salesperson adaptive selling behavior and customer orientation: A meta-analysis. *Journal of Marketing Research*, 43, 693–702.

Frazer-Winsted, K. (2000). Service behaviors that lead to satisfied customers. *European Journal of Marketing*, 34, 399–417.

Frei, R. L. & McDaniel, M. A. (1998). Validity of customer service measures in personnel selection: A review of criterion and construct evidence. *Human Performance*, 11, 1–27.

French, J. R. P. & Raven, B. (1959). The bases of social power. In D. Cartwright (ed.), *Studies in Social Power* (pp. 150–167). Ann Arbor, MI: University of Michigan.

Frenkel, S. J., Korczynski, M., Shire, K. A. & Tarn, M. (1999). *On the Front Line: Organization of Work in the Information Economy*. Ithaca, NY: Cornell University Press.

Froehle, C. M. (2006). Service personnel, technology, and their interaction in influencing customer satisfaction. *Decision Sciences*, 37, 5–38.

Fulford, M. D. & Enz, C. A. (1995). The impact of empowerment on service employees. *Journal of Managerial Issues*, 7, 161–175.

Fuller, L. & Smith, V. (1996). Consumers' reports: Management by customers in a changing society. In C. L. Macdonald & C. Sirianni (eds), *Working in the Service Society* (pp. 74–90). Philadelphia: Temple University Press.

Fullerton, R. A. & Punj, G. (2004). Repercussions of promoting an ideology of consumption: consumer misbehavior. *Journal of Business Research*, 57, 1239–1249.

George, J. M. & Bettenhausen, K. (1990). Understanding prosocial behavior, sales performance, and turnover: A group-level analysis in a service context. *Journal of Applied Psychology*, 75, 698–709.

George, J. (1991). State or trait: Effects of positive mood on prosocial behaviors at work. *Journal of Applied Psychology*, 76, 299–307.

Geurts, S., Schaufeli, W. & de Jong, J. (1998). Burnout and intention to leave among mental health-care professionals: A social psychological approach. *Journal of Social and Clinical Psychology*, 17, 341–362.

Giardini, A. & Frese, M. (2006). Reducing the negative effects of emotion work in service occupations: Emotional competence as a psychological resource. *Journal of Occupational Health and Psychology*, 11, 63–75.

Gittell, J. H. (2000). Paradox of coordination and control. *California Management Review*, 42, 101–117.

Gittell, J. H. (2001). Supervisory span, relational coordination, and flight departure performance: A reassessment of postbureaucracy theory. *Organization Science,* 12, 468–483.

Glomb, T. M. & Tews, M. J. (2004). Emotional labor: A conceptualization and scale development. *Journal of Vocational Behavior,* 64, 1–23.

Godwin, B. F., Patterson, R. G. & Johnson, L. W. (1995). Emotion, coping and complaining propensity following a dissatisfactory service encounter. *Journal of Consumer Satisfaction, Dissatisfaction and Complaining Behavior,* 8, 155–163.

Goetzinger, L., Park, J. K. & Widdows, R. (2006). E-customers' third party complaining and complimenting behavior. *International Journal of Service Industry Management,* 17, 193–206.

Goffman, E. (1959). *The Presentation of Self in Everyday Life.* New York: Doubleday and Anchor Books.

Goldberg, L. & Grandey, A. (in press). Display rules versus display autonomy: Emotion regulation, emotional exhaustion, and task performance in a call center simulation. *Journal of Occupational Health Psychology.*

Goodwin, C. (1996). Moving the drama into the factory: The contribution of metaphors to services research. *European Journal of Marketing,* 30, 13–36.

Goodwin, C. & Gremler, D. D. (1996). Friendship over the counter: How social aspects of service encounters influence consumer service loyalty. In T. A. Swartz, D. E. Bowen & S. W. Brown (eds), *Advances in Services Marketing and Management,* Vol. 5 (pp. 247–282). Greenwich, CT: JAI.

Goodwin, C., Grove, S. J. & Fisk, R. P. (1996). 'Collaring the Cheshire cat': Studying customers' services experience through metaphor. *The Service Industries Journal,* 16, 421–442.

Goodwin, C. & Smith, K. L. (1990). Courtesy and friendliness: Conflicting goals for the service provider? *The Journal of Services Marketing,* 4, 5–20.

Goolsby, J. R. (1992). A theory of role stress in boundary spanning positions of marketing organizations. *Academy of Marketing Science Journal,* 20, 155–164.

Gosserand, R. H. & Diefendorff, J. M. (2005). Emotional display rules and emotional labor: The moderating role of commitment. *Journal of Applied Psychology,* 90, 1256–1264.

Gotlieb, J., Levy, M., Grewal, D. & Lindsey-Muillikan, J. (2004). Attitude toward the service firm. *Journal of Applied Social Psychology,* 34, 825–847.

Grandey, A. A. (2000). Emotion regulation in the workplace: A new way to conceptualize emotional labor. *Journal of Occupational Health Psychology,* 5, 95–110.

Grandey, A. A. (2003). Managing emotions in the workplace. *Personnel Psychology,* 56, 563–566.

Grandey, A. A., Dickter, D. N. & Sin, H. P. (2004). The customer is not always right: Customer aggression and emotion regulation of service employees. *Journal of Organizational Behavior,* 25, 397–418.

Grandey, A. A., Fisk, G. M., Mattila, A. S., Jansen, K. J. & Sideman, L. A. (2005). Is 'service with a smile' enough? Authenticity of positive displays during service encounters. *Organizational Behavior and Human Decision Processes,* 96, 38–55.

Grandey, A. A., Fisk, G. M. & Steiner, D. D. (2005). Must 'service with a smile' be stressful? The moderating role of personal control for American and French Employees. *Journal of Applied Psychology,* 90, 893–904.

Grandey, A. A., Kern, J. H. & Frone, M. R. (2007). Verbal abuse from outsiders versus insiders: Comparing frequency, impact on emotional exhaustion, and the role of emotional labor. *Journal of Occupational Health Psychology*, 12, 63–79.

Grandey, A. A., Tam, A. P. & Brauberger, A. L. (2002). Affective states and traits in the workplace: Diary and survey data from young workers. *Motivation and Emotion*, 26, 31–55.

Grayson, K. & Shulman, D. (2000). Impression management in service marketing. In T. A. Swartz & D. Iacobucci (eds), *Handbook of Service Marketing and Management* (pp. 51–68). Thousand Oaks: Sage.

Grebner, S., Semmer, N. K., Lo Faso, L., Gut, S., Kalin, W. & Elfering, A. (2003). Working conditions, well-being, and job-related attitudes among call centre agents. *European Journal of Work and Organizational Psychology*, 12, 341–365.

Gremler, D. D. & Gwinner, K. P. (2000). Customer-employee rapport in service relationships. *Journal of Service Research*, 3, 82–104.

Gremler, D. D., Gwinner, K. P. & Brown, S. W. (2001). Generating positive word-of-mouth communication through customer-employee relationships. *International Journal of Service Industry Management*, 12, 44–59.

Griffin, K. H. & Hebl, M. R. (2002). The disclosure dilemma for gay men and lesbians: 'Coming out' at work. *Journal of Applied Psychology*, 87, 1191–1199.

Gronroos, C. (1990). Relationship approach to marketing in service contexts: The marketing and organizational behavior interface. *Journal of Business Research*, 20, 3–12.

Gronroos, C. (2001). *Service Management and Marketing: A Customer Relationship Management Approach* (Second Edition). Chichester: Wiley.

Grove, S. J. & Fisk, R. P. (1983). Impression management in service marketing: A dramaturgical perspective. In R. A. Giacalone and P. Rosenfeld (eds), *Impression Management in the Organization* (pp. 427–438). Hillsdale, NJ: Earlabum.

Grove, S. J. & Fisk, R. P. (1992). Observational data collection methods for services marketing: An overview. *Academy of Marketing Science Journal*, 20, 217–224.

Grove, S. J., Fisk, R. P. & Bitner, M. J. (1992). Dramatizing the service experience: A management approach. *Advances in Services Marketing and Management*, 1, 91–121.

Grove, S. J., Fisk, R. P. & Dorsch, M. J. (1998). Assessing the theatrical components of the service encounter: A cluster analysis examination. *The Service Industries Journal*, 18, 116–144.

Grove, S. J., Fisk, R. P. & John, J. (2000). Service as theater: Guidelines and implications. In T. A. Swartz & D. Iacobucci (eds), *Handbook of Service Marketing and Management* (pp. 21–36). Thousand Oaks: Sage.

Guerts, S. A., Schaufeli, W. B. & Rutte, C. G. (1999). Absenteeism, turnover intention and inequity in the employment relationship. *Work & Stress*, 13, 253–267.

Gustavsson, E. (2005). Virtual servants: Stereotyping female front-office employees on the internet. *Gender, Work and Organization*, 12, 400–419.

Gutek, B. (1995). *The Dynamics of Service: Reflections on the Changing Nature of Customer/Provider Interactions*. San Francisco: Jossey-Bass.

Gutek, B. A., Bhappu, A. D., Liao Troth, M. A. & Cherry, B. (1999). Distinguishing between service relationships and encounters. *Journal of Applied Psychology*, 84, 218–233.

Gutek, B. A., Cherry, B., Bhappu, A. D., Schneider, S. & Woolf, L. (2000). Features of service relationships and encounters. *Work and Occupations*, 27, 319–352.

Gwinner, K. P., Bitner, M. J., Brown, S. W. & Kumar, A. (2005). Service customization through employee adaptiveness. *Journal of Service Research*, 8, 131–148.

Gwinner, K. P., Gremler, D. D. & Bitner, M. J. (1998). Relational benefits in services industries: The customer's perspective. *Academy of Marketing Science Journal*, 26, 101–114.

Hall, E. J. (1992). Smiling, deferring, and flirting: Doing gender by giving 'good service'. *Work and Occupations*, 20, 452–471.

Hansen, H., Sandvik, K. & Selnes, F. (2003). Direct and indirect effects of commitment to a service employee on the intention to stay. *Journal of Service Research*, 5, 356–368.

Harris, L. C. & Ogbonna, E. (2002). Exploring service sabotage: The antecedents, types and consequences of frontline, deviant, antiservice behaviors. *Journal of Service Research*, 4, 163–183.

Harris, L. C. & Ogbonna, E. (2006). Service sabotage: A study of antecedents and consequences. *Academy of Marketing Science Journal*, 34, 543–558.

Harris, L. C. & Reynolds, K. L. (2003). The consequences of dysfunctional customer behavior. *Journal of Service Research*, 6, 144–161.

Harris, L. C. & Reynolds, K. L. (2004). Jaycustomer behavior: An exploration of types and motives in the hospitality industry. *The Journal of Services Marketing*, 18, 339–357.

Harris, R., Harris, K. & Baron, S. (2003). Service experiences: Dramatic script development with employees. *International Journal of Service Industry Management*, 14, 184–199.

Hartline, M. D. & Ferrell, O. C. (1996). The management of customer-contact service employees: An empirical investigation. *Journal of Marketing*, 60, 52–70.

Hartline, M. D., Maxham, J. G. III & McKee, D. O. (2000). Corridors of influence in the dissemination of customer-oriented strategy to customer contact service employees. *Journal of Marketing*, 64, 35–50.

Hatfield, E., Cacioppo, J. T. & Rapson, R. L. (1994). *Studies in Emotion and Social Interaction*. New York, NY: Cambridge University Press.

Hebl, M. R. & Xu, J. (2001). Weighing the care: Physicians' reactions to the size of a patient. *Journal of Applied Psychology*, 91, 579–593.

Hennig-Thurau, T. (2004). Customer orientation of service employees: Its impact on customer satisfaction, commitment, and retention. *International Journal of Service Industry Management*, 15, 460–478.

Hennig-Thurau, T., Groth, M., Paul, M. & Gremler, D. D. (2006). Are all smiles created equal? How emotional contagion and emotional labor affect service relationships. *Journal of Marketing*, 70, 58–73.

Hennig-Thurau, T. & Thurau, C. (2003). Customer orientation of service employees – Toward a conceptual framework of a key relationship marketing construct. *Journal of Relationship Marketing*, 2, 1–32.

Hochschild, A. R. (1983). *The Managed Heart: Commercialization of Human Feeling*. Berkeley: University of California Press.

Hoffman, K. D. & Ingram, T. N. (1992). Service provider job satisfaction and customer-oriented performance. *The Journal of Services Marketing*, 6, 68–78.

Hogan, J., Hogan, R. & Busch, C. M. (1984). How to measure service orientation. *Journal of Applied Psychology*, 69, 167–173.

Holcombe-Ehrhart, K. (2006). Job characteristic beliefs and personality as antecedents of subjective person-job fit. *Journal of Business and Psychology*, 21, 193–226.

Holman, D. J. (2003). Call centres. In D. J. Holman, T. D. Wall, C. W. Clegg, P. Sparrow & A. Howard (eds), *The New Workplace: A Guide to the Human Impact of Modern Working Practices*. Chichester, UK: Wiley.

Holman, D. J., Chissick, C. & Totterdell, P. (2002). The effects of performance monitoring on emotional labor and well-being in call centers. *Motivation and Emotion*, 26, 57–81.

Homburg, C. & Stock, R. M. (2005). Exploring the conditions under which salesperson work satisfaction can lead to customer satisfaction. *Psychology & Marketing*, 22, 393–420.

Huefner, J. C. & Hunt, H. K. (1994). Extending the Hirschman model: When voice and exit don't tell the whole story. *Journal of Consumer Satisfaction, Dissatisfaction and Complaining Behavior*, 7, 267–270.

Hurley, R. F. (1998). Customer service behavior in retail settings: A study of the effect of service provider personality. *Academy of Marketing Science Journal*, 26, 115–127.

Johlke, M. C. & Duhan, D. F. (2001). Supervisor communication practices and boundary spanner role ambiguity. *Journal of Managerial Issues*, 13, 87–101.

Johnson, D. & Grayson, K. (2005). Cognitive and affective trust in service relationships. *Journal of Business Research*, 58, 500–507.

Johnson, J. W. (1996). Linking employee perceptions of service climate to customer satisfaction. *Personnel Psychology*, 49, 831–851.

Jones, E., Busch, P. & Dacin, P. (2003). Firm market orientation and salesperson customer orientation: Interpersonal and intrapersonal influences on customer service and retention in business-to-business buyer-seller relationships. *Journal of Business Research*, 56, 323–340.

Joshi, A. W. & Randall, S. (2001). The indirect effects of organizational controls on salesperson performance and customer orientation. *Journal of Business Research*, 54, 1–9.

Kalyani, M. & Dube, L. (2004). Service provider responses to anxious and angry customers: Different challenges, different payoffs. *Journal of Retailing*, 80, 229–237.

Kasper, H., van Helsdingen, P. & De Vries, V. (1999). *Services Marketing Management: An International Perspective*. New York: Wiley.

Kelley, H. H. & Thibaut, J. (1978). *Interpersonal Relations: A Theory of Interdependence*. New York: Wiley.

Kelley, S. W. & Hoffman, K. D. (1997). An investigation of positive affect, prosocial behaviors and service quality. *Journal of Retailing*, 73, 407–427.

Kelman, H. & Hamilton, V. L. (1989). *Crimes of Obedience: Toward a Social Psychology of Authority and Responsibility*. New Haven, CN.: Yale University Press.

Kerfoot, D. & Korczynski, M. (2005). Gender and service work: New directions for the study of front-line service work. *Gender, Work and Organization*, 12, 387–399.

King, E. B., Shapuiro, J. R., Hebl, M. R., Singletary, S. L. & Turner, S. (2006). The stigma of obesity in customer service: A mechanism for remediation and bottom-line consequences of interpersonal discrimination. *Journal of Applied Psychology*, 91, 579–593.

Kop, N., Euwema, M. C. & Schaufeli, W. B. (1999). Burnout, job stress and violent behavior among Dutch police officers. *Work & Stress*, 13, 326–340.

Korczynski, M. (2001). The contradictions of service work: Call centre as customer-oriented bureaucracy. In A. Sturdy, I. Grugulis & H. Wilmott (eds), *Customer Service: Empowerment and Entrapment* (pp. 79–102). Basingstoke: Palgrave.

Kowalski, R. (1996). Complaints and complaining: Functions, antecedents and consequences. *Psychological Bulletin*, 119, 179–196.

Kraft, F. B. & Martin, C. L. (2001). Customer compliments as more than complementary feedback. *Journal of Consumer Satisfaction, Dissatisfaction and Complaining Behavior*, 14, 1–12.

Krapfel, R. E. (1988). Customer complaint and salesperson response: The effect of the communication source. *Journal of Retailing*, 64, 181–198.

Kruml, S. M. & Geddes, D. (2000). Exploring the dimensions of emotional labor. *Management Communication Quarterly*, 14, 8–49.

Landrine, H., Klonoff, E. A. & Alcaraz, R. (1997). Racial discrimination in minors' access to tobacco. *Journal of Black Psychology*, 23, 135–147.

Lashley, C. (1999). Employee empowerment in services: A framework for analysis. *Personnel Review*, 28, 169–191.

Lawler, E. J. (2001). An affect theory of social exchange. *The American Journal of Sociology*, 107, 321–353.

LeBlanc, M. M. & Kelloway, E. K. (2002). Predictors and outcomes of workplace violence and aggression. *Journal of Applied Psychology*, 87, 444–453.

Lee, J. (2000). The salience of race in everyday life black customers' shopping experiences in black and white neighborhoods. *Work and Occupations*, 27, 353–376.

Leidner, R. (1993). *Fast Food, Fast Talk: Service Work and the Routinization of Everyday Life*. Berkeley: University of California Press.

Leidner, R. (1996). Rethinking questions of control: Lessons from McDonald's. In C. L. Macdonald & C. Sirianni (eds), *Working in the Service Society* (pp. 29–49). Philadelphia: Temple University Press.

Levitt, T. (1972). Producton-line approach to service. *Harvard Business Review*, 50, 41–52.

Ligas, M. & Coulter, R. A. (2000). Understanding signals of customer dissatisfaction: Customer goals, emotions, and behaviors in negative service encounters. *American Marketing Association. Conference Proceedings*, 11, 256–262.

Lind, E. A. & Tyler, T. R. (1988). *The Social Psychology of Procedural Justice. Critical Issues in Social Justice*. New York, NY: Plenum Press.

Liu, B. S. C., Furrer, O. & Sudharshan, D. (2001). The relationships between culture and behavioral intentions toward services. *Journal of Service Research*, 4, 118–129.

Lovelock, C. H. (1983). Classifying services to gain strategic marketing insights. *Journal of Marketing*, 47, 9–21.

Lovelock, C. H. (1994). *Product Plus: How Product and Service Competitive Advantage*. New York: McGraw-Hill.

Lovelock, C. (2001). *Services Marketing: People, Technology, Strategy*, 4th ed. Sydney: Prentice-Hall.

Lytle, R. S., Hom, P. W. & Mokwa, M. P. (1998). SERV*OR: Managerial measure of organizational service-orientation. *Journal of Retailing*, 74, 455–489.

Macdonald, C. L. & Sirianni, C. (1996). The service society and the changing experience of work. In C. L. Macdonald & C. Sirianni (eds), *Working in the Service Society* (pp. 1–26). Philadelphia: Temple University Press.

Mallinson, C. & Brewster, Z. W. (2005). 'Blacks and bubbas': Stereotypes, ideology, and categorization processes in restaurant servers' discourse. *Discourse & Society*, 16, 787–807.

Marquis, M. & Filiatrault, P. (2002). Understanding complaining responses through consumer's self-consciousness disposition. *Psychology & Marketing*, 19, 267–292.

Martin, C. L. & Adams, S. (1999). Behavioral biases in the service encounter: Empowerment by default? *Marketing Intelligence & Planning*, 17, 192–201.

Maslach, C. & Jackson, S. E. (1981). The measurement of experienced burnout. *Journal of Occupational Behavior*, 2, 99–113.

Masterson, S. S. (2001). Trickle-down model of organizational justice: Relating employees' and customers' perceptions of and reactions to fairness. *Journal of Applied Psychology*, 86, 594–604.

McCallum, J. R. & Harrsion, W. (1985). Interdependence in the service encounter. In J. A. Czepiel, M. R. Solomon & C. F. Surprenant (eds), *The Service Encounter: Managing Employee/Customer Interaction in Service Business* (pp. 35–48). Massachusetts: Lexington Books.

McCrae, R. R. & Costa, P. T. (1987). Validation of the five-factor model of personality across instruments and observers. *Journal of Personality and Social Psychology*, 52, 81–90.

McGrath, H. & Goulding, A. (1996). Part of the job: Violence in public libraries. *New Library World*, 97, 4–13.

Michaels, R. E. & Day, R. L. (1985). Measuring customer orientation of salespeople: A replication with industrial buyers. *Journal of Marketing Research*, 22, 443–446.

Miller, L. C. and Berg, J. H. (1984). Selectivity and urgency in interpersonal exchange, in V. Derlega (ed.), *Communication, Intimacy, and Close Relationships* (pp. 161–206). Orlando FL: Academic Press.

Mills, P. & Margulies, N. (1980). Toward a core typology of service organizations. *Academy of Management Review*, 5, 255–265.

Mittal, B. & Lassar, W. M. (1996). The role of personalization in service encounters. *Journal of Retailing*, 72, 95–109.

Mohr, L. A. & Bitner, M. J. (1995). The role of employee effort in satisfaction with service transactions. *Journal of Business Research*, 32, 239–252.

Mohr, L. A. & Henson, S. W. (1996). Impact of employee gender and job congruency on customer satisfaction. *Journal of Consumer Psychology*, 6, 161–188.

Moisio, R. & Arnould, E. J. (2005). Extending the dramaturgical framework in marketing: Drama structure, drama interaction and drama content in shopping experiences. *Journal of Consumer Behavior*, 4, 246–256.

Molm, L. D., Takahashi, N. & Peterson, G. (2003). In the eye of the beholder: Procedural justice in social exchange. *Sociological Review*, 68, 128–152.

Morris, J. A. & Feldman, D. C. (1996). The dimensions, antecedents, and consequences of emotional labor. *The Academy of Management Review*, 21, 1986–2010.

Morris, J. A. & Feldman, D. C. (1997). Managing emotions in the workplace. *Journal of Managerial Issues*, 9, 257–274.

Mount, M. K., Barrick, M. R., Scullen, S. M. & Rounds, J. (2005). Higher-order dimensions of the big five personality traits and the big six vocational interest types. *Personnel Psychology*, 58, 447–478.

Mount, M. K., Barrick, M. R. & Stewart, G. L. (1998). Five-factor model of personality and performance in jobs involving interpersonal interactions. *Human Performance*, 11, 145–165.

Netemeyer, R. G., Maxham, J. G. III & Pullig, C. (2005). Conflicts in the work-family interface: Links to job stress, customer service employee performance, and customer purchase intent. *Journal of Marketing*, 69, 130–143.

O'Connor, S. J. & Shewchuk, R. M. (1995). Doing more with less, and doing it nicer: The role of service orientation in health care organization. *Academy of Management Journal, Best Paper Proceedings*, 120–124.

O'Hara, B. S., Boles, J. S. & Johnston, M. W. (1991). The influence of personal variables on salesperson selling orientation. *The Journal of Personal Selling & Sales Management*, 11, 61–67.

Oliver, R. L. (1997). *Satisfaction: A Behavioral Perspective on the Consumer*. New York: McGraw Hill.

Organ, D. W. (1988). *Organizational Citizenship Behavior: The Good Soldier Syndrome*. Issues in organization and management series. Lexington, MA, England: Lexington Books/D. C. Heath and Com.

Otto, S. D., Payne, C. R., Parry, B. L. & Hunt, H. K. (2005). Complimenting behavior – The complimenter's perspective. *Journal of Consumer Satisfaction, Dissatisfaction and Complaining Behavior*, 18, 1–30.

Parasuraman, A., Zeithaml, V. A. & Berry, L. L. (1985). A conceptual model of service quality and its implications for future research. *Journal of Marketing*, 49, 41–50.

Parasuraman, A., Zeithaml, V. A. & Berry, L. L. (1988). Servqual: A multiple-item scale for measuring consumer perceptions of service quality. *Journal of Retailing*, 64, 12–40.

Paules, G. F. (1996). Resisting the symbolism of service among waitresses. In C. L. Macdonald & C. Sirianni (eds), *Working in the Service Society* (pp. 264–290). Philadelphia: Temple University Press.

Pauley, L. L. (1989). Customer weight as a variable in salespersons' response time. *Journal of Social Psychology*, 129, 713–714.

Payne, C. R., Parry, B. L., Huff, S. C., Otto, S. D. & Hunt, H. K. (2002). Consumer complimenting behavior: Exploration and elaboration. *Journal of Consumer Satisfaction, Dissatisfaction and Complaining Behavior*, 15, 128–147.

Payne, S. C. & Webber, S. S. (2006). Effects of service provider attitudes and employment status on citizenship behaviors and customers' attitudes and loyalty behavior. *Journal of Applied Psychology*, 91, 365–378.

Peccei, R. & Rosenthal, P. (2001). Delivering customer-oriented behaviour through empowerment: An empirical test of HRM assumptions. *The Journal of Management Studies*, 38, 831–857.

Price, L. L. & Arnould, E. J. (1999). Commerical friendships: Service provider–client relationships in context. *Journal of Marketing*, 63, 38–56.

Price, L. L., Arnould, E. J. & Tierney, P. (1994). Going to extremes: Managing service encounters and assessing provider performance. *Journal of Marketing*, 59, 83–97.

Pritchard, R. D. (1969). Equity theory: A review and critique. *Organizational Behavior and Human Performance*, 4, 176–211.

Pugh, S. D. (2001). Service with a smile: Emotional contagion in the service encounter. *Academy of Management Journal*, 44, 1018–1027.

Rafaeli, A. (1989). When clerks meet customers: A test of variables related to emotional expressions on the job. *Journal of Applied Psychology*, 74, 385–393.

Rafaeli, A. (1989). When cashier meet customers: An analysis of the role of supermarket cashiers. *Academy of Management Journal*, 32, 245–273.

Rafaeli, A. & Sutton, R. I. (1987). Expression of emotion as part of the work role. *The Academy of Management Review*, 12, 23–37.

Rafaeli, A. & Sutton, R. I. (1989). The expression of emotion in organizational life. In L. L. Cummings & B. M. Staw (eds), *Research in Organizational Behavior*, Vol. 11, 1–42. Greenwich, CT: JAI Press.

Rafaeli, A. & Sutton, R. I. (1990). Busy stores and demanding customers: How do they affect the display of positive emotion? *Academy of Management Journal*, 33, 623–637.

Ramsey, R. P. & Sohi, R. S. (1997). Listening to your customers: The impact of perceived salesperson listening behavior on relationship outcomes. *Academy of Marketing Science Journal*, 25, 127–137.

Redman, T. & Mathews, B. P. (1998). Service quality and human resource management: A review and research agenda. *Personnel Review*, 27, 57–77.

Reichheld, F. F. & Sasser, W. E. (1990). Zero defections: Quality comes to services. *Harvard Business Review*, 68, 105–111.

Reynolds, K. L. & Harris, L. C. (2005). When service failure is not service failure: An exploration of the forms and motives of 'illegitimate' customer complaining. *The Journal of Services Marketing*, 19, 321–335.

Reynolds, K. L. & Harris, L. C. (2006). Deviant customer behavior: An exploration of frontline employee tactics. *Journal of Marketing Theory and Practice*, 14, 95–111.

Rhoads, G. K., Singh, J. & Goodell, P. W. (1994). The multiple dimensions of role ambiguity and their impact upon psychological and behavioral outcomes of industrial salespeople. *The Journal of Personal Selling & Sales Management*, 14, 1–23.

Richins, M. L. (1983). An analysis of consumer interaction styles in the marketplace. *Journal of Consumer Research*, 10, 73–82.

Roberts, K., Varki, S. & Brodie, R. (2003). Measuring the quality of relationships in consumer services: An empirical study. *European Journal of Marketing*, 37, 169–196.

Robinson, S. L. & Rousseau, D. M. (1994). Violating the psychological contract: Not the exception but the norm. *Journal of Organizational Behavior*, 15, 245–259.

Rogelberg, S. G., Barnes-Farrell, J. L. & Creamer, V. (1999). Customer service behavior: The interaction of service predisposition and job characteristics. *Journal of Business and Psychology*, 13, 421–435.

226 References

Rose, E. & Wright, G. (2005). Satisfaction and dimensions of control among call centre customer service representatives. *International Journal of Human Resource Management*, 16, 136–160.

Rosenthal, P. (2004). Management control as an employee resource: The case of front-line service workers. *Journal of Management Studies*, 41, 601–622.

Rosenthal, P. & Peccei, R. (2006). The social construction of clients by service agents in reformed welfare administration. *Human Relations*, 59, 1633–1658.

Rosse, J., Miller, H. & Barnes, L. (1991) Hiring for personality and ability: The case of service orientation. *Journal of Business & Psychology*, 5, 431–445.

Rupp, D. E., Holub, A. S. & Grandey, A. (2007). A cognitive-emotional theory of customer injustice and emotional labor. In D. De Cremer (ed.), *Advances in the Psychology of Justice and Affect* (pp. 199–226). Greenwich: Information Age Publishing.

Rupp, D. E. & Spencer, S. (2006). When customers lash out: The effects of perceived customer interactional injustice on emotional labor and the mediating role of discrete emotions. *Journal of Applied Psychology*, 91, 971–978.

Rust, R. T. & Oliver, R. L. (2000). Should we delight the customer? *Academy of Marketing Science Journal*, 28, 86–94.

Rust, R. T., Stewart, G. L., Miller, H. & Pielack, D. (2001). The satisfaction and retention of frontline employees A customer satisfaction measurement approach. *International Journal of Service Industry Management*, 7, 62–80.

Salanova, M., Agut, S. & Peiro, J. M. (2005). Linking organizational resources and work engagement to employee performance and customer loyalty: The mediation of service climate. *Journal of Applied Psychology*, 90, 1217–1227.

Saura, I. G., Berenguer, G., Taulet, C. A. & Velázquez, B. M. (2005). Relationships among customer orientation, service orientation and job satisfaction in financial services *International Journal of Service Industry Management*, 16, 497–525.

Saxe, R. & Weitz, B. A. (1982). The SOCO scale: A measure of the customer orientation of salespeople. *Journal of Marketing Research*, 19, 343–351.

Sayer, A. (2005). Class, moral worth and recognition. *Sociology: The Journal of the British Sociological Association*, 39, 947–963.

Scalora, M. J., Washington, D. O., Casady, T. & Newell, S. P. (2003). Nonfatal workplace violence risk factors: Data from a police contact sample. *Journal of Interpersonal Violence*, 18, 310–327.

Schaufeli, W. B. (2006). The balance of give and take: Toward a social exchange model of burnout. *The International Review of Social Psychology*, 19, 87–131.

Schaufeli, W. B., van Dierendonck, D. & van Gorp, K. (1996). Burnout and reciprocity: Towards a dual-level social exchange model. *Work & Stress*, 10, 225–237.

Schlesinger, L. A. & Heskett, J. L. (1991). Breaking the cycle of failure in service. *Sloan Management Review*, 32, 17–28.

Schmidt, M. J. & Allscheid, S. P. (1995). Employee attitudes and customer satisfaction: Making a theoretical and empirical connection. *Personnel Psychology*, 48, 521–537.

Schneider, B. (1980). The service organization: Climate is crucial. *Organizational Dynamics*, 9, 52–65.

Schneider, B. & Bowen, D. E. (1985) Employee and customer perceptions of service in banks: Replication and extension. *Journal of Applied Psychology*, 70, 423–433.

Schneider, B. & Bowen, D. E. (1993). The service organization: Human resources management is crucial. *Organizational Dynamics*, 21, 39–52.

Schneider, B. & Bowen, D. E. (1995). *Winning the Service Game*. Boston: Harvard Business School Press.

Schneider, B., Erhart, M. G., Mayer, D. M., Saltz, J. L. & Niles-Jolly, K. (2005). Understanding organization-customer links in service settings. *Academy of Management Journal*, 48, 1017–1032.

Schneider, B., Parkington, J. J. & Buxton, V. M. (1980). Employee and customer perceptions of service in banks. *Administrative Science Quarterly*, 25, 252–267.

Schneider, B., Wheeler, J. K. & Cox, J. F. (1992). A passion for service: Using content analysis to explicate service climate themes. *Journal of Applied Psychology*, 77, 705–716.

Schneider, B., White, S. S. & Paul, M. C. (1998). Linking service climate and customer perceptions of service quality: Test of a causal model. *Journal of Applied Psychology*, 83, 150–163.

Schwepker, C. H. & Hartline, M. D. (2005). Managing the ethical climate of customer-contact service employees. *Journal of Service Research*, 7, 377–397.

Scott, E. D. (2003). Plane truth: A qualitative study of employee dishonesty in the airline industry. *Journal of Business Ethics*, 42, 321–337.

Sergeant, A. & Frenkel, S. (2000). When do customer contact employees satisfy customers? *Journal of Service Research*, 3, 18–34.

Shamir, B. (1980). Between service and servility: Role conflict in subordinate service roles. *Human Relations*, 33, 741–756.

Shields, G. & Kiser, J. (2003). Violence and aggression directed toward human service workers: An exploratory study. *Families in Society*, 84, 13–20.

Siehl, C., Bowen, D. E., Pearson, C. M. (1992). Service encounters as rites of integration: An information processing model. *Organization Science*, 3, 537–555.

Sierra, J. J. & McQuitty, S. (2005). Service providers and customers: Social exchange theory and service loyalty. *The Journal of Services Marketing*, 19, 392–400.

Singh, J. (1993). Boundary role ambiguity: Facts, determinants, and impacts. *Journal of Marketing*, 57, 11–31.

Singh, J. (1998). Striking a balance in boundary-spanning positions: An investigation of some unconventional influences of role stressors and job characteristics on job outcomes of salespeople. *Journal of Marketing*, 62, 69–86.

Singh, J. (2000). Performance productivity and quality of frontline employees in service organizations. *Journal of Marketing*, 64, 15–34.

Singh, J., Goolsby, J. R. & Rhoads, G. K. (1994). Behavioral and psychological consequences of boundary spanning burnout for customer service representatives. *Journal of Marketing Research*, 31, 558–569.

Singh, J., Verbeke, W. & Rhoads, G. K. (1996). Do organizational practices matter in role stress processes? A study of direct and moderating effects for marketing-oriented boundary spanners. *Journal of Marketing*, 60, 69–86.

Singh, J. & Rhoads, G. K. (1991). Boundary role ambiguity in marketing-oriented positions: A multidimensional, multifaceted operationalization. *Journal of Marketing Research*, 28, 328–338.

Smets, E. M. A., Visser, M. R. M., Oort, F. J., Schaufeli, W. B., Hanneke J. C. & de Haes, J. M. (2004). Perceived inequity: Does it explain burnout among medical specialists? *Journal of Applied Social Psychology*, 34, 1900–1918.

Snipes, R. L., Thomson, N. F. & Oswald, S. L. (2006). Gender bias in customer evaluations of service quality: An empirical investigation. *The Journal of Services Marketing*, 20, 274–284.

Solomon, M. R., Surprenant, C., Czepiel, J. A. & Gutman, E. G. (1985). A role theory perspective on dyadic interactions: The service encounter. *Journal of Marketing*, 49, 99–111.

Sparks, B. A., Bradley, G. L. & Callan, V. J. (1997). The impact of staff empowerment and communication style on customer evaluations: The special case of service failure. *Psychology & Marketing*, 14, 475–493.

Spiro, R. L. & Weitz, B. A. (1990). Adaptive selling: Conceptualization, measurement and nomological validity. *Journal of Marketing Research*, 27, 61–691.

Spreitzer, G. M. (1995). Psychological empowerment in the workplace: Dimensions, measurement, and validation. *Academy of Management Journal*, 38, 1442–1465.

Sprigg, C. A. & Jackson, P. R. (2006). Call centers as lean service environments: Job-related strain and the mediating role of work design. *Journal of Occupational Health Psychology*, 11, 197–212.

Stead, B. A. & Zinkhan, G. M. (1986). Service priority in department stores: The effects of customer gender and dress. *Sex Roles*, 15, 601–611.

Stephens, N. (2000). Complaining. In T. A. Swartz & D. Iacobucci (eds), *Handbook of Service Marketing and Management* (pp. 287–298). Thousand Oaks: Sage.

Sternberg, L. E. (1992). Empowerment: Trust vs. control. *Cornell Hotel and Restaurant Administration Quarterly*, 33, 68–72.

Stewart, G. L., Carson, K. P. & Cardy, R. L. (1996). The joint effects of conscientiousness and self-leadership training on employee self-directed behavior in a service setting. *Personnel Psychology*, 49, 143–164.

Stiles, J. L. (1985). Servicing alternatives. *Mortgage Banking*, 45, 81–82.

Stock, R. M. & Hoyer, W. D. (2005). An attitude-behavior model of salespeople's customer orientation. *Academy of Marketing Science Journal*, 33, 536–552.

Strutton, D. & Pelton, L. E. (1998). Effects of ingratiation on lateral relationship quality within sales team settings. *Journal of Business Research*, 43, 1–12.

Strutton, D., Pelton, L. E. & Lumpkin, J. R. (1995). Sex differences in ingratiatory behavior: An investigation of influence tactics in the salesperson-customer dyad. *Journal of Business Research*, 34, 35–45.

Strutton, D., Pelton, L. E. & Tanner, J. F. (1996). Shall we gather in the garden: The effect of ingratiatory behaviors on buyer trust in salespeople. *Industrial Marketing Management*, 25, 151–162.

Suprenant, C. F. & Solomon, M. R. (1987). Predictability and personalization in the service encounter. *Journal of Marketing*, 2, 86–96.

Sutton, R. I. (1991). Maintaining norms about expressed emotions: The case of bill collectors. *Administrative Science Quarterly*, 36, 245–268.

Sutton, R. I. & Rafaeli, A. (1988). Untangling the relationship between displayed emotions and organizational sales: The case of convenience stores. *Academy of Management Journal*, 31, 461–487.

Swan, J. E., Bowers, M. R. & Richardson, L. D. (1998). Customer trust in the salesperson: An integrative review and meta-analysis of the empirical literature. *Journal of Business Research*, 44, 93–107.

References 229

Taris, T. W., Peeters, M. C. W., Le Blanc, P. M., Schreurs, P. J. G. & Schaufeli, W. B. (2001). From inequity to burnout: The role of job stress. *Journal of Occupational Health Psychology*, 6, 303–323.

Taylor, P. & Bain, P. (1999) 'An assembly line in the head': Work and employee relations in the call centre. *Industrial Relations Journal*, 30, 101–117.

Taylor, S. & Tyler, M. (2000). Emotional labor and sexual difference in the airline industry. *Work, Employment & Society*, 14, 77–95.

Testa, M. R. (2001). Organizational commitment, job satisfaction, and effort in the service environment. *The Journal of Psychology*, 135, 226–236.

Testa, M. R. & Ehrhart, M. G. (2005). Service leader interaction behaviors: Comparing employee and manager perspectives. *Group & Organization Management*, 30, 456–486.

Thakor, M. V. & Joshi, A. W. (2005). Motivating salesperson customer orientation: Insights from the job characteristics model. *Journal of Business Research*, 58, 584–592.

Thomas, K. & Velthouse, B. (1990). Cognitive elements of empowerment: An 'interpretive' model of intrinsic task motivation. *Academy of Management Review*, 15, 666–681.

Tolich, M. B. (1993). Alienating and liberating emotions at work: Supermarket clerks' performance of customer service. *Journal of Contemporary Ethnography*, 22, 361–381.

Totterdell, P. & Holman, D. (2003). Emotion regulation in customer service roles: Testing a model of emotional labor. *Journal of Occupational Health Psychology*, 8, 55–73.

Troyer, L., Mueller, C. W. & Osinsky, P. I. (2000). Who's the boss? A role-theoretic analysis of customer work. *Work and Occupations*, 27, 406–429.

Truchot, D. & Deregard, M. (2001). Perceived inequity, communal orientation and burnout: The role of helping models. *Work & Stress*, 15, 347–356.

Tsai, W. C. (2001). Determinants and consequences of employee displayed positive emotions. *Journal of Management*, 27, 497–512.

Tsai, W. C. & Huang, Y. M. (2002) Mechanisms linking employee affective delivery and customer behavioral intentions. *Journal of Applied Psychology*, 87, 1001–1008.

Tuten, T. L. & Neidermeyer, P. E. (2004). Performance, satisfaction and turnover in call centers: The effects of stress and optimism. *Journal of Business Research*, 57, 26–34.

van Dierendonck, D. & Mevissen, N. (2002). Aggressive behavior of passengers, conflict management behavior and burnout among trolley car drivers. *International Journal of Stress Management*, 9, 345–355.

van Dierendonck, D., Schaufeli, W. B. & Buunk, B. P. (1996). Inequity among human service professionals: Measurement and relation to burnout. *Basic and Applied Social Psychology*, 18, 429–451.

van Dierendonck, D., Schaufeli, W. B. & Buunk, B. P. (1998). The evaluation of an individual burnout intervention program: The role of inequity and social support. *Journal of Applied Psychology*, 83, 392–407.

van Dolen, W., de Ruyter, K. & Lemmink, J. (2004). An empirical assessment of the influence of customer emotions and contact employee performance on encounter and relationship satisfaction. *Journal of Business Research*, 57, 437–444.

van Dolen, W., Lemmink, J., de Ruyter, K. & de Jong, A. (2002). Customer-sales employee encounters: A dyadic perspective. *Journal of Retailing*, 78, 265–279.

Van Horn, J. E., Schaufeli, W. B. & Enzmann, D. (1999). Teacher burnout and lack of reciprocity. *Journal of Applied Social Psychology*, 29, 91–108.

Van Horn, J. E., Taris, T. W., Schaufeli, W. B. & Schreurs, P. J. G. (2004). The structure of occupational well-being: A study among Dutch teachers. *Journal of Occupational and Organizational Psychology*, 77, 365–375.

Van Yperen, N. W. (1996). Communal orientation and the burnout syndrome among nurses: A replication and extension. *Journal of Applied Social Psychology*, 26, 338–354.

Van Yperen, N. W. (1998). Informational support, equity and burnout: The moderating effect of self-efficacy. *Journal of Occupational and Organizational Psychology*, 71, 29–33.

Van Yperen, N. W., Buunk, B. P. & Schaufeli, W. B. (1992). Communal orientation and the burnout syndrome among nurses. *Journal of Applied Social Psychology*, 22, 173–189.

Verbeke, W. (1997). Individual differences in emotional contagion of salespersons: Its effect on performance and burnout. *Psychology & Marketing*, 14, 617–636.

Vilnai-Yavetz, I. & Rafaeli, A. (2003). Organizational interactions: A basic skeleton with spiritual tissue. In R. A. Giacalone & C. L. Jurkiewicz (eds), *Handbook of Workplace Spirituality and Organizational Performance* (pp. 76–93). Armonk, New York: Sharpe Publications.

Viswesvaran, C., Ones, D. S. & Schmidt, F. L. (2005). Is there a general factor in ratings of job performance? A meta-analytic framework for disentangling substantive and error influences. *Journal of Applied Psychology*, 90, 108–131.

Vonk, R. (2002). Self-serving interpretations of flattery: Why ingratiation works. *Journal of Personality and Social Psychology*, 82, 515–526.

Walster, E., Walster, G. W. & Berscheid, E. (1978). *Equity: Theory and Research*. Boston: Allyn & Bacon.

Walters, A. S. & Curran, M. C. (1996). 'Excuse me, sir? May I help you and your boyfriend?': Salespersons' differential treatment of homosexual and straight customers. *Journal of Homosexuality*, 31, 135–152.

Weatherly, K. A. & Tansik, D. A. (1993). Tactics used by customer-contact workers: Effects of role stress, boundary spanning and control. *International Journal of Service Industry Management*, 4, 4–17.

Weitzer, R. (1997). Racial prejudice among Korean merchants in African American neighborhoods. *The Sociological Quarterly*, 38, 587–606.

Wharton, A. S. (1993). The affective consequences of service work: Managing emotions on the job. *Work and Occupations*, 20, 205–232.

Wharton, A. S. & Erickson, R. J. (1993). Managing emotions on the job and at home: Understanding the consequences of multiple emotional roles. *Academy of Management Review*, 18, 457–486.

White, W. (1949). *Men at Work*, Irvin-Dorsey series in Behavioral Sciences. Homewood, III: The Dorsey Press and Richard Irwin.

Wilk, S. L. & Moynihan, L. M. (2005). Display rule 'regulators': The relationship between supervisors and worker emotional exhaustion. *Journal of Applied Psychology*, 90, 917–927.

Williams, A. & Anderson, H. H. (2005). Engaging customers in service creation: A theater perspective. *Journal of Services Marketing*, 19, 13–23.

Williams, M. R. & Attaway, J. S. (1996). Exploring salespersons' customer orientation as a mediator of organizational culture's influence on buyer-seller relationships. *The Journal of Personal Selling & Sales Management*, 16, 33–52.

Withiam, G. (1998). Customers from hell. *Cornell Hotel and Restaurant Administration Quarterly*, 39, 11.

Witt, L. A., Andrews, M. C. & Carlson, D. S. (2004). When conscientiousness isn't enough: Emotional exhaustion and performance among call center customer service representatives. *Journal of Management*, 30, 149–160.

Yagil, D. (2001). Ingratiation and assertiveness in the service provider-customer dyad. *Journal of Service Research*, 3, 345–353.

Yagil, D. (2002). The relationship of customer satisfaction and service workers' perceived control: Examination of three models. *International Journal of Service Industry Management*, 13, 382–398.

Yagil, D. (2006). The relationship of service provider power motivation, empowerment and burnout to customer satisfaction. *International Journal of Service Industry Management*, 17, 258–270.

Yagil, D. & Gal, I. (2002). The role of organizational service climate in generating control and empowerment among workers and customers. *Journal of Retailing and Consumer Services*, 9, 215–226.

Yen, H. R., Gwinner, K. P. & Su, W. (2004). The impact of customer participation and service expectation on Locus attributions following service failure. *International Journal of Service Industry Management*, 15, 7–26.

Yoon, M. H., Beatty, S. E. & Suh, J. (2001). The effect of work climate on critical employee and customer outcomes: An employee-level analysis. *International Journal of Service Industry Management*, 12, 500–521.

Yoon, M. H. & Suh, J. (2003). Organizational citizenship behaviors and service quality as external effectiveness of contact employees. *Journal of Business Research*, 56, 597–611.

Zabava Ford, W. S. (1995). Evaluation of the indirect influence of courteous service on customer discretionary behavior. *Human Communication Research*, 22, 65–89.

Zabava Ford, W. S. (1998). *Communicating with Customers: Service Approaches, Ethics and Impact*. Cresskill, NJ: Hampton Press.

Zabava Ford, W. S. (2001). Customer expectations for interactions with service providers: Relationship versus encounter orientation and personalized service communication. *Journal of Applied Communication Research*, 29, 1–29.

Zapf, D. (2002). Emotion work and psychological well-being. A review of the literature and some conceptual considerations. *Human Resource Management Review*, 12, 237–268.

Zapf, D. & Holz, M. (2006). On the positive and negative effects of emotion work in organizations. *European Journal of Work and Organizational Psychology*, 15, 1–28.

Zapf, D., Isic, A., Bechtoldt, M. & Blau, P. (2003). What is typical for call centre jobs? Job characteristics, and service interactions in different call centers. *European Journal of Work and Organizational Psychology*, 12, 311–340.

Zapf, D., Vogt, C., Seifert, C., Mertini, H. & Isic, A. (1999). Emotion work as a source of stress. The concept and development of an instrument. *European Journal of Work and Organizational Psychology*, 8, 371–400.

Zeithaml, V. A. & Bitner, M. J. (1996). *Service Marketing*. New York: McGraw-Hill.

Zemke, R. & Albrecht, K. (1985). Service management: A new game plan for the post-industrial era. *Training*, 22, 54–60.

Zinkhan, G. M. & Stoiadin, L. F. (1984). Impact of sex role stereotypes on service priority in department stores. *Journal of Applied Psychology*, 69, 691–693.

Index